False Gods

The Jerusalem Memoirs

by

Adolf Eichmann

False Gods

The Jerusalem Memoirs

by

Adolf Eichmann

Translated

by

Dr Alexander Jacob

Copyright © 2015 Black House Publishing Ltd
ISBN-13: 978-1-910881-11-8

All rights reserved. No part of this book may be reproduced in any form by any electronic or mechanical means including photocopying, recording, or information storage and retrieval without permission in writing from the publisher.

Black House Publishing Ltd

Kemp House

152 City Road

London

United Kingdom

EC1V 2NX

www.blackhousepublishing.com
Email: info@blackhousepublishing.com

False Gods

The Jerusalem Memoirs

by

Adolf Eichmann

Translated

by

Dr Alexander Jacob

SS Obersturmbannführer Adolf Eichmann 1906-1962.

Contents

Preface	1
Foreword	7
Part I	9
My Early Life	9
Transfer to the SS Intelligence Service	13
Transfer to Vienna	36
Hitler Gives His Warning	46
Assignment to Prague	51
Theresienstadt	55
Invasion of Poland	58
Assignment to Gestapo Office IV	61
Resurgence of the Madagascar Plan	72
The Attack on the USSR	74
Hitler's Order for Physical Annihilation	75
The Gassing of Jews at Lublin	77
Eichmann Witnesses the Murders	79
The Killings in Minsk	87
The Wannsee Conference	94
The Gassing of Jews at Auschwitz	101
The Strasbourg Skeletons	111
Burning the Evidence	115
The Meaning of Special Treatment	118
Himmler and the Demand for Obedience	130
Part II	135
France	136
Holland	154
Belgium	158

Contents

Italy	161
Norway	165
Denmark	165
Slovakia	168
Greece	174
Yugoslavia	176
Slovenia	177
Serbia	178
Croatia	184
Romania	185
Bulgaria	190
Hungary	192
Part III	225
My Capture and Trial	225
On Knowledge and Will	230
Of Blood and Soil	245
The End of Nationalism	255
A Cosmic World View	259
The Letter from Pastor Achenbach	261
Testament	265

Preface

Adolf Eichmann (1906-1962) was born in Solingen in Germany to Adolf Karl Eichmann and Maria Eichmann, née Schefferling. After his mother died in 1914, his family moved to Linz in Austria. Eichmann began working in his father's mining company in 1923 and, from 1925 to 1927, worked as a sales clerk for the Oberösterreichische Elektrobau company. He also served as district agent in the Vacuum Oil Company.

As a young man, Eichmann joined the German Austrian Young Frontline Soldiers' Association, which was the youth wing of the paramilitary Frontline Soldiers' Association of Hermann Hiltl. On the advice of his family friend Ernst Kaltenbrunner, he joined the Austrian branch of the NSDAP and was enlisted as a member of the SS in 1932. Shortly after the National Socialists came to power in January 1933, Eichmann was dismissed from the oil company and so he devoted all his time to working with the National Socialist party. He was promoted to SS Scharführer in November 1933 and served as an administrator in the Dachau concentration camp. In 1934 he moved to the Security Service and, after briefly working in the Freemasonry department, moved to the Jewish department in Berlin in November 1934.

In 1937, he travelled with his superior Herbert Hagen to the British Mandate territory of Palestine to assess the possibility of Jewish emigration from Germany to Palestine. In 1938, after the Anschluss, Eichmann was posted to Vienna and was entrusted with the establishment of a Central Office for Jewish Emigration. In the course of this assignment Eichmann developed numerous contacts with Jewish authorities who helped him speed up the emigration of Jews from Austria. In December 1939, he was made head of the Gestapo division IV-B4 of the newly formed Reich Security Head Office (RSHA) and worked, under Heinrich Müller, on Jewish matters. By 1941 Eichmann had been promoted to SS Obersturmbannführer (Lieutenant Colonel) and was entrusted with the organisation of the deportation of the European Jews to various concentration camps in the Greater German Reich.

Preface

Though arrested at the end of the war by the U.S. army, Eichmann succeeded in escaping from U.S. custody early in 1946 and lived unnoticed in Germany and Austria until 1950, when he travelled to Argentina, through Italy, under the false name of Ricardo Klement. For the next ten years he worked at mechanical jobs in Buenos Aires and, in 1952, brought his family over to Argentina from Germany. However, in 1953, Simon Wiesenthal obtained a letter to an Austrian baron Mast from a German officer in Argentina who reported that he had met Eichmann, who was working at that time in a power plant near Buenos Aires. Although this information was conveyed to the Israeli consul in Vienna as well as to Dr. Nahum Goldmann of the World Jewish Congress in New York, it was 1957 before the Mossad was involved in the search for Eichmann. Walter Eyan of the Israeli Foreign Ministry was informed by the German public prosecutor Fritz Bauer that Eichmann was living in Argentina and he then relayed this information to Isser Harel, the head of Mossad, whose agents succeeded in tracing Eichmann in Argentina and capturing him, three years later, on May 11, 1960. On May 21 he was flown to Israel, where he was tried by the Israeli Court in 1961, found guilty and hanged on May 31, 1962.

In Argentina, from 1951 until 1959, Eichmann made a series of tape-recorded interviews with the former SS Dutchman Willem Sassen. When the Israeli prosecutor Gideon Hausner wished to have the full Sassen transcripts admitted into evidence during Eichmann's trial in 1961, Eichmann opposed this claiming that this record was mere "pub talk" since he had been drinking red wine during the interview and Sassen had constantly encouraged him to embellish his accounts for journalistic sensation and had even falsely transcribed the interview. Portions of the Sassen interview were sold by Sassen to Life magazine, which published them in December 1960 (*Life*, Vol.49, no.22, November 28, 1960 and no.23, December 5, 1960), that is, when Eichmann had already been taken to Israel.

Another copy of the transcription of Eichmann's original recordings and handwritten notes, was taken by Eichmann's widow Veronika to the Nuremberg lawyer, Dr. Rudolf Aschenauer, whom she commissioned to act on her behalf in regards to their publication. This edition was published by the German publisher Druffel Verlag as *Ich, Adolf Eichmann: ein historischer Zeugenbericht*, and my English translation of this edition entitled *The Eichmann Tapes - My Role in the Final Solution* is also available from Black House Publishing, and is a companion to this volume.

False Gods

Adolf Eichmann arrived in Argentina in 1950 under the name of Riccardo Klement.

After his courtroom testimony, in August 1961, Eichmann wrote another handwritten testimony that he called "Götzen" (False Gods). These final memoirs of Adolf Eichmann are more concise than the original version he wrote in Argentina, although they follow the same plan of an initial biographical sketch followed by a country-wise record of the deportations he conducted. Like the earlier memoirs, the latter also provides a detailed account of his career in the SS and Gestapo as the divisional head in charge of the numerous deportations of the European Jews. Through a perusal of Eichmann's memoirs, the reader will undoubtedly be able to ascertain the scope of the anti-Jewish measures undertaken in the Third Reich.

However, compared to the Argentinean memoirs, the present memoirs reveal an extremely sharp disillusionment with the National Socialist goals he championed during the Reich as well as a greater sympathy with the post-war attempts to establish a non-nationalistic one-world order. Although he had joined the NSDAP in order to defend Germany from the humiliation of Versailles, incidents such as the Night of Broken Glass caused him early in his career to realise that he had followed "false gods", a suspicion that was confirmed by his visits to Lublin and Auschwitz to witness the mass killings of Jews. It is interesting also, that in this version of his memoirs, he is more honest in his account of certain events such as, for example, the development of the ghetto in Theresienstadt. For, whereas in the

Preface

Argentinean memoirs he had suggested that it was actually a model old-age home that he himself had done much to develop, he now admits that it was not really meant by Himmler to be an exemplary ghetto but was rather a "camouflage" to deceive the outside world on the manner in which the Reich was dealing with its Jewish problem.

In his Argentinean memoirs, besides, Eichmann had pointed to the contrary effects of the post-war democratic propaganda and re-education on former National Socialists in a derisory manner:

> Twelve years of re-education propaganda and occupation-dictatorship have made people who would be considered as witnesses for the defence, if they are not dead or have not been killed, so afraid that they do not wish to know anything at all, or remember about anything anymore. Very many would have been, in 1945 and 1946, still ready for a clear statement even under the pressure from the occupation powers, for every pressure releases a counter-reaction. But, today, that option is no longer available. For, the good life and "democratic re-education" have borne fruits, so that today, as a defendant, I would not know which witnesses for the defence would actually be pertinent. In 1945, I would, as a defendant, have had all my colleagues; today, I am no longer sure of that; one part of them will not come into question at all as witnesses for the defence because they are concerned for their survival. And another part has had to lead such a hard life in the meantime that they curse the past and the "stupidity" of having been a National Socialist.

Now, in the present memoirs, Eichmann himself shows very little sympathy for the National Socialist world-view, which he now considers to have been "something half-baked, something cobbled together from all possible ideas and imaginations" and held together as a totalitarian "collective" system through the military principles of command and obedience. In the Argentinean memoirs he had indeed expressed a strong sympathy for Zionist ideals as a mirror-image of National Socialist ones:

> Generally, Ben Gurion follows nothing but what the SS Reichsführer also did; the Jewish "Pioneers" root themselves in the soil and have, next to the plough, their gun ready at hand; they are the Israeli translation of our idea of "soldier peasants". The National Socialist ancestral farm legislation represented similar norms as the "Jewish Development League", for example, the inalienability of farming

land. The organised youth presents a similar image as our National Socialist youth and is likewise the youth of a people in a state of emergency. So I often said to the Jewish representatives well known to me: "If I were a Jew, then I would be the most committed Zionist that you could imagine." Already as the specialist in the SDHA on the World Zionist Organisation I recognised the parallels between the goals of the SS with its blood and soil ideas and Zionism; in this goal SS and Zionism are siblings.[1]

Now, he abjures nationalism itself as a primitive instinct and considers that:

> Mutual mistrust, the striving for domination of one over the other, grouping of men according to values and classifications, all this is from now on part of the old rubbish.

He goes so far as to suggests that such ideologies must be totally eradicated:

> That is why I said that evil must be extirpated basically, radically. The organisational form that can bring men to such conflicts must be removed. In mutual coexistence man does not have to accommodate himself to the organisational form but the organisational form must be tailored to man. This alone seems to be a practical application based on the bleak experiences up to now; the other is, I think, heretical nonsense. Good perhaps for inner edification, but what is the use of this when murder and annihilation can continue to be ordered by the state.

The remedy for nationalism is of course internationalism: "only an internationalisation of peoples overcomes the existing basic instincts, at least one part of the additional hotbeds artificially created by men through nationalisation." Eichmann even goes so far as to embrace what we now recognise as the globalist ideal of a world-government:

> The task of regional governments, which will then have only a provincial character, will be to make the nations of the earth happier in union with the central authority. And the sooner such a thing is achieved the more the personal security and independence of the individual is provided for, and every oppression of him will be prevented.

---

1 See ""Unity of Jewry in the world?", in Adolf Eichmann, *op.cit.*,

Preface

This abjuration of National Socialism seems not to be the mere result of the broad public discussion of the events of the Reich during his trial or of his fear of a death sentence. For, the final part of the memoirs in which he meditates on political and philosophical issues also evokes the serenity that he seems to have discovered in the last days of his extraordinary life. As he states, "I have finally found a world-view for myself which satisfies me". For,

> Today, having an open mind, no anxious skulking, a lack of prejudice, no envy and no hatred are the most important advantages. Of course, I am still an egoist, but this time not at the cost of others. Now even my fellow human beings take part in this egoism with advantages to themselves.

Whatever the reasons for the aversion that he developed to nationalism between the writing of the Argentinean memoirs and that of his final manuscript, a common strand in both memoirs is Eichmann's consistent insistence on his absolute freedom from "legal guilt" - even though he may well have had reason to feel personal "moral guilt". For, as he repeatedly declares, even though he had, in the course of his extraordinary life, been forced to witness what he calls "death and the devil", he had never on any occasion participated more closely in this "hell" than as a mere "recipient of orders".

Dr Alexander Jacob.

Foreword

I am in prison in Israel. The hearing of evidence has concluded and in a week there will follow the pleadings of the attorney general and my defence. Then some two or three months will pass before the court reaches a judgement. Possibly it will then go to the higher court; possibly also not. 'However it may be', I once said during the trial to a question of the prosecutor in the cross-examination; 'I shall say that, if I sit down one day to write some chapters for the present and future youth, as a warning to them, provided that I receive the approval for that, then I shall "call a spade a spade".

Now, the president of the court demanded this from me already during the trial. I obeyed and said that the events related to the Jews which the then German Reich government instituted during the years of the last great war represent the greatest crime in the history of mankind. So I have decided to use or, better, to take advantage of the time of waiting for the judgement and to realise that which I had announced. It can hardly harm, rather, on the other hand, it may provoke reflection, how things could have happened in this way to a man. I was inspired by a thousand ideals and slid in many others into a matter from which one could no longer find one's way out. Today I have a temporal distance from the events that lie 16-29 years in the past. And much that was valid then has become invalid. Former "worldview values" I have gradually, in the course of the years, thrown overboard as rubbish.

Because I saw hell, death and the devil, because I had to look on at the madness of the annihilation, because I was harnessed as one of the many horses and, following the will and order of the coachman, could break out neither to the left nor the right, I find myself called upon here and have the desire to narrate and proclaim what happened.

It is certainly a sad summary that I am in a position to only give an outline of the organisational requirements that the events made possible. Most of those actors who will now indeed enter history in one way or the other I knew, in part communicated with them, and can judge them in detail.

Foreword

I shall describe the life of that time, as I experienced it and saw it. I shall try to spare nothing. I write for nobody's fame and honour - what mendacious, self-adulatory concepts these are! What I thought I had to adore yesterday lies today in the rubble of that which has been destroyed.

I shall describe the genocide of the Jews, how it happened and give, in addition, my thoughts of the past and of today. For not only did I have to see with my own eyes the fields of death, the battlefields on which life died away, I saw much worse. I saw how, through a few words, through the mere concise order of an individual to whom the state gave the authority of commander, such fields of the extinction of life were created.

I saw the machinery of death. Grasping cogs within cogs, like clockwork. And I saw those who observed the process of the work. I saw them always repeating the work and they looked at the seconds-hand, which hurried; hurried like life to death. The greatest and cruellest dance of death of all time. That I saw, and I prepare to describe it, as a warning.

Adolf Eichmann

6 September 1961

Part I

My Early Life

I came into the world on 19 March 1906. I was born in Solingen, in the Rheinland, as the first son of the married couple Wolf and Maria Eichmann. A few days after my birth I was baptised Adolf Otto according to the ritual of the Evangelical faith of the Helvetian confession. As a small child I moved with my parents to Linz on the Danube, Upper Austria, where my father was trade director of the Linz Railway and Electricity Company, and later retired I think in the twenties to found an electric wares enterprise.

After attending a primary and secondary school, I graduated after two years at a federal technical academy. From 1925 until 1927 I was active as a sales officer of the "Upper Austrian Electrical Co. Inc". in Linz on the Danube and then, until June 1933, as sales officer of the Austrian Vacuum Oil Company Inc., in the Linz and Salzburg branch.

The Linz on the Danube of that time was a dreamy, small, lovely and clean provincial capital in the centre of the predominantly peasant Upper Austria. With it's wheat-rich Inn region, the kale-rich Hansruck region, the Traun region already then closed to foreign traffic with its pearl, Gmunden on the Traun Lake, and the Upper Austrian Hausberg with Traunstein, the watchman of the region of the beginning High Alps. But I was especially in love with the attractive Mühl region. The region with many ruins and fortresses wrapped in sagas. And here it was the upper Mühl region that I especially cherished in my heart.

My Early Life

Franz Josef-Platz in the Austrian city of Linz.

The homeland of Adalbert Stifter,[1] the eternal Bohemian woods whose offshoots reach deep into the upper Mühl region with its small romantic brown-water tributary streams. The many swift trout-filled streams, which have found their way, from times immemorial, to the great collection of water, the Danube, through the Bohemian-Moravian granite plateau that is very steeply sloped against the Danube.

This gorgeous spot of earth I could call my second homeland and in this jewel of Upper Austria I spent, thanks to the constant care of my parents, a wonderful carefree youth.

And even as a young man – as one tends to say – it was days of love, springtime and life that were offered to me. Motor sports, mountain sports, work, coffee-house, friends and also girlfriends – why not – filled my days and years.

Many cosy wine taverns encouraged one's entry and one sat very comfortably within their old walls. I knew one such wine tavern whose existence was traced back to the thirteenth century. And the "Gumpoldskirchner" had the flavour of every region even without Schrammel[2] and gypsy music.

---

1   Adalbert Stifter (1805-68) was an Austrian writer whose novels are imbued with middle-class, 'Biedermeier' ideals of morality and humanism.

2   A type of Viennese folk music made popular in the late nineteenth century

False Gods

We lived in the land of well-off Austrians in Upper Austria. And if we drove to the Postlingberg, the landmark of Linz, the first trip was, with my little girlfriend, to Master Bugele, the head gardener of the wonderfully beautiful garden parks on this mountain with its thousand or more rose bushes. To be requested a bouquet of roses for one's beloved was always a great joy for this master of flowers, shrubs and trees, even if he knew me as a little kid when I visited the parks on Saturdays holding my father's hand. My old man had in his time done much for the improvement of this beautiful spot which at that time belonged to the property of the Linz Highway and Electricity Company and appointed my friend Bugele as head gardener of this paradise.

Nothing could have disturbed this gay and carefree love of life if the "gods" had not come as far as Upper Austria. They knocked on my door from 1931, and on and off even earlier, they then caught me on 1 April 1932. Yes, my friends, looking back it is almost 30 years, and I must say, "when the donkey is happy it goes on the ice to dance". Now, there were at that time different sorts of recruits, as there may have been at all times and always will be. Through the school and company in which I moved, in short through the environment that influenced me – and which environment does not form a young man – I was led in the nationalist direction, and which nationalist did the word "Versailles" at that time not set on fire.

Of course at first one did not understand anything of it. But an understanding of it was already awakened, newspapers, conversations and books took care of that. And a man inclining in this direction was told of national disgrace, betrayal, the stab in the back that was meted out to the German army, national distress and misery. God, one wanted a stop, one flew into a rage. And then one heard through the propaganda that there was one party that had inscribed the removal of the disgrace on its banner. Promised an end to the national distress, prepared to remove the dagger from the wound, sought to combat equal opportunity in the military sector, and condemned the unemployment in the lowest hellish stratum. And then one sat in such a wine tavern, called "the quarter", or in the beer pub called "Krügerl", or in the café called "the Black" and read the *Völkische Beobachter*.[3]

---

by the violinists Johann and Josef Schrammel.

3   The *Völkische Beobachter* was the official newspaper of the NSDAP from 1920. It was first edited by Dietrich Eckart and then, from 1923, by Alfred Rosenberg.

My Early Life

one read of the death of an SA man or men; one read heroic words about heroic deeds, about manly striving and fearless loyalty. And I repeat, which young man of nationalist tendency was not "captivated" by that?

There was not a word about the Jews and Jewry; and if one read on and off about it in certain articles, who took such things seriously? Who in general pondered on account of this? Perhaps the senior and old people. We young men were only, and exclusively, interested by the heroic. To help in the removal, the destruction, of the distress.

One saw red at the word "Versailles". Ready for everything, to destroy, to trample down this word, and even to suffer for this if necessary. It must be expunged. And those who were called to this were our gods. So must it have been in ancient times, if one may believe the heroic sagas. But why should one not have believed them?

The "dukes", the "followers", the loyalty to the duke and the loyalty to the followers. I dedicated myself to the gods completely. Indeed, partly for the sake of these gods I left the "region of Enns", my beloved Upper Austria. Of course, the farewell from the region was difficult, the farewell from parents and siblings, the farewell from my beloved. The regular joyous togetherness at weekends, whether it was in South Bohemia, or in Upper Austria, was over. Being the master of one's own time was over. Something alien, unknown, lay before me. But service to the gods, for the sake of my fatherland, seemed to me to be of equal weight, for otherwise I would indeed have stayed behind.

Thousands of cords pulled me to remain, but as many pulled me to the gods. And I served them. I served them with all the faith that I could bring forth, no sacrifice seemed to me to be too small. No effort too great. Yes, the greater the sacrifices and the efforts and hardships so much greater seemed to me the activity for the work that the gods promised to accomplish.

Sleeping on the bare ground, on straw, on straw-sacks, harder and ever harder exercise, training with the troops, crawling on strained elbows and knees; blind obedience and limitation of freedom I exchanged for the middle-class comfortable parental house, for the coffee-house and wine tavern, for motor sports, mountain sports and the togetherness of young lovers. Truly I served the gods of my own accord; truly I offered too much in sacrifice to them. But what did it matter if the fatherland could become free, and distress and misery found an end.

Transfer to the SS Intelligence Service

In 1934, on a sunny autumn morning, I arrived at the Anhalt station on transfer from the first battalion of SS Regiment 1 to Berlin, to the SD Head Office.[4] After an all-night train journey a little freshening up was very important and useful. I went to a barber's shop opposite the railway station, and, after a shave, I had hot towels placed on my face to banish the overnight strain. I then strolled thereupon to a "Anschinger" bar right next to the barber's. Some light lagers and as many schnapps and, in between, a good goulash with fresh crisp bread were just the right breakfast for a junior officer in the SS reserve troop, the precursor of the later Waffen SS.

I had reported voluntarily to the Security Service of the SS Reichsführer. Security escort for the gods. Why not; I imagined that it would be very interesting. Only later would I realise that I had made a mistake. The security escort for the gods was the *Reich* Security Service. The Security Service of the SS Reichsführer was something quite different.

At first however I did not yet have any idea. At first I looked for a coffee-house. Coffee was good for everything. Good for snoozing, good to kill the odour of Aschinger's Berlin beer, and with the troops we used it daily and yearly for cleaning stains from our uniforms. Of course, for training we had field-grey or, what was most annoying, canvas that was light grey or bordering on white which got dirty easily. With the sovereign calm of a junior officer I went to the office that I was commanded to, a palace at 102 Wilhelmstraße, to report for duty. Whether I was married or single - that was the first question which the serving officer asked me. Single. My fiancé was in South Bohemia and a wedding was not to be thought of at that moment. 'Single men are barracked; when they marry they can live outside', I was told. Well, I thought to myself, one must belong somewhere. To one's parents, the barracks or one's wife.

So I went to the quartermaster sergeant. Previously we junior officers always had at our disposal orderlies for personal service who were silently tolerated, every four junior officers had an orderly. He drank and smoked freely at our cost, and he had his four junior officers as friends who would defend him against death and the devil if he did

---

4   Sicherheitsdient, the Security Service, was the intelligence agency of the NSDAP formed in 1931 by Heinrich Himmler and headed by Reinhard Heydrich. In 1939 it became part of the Reichssicherheitshauptamt (RSHA), the Reich Security Service Head Office, also headed by Heydrich.

Transfer to the SS Intelligence Service

something against the service rules. Besides he had only the lightest drill, but mostly he was able to squeeze himself out even from this. But here the quartermaster sergeant threw my blue and white checked bed clothes at my own head; blanket and sheet followed and, with that, to the barrack room. The remainder of the outfit was the usual barrack rubbish, familiar and nothing new.

In the afternoon I was sworn in. Of course I had, already at the death of the Reich president Field-Marshal General von Hindenburg, taken the oath of allegiance to the Führer, the Reich Chancellor and the fatherland; so now once again, but in another form, with a pledge to secrecy.

In itself it had already more than puzzled me when I was led for the swearing-in in service uniform and with steel helmet to an SS officer and, in doing so, had to cross some museum-like rooms; I also saw in one of these rooms a sarcophagus with a glass plate in which lay a human skeleton, but I had to take great care of my feet, for my hard boots did not suit the smooth waxed floor and I had difficulty not slipping on a bend.

I thought that it was remarkable; everything was quite remarkable. 'Perhaps the staff are accommodated in a museum', went through my head. The offices at that time were indeed found in all corners and ends where one would never have suspected them. Besides, I came from the troops and did not have to worry about such stuff. Anyway I was treated as a recruit who had only just been drafted. And it is surprising to what extent drilled total obedience coupled with a proper shot of idealism leads to suffering. Naturally it must be hard, very hard for every *upright* junior officer if he, in the company of eleven more barrack-room fellows, together with whom he lived, of whom only two were likewise serving junior officers, the rest however knew a barracks at most by hearsay – at best on the basis of a "quick boiled-fodder course".

Saturday after Saturday, scrub the stools and tables, and lay the bedclothes in the locker in a different, new order. To be commanded by a sergeant of the "general SS", thus the civil SS, who likewise had not even begun his service as a "weapons-bearer of the nation" but brought with him a rank in the SD from the *general* SS, thus the civil SS, whereby his satisfaction in being able to "give it" to the junior officer gentlemen from the troops was visible from a distance of a thousand metres.

False Gods

It was no joy to fall in for exercise early in the morning in the park of the palace. Not on account of the exercising; on the contrary, this was the only enjoyable thing in the entire service organisation. No, the rankling and gnawing anger came from the fact that clowns to whom the handling of a machine gun was alien, that is, Sunday exercise leaders of the general SS, had us do the most tedious and stupid movements here; we three serving officers, of "barrack room 12" were driven to the limits of our patience by these tactics, but we tolerated it, we obeyed. After a few days I figured out that I had come to the wrong place, and a departure to the Reich Security Service was not permitted.

Once the galley slavery was over. I found myself bound with invisible chains to a file-tray and had the task, along with half a dozen other comrades, of writing out, ordering and classifying the Freemasonry cards which comprised ten thousand cards. The hardest battle that had to be fought in those days was the battle against boredom.

Good God, if, as a free man, I were roped in somewhere against my will to a job that went against the grain, one should simply stop it or one is a wimp who indeed deserves nothing better. In the barracks, yes, well, one has to obey, everybody knows that. But in an office, in a bureau, I should put my foot down, speak my mind and scoot from the temple. Especially when one is a young man of twenty-eight.

These were the thoughts I had at that time, and along with me a number of my barrack-room fellows. But there were the gods whom I wished to serve. And the political schooling which we were subjected to at the beginning drew us closer to them. The life of the Prussian king, Frederick the Great, was brought to us in a true-to-life manner, in the most vivid forms, by masters in this field. The national bond and the blood bond were idealised in the most glowing colours.

The service to the nation, service to the Führer, was preached as a sacred privilege. The dedication of *everything* for the liberty of the nation hammered in as the highest duty and as a joyful, constant desire. And I believed it with every fibre of the faith that I was in a position to muster.

In this way then I performed my service; a writing-desk service, which suited me neither physically nor psychologically, which meant for me a torture, for which I had to master myself every day anew through struggle before I set out on the commanded day's work.

Transfer to the SS Intelligence Service

Man gets used to everything when he has to. And after the force of custom had swallowed up great parts of the aversion to the unpleasant activity and the world-view teachings swept another part of it under the table, there remained superficially only relatively little resistance of repugnance and even this was soon whitewashed by the undeniable successes that the leadership of the Reich had obtained for the German people. The likes of us did not see the large political outlines. Foreign announcements through the press and radio did not yet reach us; for that we were too small servants of the nation and the state. The international interrelations in political events were at that time all Greek even to me. But even I saw the disappearance of the armies of the unemployed and the militarisation of the Rhineland zone, the re-establishment of the sovereign defence, the frenetic jubilation of the masses of millions when the gods revealed themselves. And my captivation by this was always perceptible.

But they were finally only *earthly* gods. Consciously and unconsciously I guarded against becoming enslaved to them in my innermost self.

The fatherland, freedom, yes, unconditionally!

The soul - which enters when it is time, and these earthly values cease to be the object of hope, belief and action - this I retained as a private possession on which finally only I could and wished to decide. Here I did not allow even the gods to approach, no matter how I had fallen for them in faith. Here the parental education and the inner binding to values transmitted from generation to generation was still too strong to yield to the attempts at inroads. Here I was stubborn. Stubborn like the new heavy tanks which appeared for the stirring up of joy and as visible guarantors of freedom. Stubborn like the flights of the new bomb squadrons which unswervingly thundered in the Berlin skies.

My bond to the Church! Almost all my comrades had long withdrawn from the religious communities and only ground their nose in dirty jokes and smears against the Church and the clergy. If they had alcohol in their stomach then they wished to surpass one another in a contest of their stupidity. Naturally, I was then always an especially welcome target of the mockery of comrades, to be sure, not meant in a bad way. It began already in the barracks. It was the new fashion to get a de-registration certificate. Not that that was forced by the superiors; that would be untrue. It may be that this was customary in the party life. Among the SS reserve troops and even also in the SD Head Office it was not customary. But the comradely mockery, coarse, indeed filthily coarse, to be sure good-humoured in an infantry manner, but not without sting and prickle, saw to it, and even the hope of quick promotion did its part to obtain these de-registration certificates as quickly as possible. Among the troops I soon had peace on this account. For, as is indeed customary among young men, often everything else did not matter half as much when the person concerned was a good sport.

The feared object at that time was the scaling wall. A two-metre solid, high and strong boarding over which one had to run in a more or less elegant manner. Here one's behind, knees and front of the foot worked desperately with the musculature of the arms to heave the around-70 kilogram live weight of the infantry man onto the other side. The "good for nothings" were entered into the memorandum book of the sergeant major for the purpose of service in the kitchen for the hated potato bowl, for cleaning of toilet seats, for there were only too few, or no, expert cleaners and this activity was then mostly demanded of these good for nothings when the remaining company had leave to go out and could scamper into the meadow with Miss Wife.

I had the advantage – at that time I still had a gymnastic and sporty "streak" – of going over that wall effortlessly and even elegantly and was, on account of my excellence, reserved by the company leader for the purpose of lighter help which could be performed with the fingertips. This was a customary alleviation. But as a rule those who had to support derived their greatest joy in obstruction or aggravation instead of the opposite. This was indeed part of the general "bullying" and teasing. Joy at the expense of others. Yes, the barrack life was indeed rough but hearty. Indeed, I used to do excellent support work. Most often a light pressure on the lower back grinding in the air was enough and the fellow was over it. The tipping of the scales, so to speak. And since it was indeed forenoon on Saturday and the staff sergeant had to make no notes, the masters of the company all came with their girlfriends for their weekend enjoyment.

Since that time I was - however little the matters were connected to each other - no longer harassed about religious matters . When in 1935 I married, it took place in the Evangelical Church in Passau, in uniform. Here naturally superiors at that time tried to intervene and pointed to the impossibilities. But I was stubborn. Only in autumn 1937 – I had already for a small eternity been first sergeant – did I leave the Evangelical community, without pressure or force, of my own accord and with fullest consideration and I designated myself

Transfer to the SS Intelligence Service

since that time as a "believer in god". Nothing has changed in that even today. I did not become hostile to the Church nor was I ever anti-clerical. I considered the need of religious communities as important for ethical and educational reasons but *I* wished to be free and without church connections in the communication between my God and myself. Moreover the strife at that time within the Evangelical Church disgusted me so much that I did not want to hear anything more of it. One side of it was all on fire for the new gods and their actions, the other side opposed them to the death.

It was not the fact of the battle against the state of the time that forced me to distance myself so much as, rather, the consideration "that it could hardly correspond to any divine wish" that his ordained servants allowed themselves to become involved in earthly matters and get into fights with one another. In addition, there were my doubts regarding religion, which I touch upon in another passage.

At that time the Roman Catholic Church commended itself to me. Its value standards were not conjured up just recently. It was used to thinking, evaluating and weighing in terms of centuries. If I had at that time been a Catholic and not a Protestant, I would have remained stubbornly in the Church community. People had got used to it for three long years that I was one of the few, if not the only one, who remained stubborn in this for so long. Of course, I must as a qualification add that I was however not active, on the other hand, in any form as a missionary, or preaching in any other way. Such things I would never have done. I defended exclusively my own personal attitude to the values and customs acquired by me until the day when, through personal knowledge, I saw things in an inwardly more satisfying light.

Yes, and how was it with the Jewish question at that time and what was my attitude to it? When I was transferred in autumn 1934 to the SD Head Office, there was not yet a departmental head there and no specialist who had to deal with Jews. This was the case only in the course of 1936. During the trial and particularly within the cross-examination lasting for some 10 days, one of the three judges – or was it the attorney general – questioned me with regard to my attitude at that time to the programme of the "National Socialist German Workers' Party", whether it was known to me, and I must doubtless have known, that this party had regarded the battle against Jewry as a major issue, and so I must also have been an anti-Semite.

False Gods

I could answer this question very easily and truthfully by saying that I indeed knew the Jewish programme but I was never an anti-Semite. Now, those of the Israeli authorities with whom I had to deal continually were aware of the detailed circumstances that justified me in giving such an answer. I discussed this question also with a psychiatrist. It is customary that persons accused in big trials sit down in the course of the preliminary examination with such specialist doctors who then make their tests on the basis of the discussion. This discussion naturally presupposes a voluntary readiness on the part of the accused, for otherwise the test would finally be worthless.

Now, I wish to express my position with regard to this question; and I must return for a few moments to my parental house. My first mother died very early, my father married a second time. He had to do it, for we were five small children and there was much trouble with the housekeeper, the cook and parlour maid who had to conduct the household of my father during a two-year "motherless" period. As it happens, with my step-mother – who herself did not come directly from any Jewish family – Jewish relatives entered our family. Aunts, uncles, later cousins. When one is small, one automatically grows into one's environment. Our family, not only the immediate one, I mean the entire clan, belonged to the rare family groupings of which one could maintain that no one muddied the other's waters. It was a cheerful, warm association without malice, lies or deception. No matter whether it was a Jew, a person of Jewish origin, or a non-Jew.

My parents and my wider family were neither philo-Semites nor anti-Semites. The concept as such was fully alien to my family; it was never discussed in any form. My father also had Jews, among others, as friends. If they were Jews or not, they would have been befriended. My father worried as little about these things as about what was for dinner, so to speak. I still remember the Jewish hops merchant Taussig from Urfahr near Linz. He had an adjoining garden to ours on the slopes of the Pöstlingberg at that time, where we children went during the strawberry season into Taussig's compound and with his agreement and invitation, we children picked all his strawberries empty.

I was still a kid but I remember very well another Jewish friend of my father's, who, when he was the guest of my parents, always acted out the Marseillaise to me very fierily and sang, "Allons enfants de la patrie". He was a Frenchman by birth but for a long time a naturalised Austrian. In the primary school I came to sit with a Jew and we became friends. I in his parents' house, he in mine. Actually the friendship

Transfer to the SS Intelligence Service

lasted for a long time. To be precise, until we lost sight of each other through my departure from Linz on the Danube in 1933. Sometimes we met during travels, the last time in Grünau in the Alm valley at a barber's. It clearly made no impression on him that I had affixed the insignia of the NSDAP and it made no difference to me that he was a Jew. In the pub we drank our drinks and did not care at all about anything, whether it was about a Jew or a non-Jew.

My religious teacher, the Evangelical priest Tiebel in Linz, a celibate from East Prussia, often narrated to us during religious instruction about his counterpart comrade – as he often called him – the rabbi. Even as an SS lieutenant colonel I warmly kissed my half-Jewish cousin who visited me along with her father in my office and in the evening we emptied some nice bottles in a wine tavern in Berlin. And why should I not kiss my picture-perfect twenty year old half-Jewish cousin, I said to my regular deputy, SS major Günther; something like that cannot possibly be a national treason, but he had stricter ideas concerning this.

In Budapest I had distant relatives over for drinks. My cousin there, a psychiatrist, was married to a Jewish shoe industrialist from whom however she was divorced and just at the time when I was ordered to Budapest in 1944 she had fallen in love with a Jewish lecturer at the University of Budapest.

We sat together at table in the evening. My aunt, my cousin, her Jewish lover and I in the uniform of an SS lieutenant colonel. Just as I dealt with the Jews among the relations of my second mother, so I did with my wife's relations who were Czechs. Moreover I celebrate here in prison in Israel in a few day the thirtieth anniversary of our engagement; I have been married for 26 years. The relatives of my wife consist of Czech and former Austrians, that is, from Bohemia, with German as their mother-tongue. Her family has been settled in southern Bohemia since 1648 and a wooden beam in the yard reveals a still earlier date.

When I was officially transferred to Prague in 1939, I took up again the same cordial life along with my Czech brothers-in-law (they were the husbands of my wife's sisters). One of them had been an artillery officer during the time of the Czechoslovakian Republic, the other during the period of the occupation by us an active resistance member and Communist. His daughter, so my niece, was studying international trade in Moscow sometime after 1945.

False Gods

I know that both my brothers-in-law were fervent Czech patriots and I respected their nationalism. I would rather have bitten my tongue than exposed them or undertaken an arrest myself, which I would have been justified in doing. The bonds of family relationships were stronger than that to my gods although they too were not weak at all.

I did not hate either the Czech or the Jew, or anybody else. I also never experienced personal injury from anybody. Besides, my entire education and upbringing protected me from such feelings. I just did not have them. I lived in a world which was, for example, contrary to the close bonds of young corps cadets. Here the spirit of a Ritter von Schönerer[5] attended with his anti-Semitic songs and sermons. Here the word Aryan was pronounced with emphasis and clearly, a word that generally entered my vocabulary only later, very much later.

If I had not lived within such a personal and cordial family relationship, a relationship to which the family of my wife then allied itself, it is possible that I too would have been infected by such ideas. But I was not, and this is decisive.

Once in Linz, when scout leaders, coming from some convention, spent some days in our beautiful little provincial capital and the individual foreign scout leaders were distributed to local families, my father brought home a French scout leader as guest. At that time I spoke French very well – exactly like my second oldest brother Emil – since our mother spoke good French and English and wished to funnel the language effortlessly through conversation.

This young Frenchman was a wonderful person and, in the way of adolescents, I felt fortunate to regard him as a friend. We spent joyful carefree days together luxuriating in Romanticism, boyhood friendship and Pöstlingberg rose gardens and exchanged our association songs from the *Zupfgeigenhansel*,[6] the Wandervogel,[7]

---

5 Georg Ritter von Schönerer (1842-1921) was an Austrian anti-Semitic politician who, in his pan-Germanism, also opposed Catholicism in favour of Lutheranism.

6 A collection of folk songs published in 1909 that was popular among members of the Wandervogel and .other youth movements.

7 The Wandervogel (wandering bird) movement was established in 1901 by Herman Fölkersamb as a youth organisation that combined a love of Nature with a love of the fatherland. There was also a Jewish version of this movement called "Blau-Weiss" (blue-white).

Transfer to the SS Intelligence Service

and from elsewhere. And later, when the French became even for me simply the embodiment of Versailles, even then no power succeeded in producing in me even the slightest feeling of hatred against even an unknown Frenchman as such. And I learnt really quickly that the individual is not to be identified in any way with the nation or religion or politics. The terms race, nationality and such entered only relatively late into my vocabulary, as I have already stated in relation to the word "Aryan". And even there I understood the relationship between the individual and the concept no differently than I did that between the individual and the nation until then.

Obviously I am no saint; when during the war, from bomb attacks our entire city quarters lay in rubble and ashes and thousands of Germans perished and were scorched and shredded I launched innumerable coarse, and worse, curses against the bombers in the heat of passion. I also used rough, and worse, words in the heat of the passions unleashed by the press when the Israelis with the French and the English attacked Egypt. I am not different from others. But this is indeed a triggered reaction, to which one yields according to one's temperament and which then finds its end in words. This is related neither to the individual Englishman, Frenchman or Jew or North American, nor to the individual Russian, Pole, Yugoslav or to any other individuals.

It is – in any case it seems to me to be so - somehow natural, for only sick or apathetic men, or the wise, are immune to these human weaknesses, others are not, especially when these are, in the case of the examples I mentioned, aroused in a person practically through destruction and artificially through the press. So I could say that I was never an anti-Semite, for this is true.

During the so-called struggle time of the NSDAP, neither I nor the people who were intellectually connected to me took the party point about the battle against the Jews seriously even in the slightest way. I can say one did not even pay any attention to it. One did not feel bound to the party simply for the sake of its anti-Semitism. The points of attraction, as I already mentioned, lay even for me in an entirely different area. At least it was so in the Austrian Bergland.[8] I paid as little attention and it was for me so meaningless as the "battle" against the Church and the clergy.

---

8   Bergland is a municipality in Lower Austria.

False Gods

So this was my "self" when I spent my initial period in the SD Head Office in Berlin. Unspoiled, uncomplicated, neither lazy nor industrious; and a thick barracks-skin on the outside protected my inner life. Of course my activity was not to my liking but the constant world-view pointers to oath and obligation gradually permitted no other considerations to arise in me. I obeyed and remained bound to my gods in that I allowed myself to be ordered and did not kick against the pricks.

Half a year after my transfer to Berlin I married. I had been engaged since 15 August 1931 and the wedding took place on 21 March 1935 in Passau. Until my wife's furniture van came to Berlin from Czechoslovakia and the customs and other formalities were dealt with, we lived – it was for some three weeks – in a guesthouse and then moved into a nice small, one-floor, single-family house with garden in which we could live peacefully and comfortably.

During the day I did my service with the monotony of clockwork and during the evenings and weekends I worked in the garden, or we reconnoitred around Berlin and the neighbouring surroundings. Through a friend I had many small barrels of Pfalz wine supplied from his home district, and according to the weather and season I squeezed many a drop under the shadow of a Japanese beech tree or amongst the tasteful furnishings, the furniture of my wife, in the living room. The moment my service was over I let the gods lie where they were, and my exclusive interest was in the familiar togetherness. My official activity was also – as I frequently said – a drudgery. I had to catalogue and classify thousands of Freemasonic seals and coins; my sparse grasp of Latin was of some help. My boss was a lazy but, equal in rank, student at the Berlin university and had done no service and never been in the troops, and came from the civil, or general SS.

As "museum director" he was appointed departmental head of the Freemasonry Museum at 102 Wilhelmstraße, and I was assigned to him as his "specialist". Many distinctions and keeping a distance of three steps from anybody were the most outstanding characteristics of the "director", and we products of the barracks took the Mickey out of him forcefully. Especially when he, with ferocious seriousness formed a surrealistic "half-decomposed" body out of modelling clay and decorated it with larger than life worms and woodlice. And when he succeeded in making such a showpiece, it was put into a sarcophagus and exhibited on display in the "Andreas Hall".

Transfer to the SS Intelligence Service

Professor Schwarz-Bostaunitzel, pointed out, in his thundering Russian German accent, to the visitors of the museum the "tastelessness and the muddled decadence of the Freemasonic corruption", "and such people were then responsible for the education of our children", was his sarcastic conclusion and his physiognomy strongly recalled a bigoted Babylonian-Assyrian priest.

I saw how such nonsense was conducted here in order to make Freemasonry absurd and I thought to myself: if they find nothing else and must prepare a worm-ridden corpse with clay and plasticine, then there does not seem to be much behind it. I had heard the word "Freemasonry" for the very first time in April 1932. I mean I heard it for the first time academically and that occurred in this manner:

I was introduced by colleagues around the beginning of 1932 as a guest of the Linz "Schlaraffia", to the clubhouse in Linz of a regional association of the so-called "Mother Prague". Businessmen, doctors, lawyers, artists counted among their members. The tone there was witty and the people were harmlessly humorous. Dunce-cap-like headdresses with many orders and association decorations adorned the heads of the members. One had to greet a stuffed bird, an owl, which was mounted in a corner in a special place, on entry with one's hands on one's breast and bowing. An arch-marshal led the official part of the get-together and the piano was a harpsichord. Well, as I already said, harmlessly humourousy; Jews and Christians sat at the tables drinking beer and wine, that is, one would not have known who was a Jew and who a Christian, but in a small city anyway many already knew such things.

On 1 April 1932 I entered the SS. The then SS Oberscharführer,[9] Dr. Ernst Kaltenbrunner, lawyer in the chancellery after his father, was already a significant personality within the Austrian NSDAP. He wanted to know if I was in any union or association, and if so, in which and why. And I said to him that I socialised with the Schlaraffen. 'The Freemasonic bunch are a very dangerous group', he said to me.

Now he was at that time not yet the chief of the Security Police and the SD, nor a general of the Police and the Waffen SS and not yet member of the parliament. So I could tell him that I knew nothing of Freemasonry since I had never heard of it up to that time, but it was certainly not a dangerous group, that much I already knew.

---

9   SS first sergeant

False Gods

Kaltenbrunner and I knew each other already a long time from the streets. We greeted each other and spoke about the events of the day and hour. Our fathers often had to deal with each other on business. But I could dismiss the entire matter since I explained that no more importance was to be placed on my attendance at the Linz Schlaraffia because I had at a late hour and in a mellow mood invited the Upper Austrian humorous writer Franz Resl, who was at that time likewise in a mellow mood, for a bottle of wine in the Rose tavern in Linz. He was an arch Schlaraffer. I was just a minor guest, I was 26 years old at that time, and he somewhere between fifty and sixty; I was a nobody but he was a significant writer, even if actually little known beyond Austria's borders. But in spite of everything: this insolence of mine overstepped the limits of that which was normal. That was my first experience of "Freemasonry".

Thus, although Anti-Semitism was fixed in the party programme, I remained unreceptive to it, not through knowledge or desire, but simply for the reason that it did not belong to the world of my ideas, I was not able to do anything with it. I had not got round in those years to reading many books. Much to the worry of my father. I had not, through indolence, grappled with any "isms" and personally I had no enemies, either Jews or non-Jews.

I had not read the racial doctrine of Günther[10] and Rosenberg's *Mythos of the twentieth century*[11] or Mathilde Ludendorff.[12] I had never fallen for mysticism. For me up to the present neither have the light-eyed Nordic racial representatives embodied light nor the dark-eyed Semites darkness. I have always considered, and still consider, such things as rank nonsense. To be sure, Himmler and others burrowed and drilled into these concepts. Even small servants like the afore mentioned Professor Schwarz-Bostaunitzel revelled in his world of mystical ideas and oscillated among his various geometric figures to make this entire matter attractive in the manner of the old alchemists.

---

10 Hans F.K. Günther (1891-1968) was a racial theorist who held professorships during the Weimar Republic as well as the Third Reich. He championed the Nordic race as the most gifted of the European races.

11 Alfred Rosenberg's *Mythos of the Twentieth Century* was a racialist survey of history and culture that was published in 1930.

12 Mathilde Ludendorff (1877-1966) was the wife of General Erich Ludendorff and participated in the nationalist movements of her time especially through the formation of a society called 'Bund für Gotteserkenntnis' (Association for the Knowledge of God). She was, as a trained psychiatrist, opposed to occultism and, as a Germanic racialist, opposed to Christianity.

Transfer to the SS Intelligence Service

His diagrams, pentagrams and hexagrams, represented in the most diverse forms and significances, decorated with dozens of further symbols, found no place in my soldier's mind which was delighted by wine and beer.

When I was at that time in the SD Head Office, Himmler had set up for one such modern alchemist a small laboratory in the park where we did our morning exercises. He was supposed to make gold there. He was said to be able to do this. This gold-maker was remarkably called Tausend.[13]

Himmler was on the way to forming the SS into an order with special traditions in which ideas of the old Teutonic Knights mingled with Romanticism, belief in god and many other things. The brewers of this mixture sat in the SS Race and Settlement Head Office and these ideas were pumped into the order from there.

In 1936 I spoke with SS Untersturmführer von Mildenstein who had been working for a short while in the SD Head Office. He had established a Jewish department and now sought personnel to help him in this expert field. He told me that by profession he was an engineer, had been in Palestine and now needed another expert. He asked me whether I would be interested in performing this task. I was interested. At that time I would have accepted anything if only I were released from my damned seals and coins which hung round my neck.

The department was called II 112; the chief departmental head remained the same as before, so the personnel department of the SD Head Office did not have to be consulted in a major way but just an order report needed to be made to it. Mr. von Mildenstein retained for himself the handling of the Zionists, I had to deal with the Jewish orthodoxy and a third man with the assimilated Jews. In addition, there were three more assistants as secretaries and file-clerks. Mr. von Mildenstein directed it all.

My first activity in this new office was the reading of a work by Adolf Böhm. It was a detailed description of the work and aims of the World Zionist Organisation. I had to prepare a short synopsis of the contents. This was my first conscious contact with Jewry.

---

13 The name means 'Thousand'. Franz Tausend (1884-1942) was a self-proclaimed alchemist who initially obtained finanical backing for his fraudulent projects from some National Socialist members but was in 1931 sentenced to jail for fraud and again in 1938.

False Gods

Mildenstein had a liberal and tolerant mind, far from all fanaticism, mysticism and radicalism. Originally from the Znojmo region of Moravia, he was always friendly, calm and had a mild temper. He did not consider the Jewish question from the racial and religious standpoint but solely from a political viewpoint. He was my first and, at the same time, most important master and teacher in this field and I made his views of things my own since they impressed and convinced me. I retained this view until the end.

Unfortunately von Mildenstein left a few months later. He was one of the few who succeeded in doing so. To be sure, his profession came to his aid thereby, otherwise it would certainly not have worked. He was an expert in road-building; as such he received an order to study the highways in North America. When he returned from his study tour, he was co-opted by some other ministry since at that time the national highway construction had to be expedited with all force.

His position as departmental head was taken over by a young man who however was after a short while drafted for the military and, with the takeover of the Jewish department of the SD Head Office by Wisliceny, and later by Six, a period of stability entered the office for a long time. Then, in the following period, the departmental heads changed one after the other in quick succession. Each one had issued his own system as well as standards, then he was removed and another entered in his place. Finally, Dr. Six took over the central department and appointed one of his confidants as head of the Jewish department.

In the course of this period the arrangement of case files began, one case-card index was set up, a general file storage was established, and running reports for the superiors were the main work that we had to perform. All other work was subordinated to the submission of reports.

Himmler and Heydrich must at that time have been very proud of their information apparatus, the SD Head Office. A document that I have before me from that time shows the visits that took place and one sees that, within a few days, the office was visited by 150 officers of the war academy, that Heydrich then showed the SD Head Office to the Reich Foreign Minister von Ribbentrop, a further 150 officers of the Reich War Ministry are recorded, as well as the visit of the Chief of the Jugoslav Secret Police.

Transfer to the SS Intelligence Service

At that time my main work consisted of reading specialist newspapers and journals as well as in the assimilation of relevant works. The newspapers were laid out in piles and I was always annoyed when I saw the Yiddish newspapers printed in Hebrew letters, for nobody could read them. So I set out one day to buy from a bookshop a textbook for the study of the Hebrew language. It was called *Hebrew for Everybody* and a certain Samuel Kaleko had written it. After a year of self-study I could not advance further and the solo cramming had become boring for me, so I asked for approval through official channels of a grant for further instruction from a rabbi for the customary hourly payment of three marks. Apparently for political reasons this grant was not approved. Possibly the decision would have been a positive one if I had suggested they instead lock up a rabbi until he had communicated the language to me. Indeed at that time people were locked up continuously by the Secret State Police, but the idea of such an action did not even occur to me, let alone that it would have given me pleasure to gain the deficient knowledge in this way.

Once every year, in autumn, the gods held a military parade. They descended from their Olympus and showed themselves broadly to the masses whom they mobilised. Military parades, SA and SS parades, marches of the other party organisations. Conferences, congresses, resolutions, speeches, and the issuing of slogans. The leadership informed their believers what it had achieved and what it planned.

It would be wrong to say that they had done nothing. They really did not laze around, and they had within the shortest time done so much for the German people, especially in economic terms, that the powerful jubilant applause of the masses was genuine. Even Goebbels could not conjure up artificially such a noisy, impulsive enthusiasm.

I was for the first time at such a Party-Day, which took place always in Nuremberg; I was sent there officially. Not to take part in the parades and march-pasts, not to listen to speeches and attend conferences, but to serve in an information-gathering capacity. For the SD Head Office was at that time nothing but a single large strictly directed and organised espionage organisation. It was under nobody else but Himmler, and its founder Heydrich had to direct it on his orders. A large boycott movement with its headquarters in North America fought against the National Socialist German Reich. Not without reason; this was, already at that time, clear even to me. When, during the troop training period, we were drilled to such an extent that we were flayed, as we used to say in the crude infantrymen's jargon, the

False Gods

Enthusiastic crowds greet Hitler, Nuremberg 1936.

momentary sufferings produced in us infantry men frightful thoughts relating to retaliation after the service period against the instructors drilling us. Of course, at the end of the daily activity, following the saying, "one tolerates sufferings that one has already undergone", these resolutions completely cooled again just as quickly as they had arisen and burned out with one or more litres of beer in the canteen.

But when I saw, and read what the Jewish laws department of the Reich Foreign Ministry had issued since 1935 I was able to understand the boycott movement quite well. It was a quite natural reaction. When I consider that, at that time, a Berlin rabbi called Prinz departed from his community to emigrate to North America and said that he wished to collaborate there in the creation of a powerful reservoir from which Jewry would receive force and aid, I, who was according to orders always one of his audience, knew very well what Prinz meant by that and I could not at all disagree with him.

The regional criminal secretary of the Berlin Secret State Police office who had to supervise the meeting according to orders relied on me, and I on him in case of a possible necessary dispersal and arrest of the speaker. I did nothing of the sort, for my thoughts prohibited me to turn to the criminal officer in this regard since I, as mentioned, had to agree with the speaker when considered from his point of view, and there were thousands upon thousands of Prinz's, so that the arrest of

Transfer to the SS Intelligence Service

a single one would not have solved the problem anyway. According to the order that I received, I later made my report describing everything truthfully and even giving my considerations broad space. I never heard anything about it again; Prinz emigrated to North America.

Indeed I did not create the Nuremberg Laws, and did not help in doing so. I had nothing to do with it since I belonged to an information institution and not to any police apparatus with executive powers.

That the gods had fallen victim to a disastrous mistake seemed clear, but there are and were negative effects after every revolution and then one always said to oneself that a barking dog seldom bites. The goal of the measures seemed to be to promote the emigration of the Jews from the Reich, but of course these measures were not very suited for that. The solution of a *systematically* directed emigration went through my mind too. For, in the mean time, I had now read that the Jews in the course of history in many European countries always had to serve as scapegoats when the masses could be distracted at their expense from momentary difficulties or ills of some sort.

So a directed and systematically organised emigration was of all evils the least; and the laws would no longer harm the Jews who had emigrated. Much worse was the distress that they were subjected to *until* the time of emigration. But here I could not restrain either the gods or the demigods, I did not have any possibility of doing so. I had to work in my sector on information services and to transmit the received announcements and communiqués officially in the form of reports. My superiors put together these mosaic pieces coming from many departments, with their revisions, into an image and presented it to the demigods to be acknowledged according to their pleasure. In this form even the gods could observe "images" amongst themselves.

So I was now in Nuremberg. It was 1937. There was a festive party-day atmosphere, massive sports fields, stadiums holding hundreds of thousands, noisy throngs in the old intimate alleys and lanes within the walls of mediaeval Nuremberg. The red colour of thousands of flags glowed in the light of the splendid early autumn sun.

A policeman must - if he wants to hear something and obtain agents, co-workers, confidants or informers, whatever the specialist terms in this field may be called - creep in everywhere. At that time for our sort it was particularly the nice small smoky beer-filled beer pubs in which entire groups of foreign helpers placed at their disposition were

False Gods

hosted, managed and well taken care of. Here therefore, with some luck, one came into contact, through connections and relationships, with visitors from distant countries.

From a document that I have before me I quote the following words which I at that time used among others in my official travel report: "The large part gave the impression of being more or less questionable persons some of whom are obsessed with the *idée fixe* that they were at one time called to be leaders of parties and organisations in their countries." Only a single person found "favour in my eyes", a North American citizen who wished to have excellent relations with the leaders of the "Anti-Nazi League", the command office of the boycott organisation against Germany.

But since this case too was not very clear, especially in relation to the question whether the SD Head Office was indeed responsible for this, I observed in conclusion that I requested instructions on whether the SD should itself deal with this matter or whether it should delegate it to the Propaganda Ministry. I never heard anything more about that, so that I assume that my superiors decided in their counsel to delegate the matter.

Some days later I and my superior departmental chief undertook an official trip to Palestine and Egypt. The train brought us through Poland and Romania to Constanța[14] and from there we sailed on the "Romania" to Constantinople, Piraeus, Beirut, Haifa and Alexandria. Mosques, the Acropolis, Mt. Carmel, the Graeco-Roman Museum in Alexandria were visited, and likewise the Egyptian Museum in Cairo. We saw the pyramids of Giza as well as those of Sakkara, the former sacred animal graves; an excursion into the Egyptian desert was undertaken, another into the Libyan desert. The Pharaoh Tutankhamen who died three and a half thousand years ago, along with his treasures, which were drawn out of their long sleep thanks to the skill of the archaeologists and exhibited to an amazed posterity, gladdened my eyes and understanding, and I too could only be awed. Be awed by the high culture of the men of that grey antiquity and my thoughts lost themselves far from that which "affirmed the state and the present" in zones and regions in which the changeability and the eternal becoming and passing of life, indeed of all being, played the leading role. All vain hope and effort seemed, on glimpsing the past millennia, nothing but a fleeting human condition and I envied at that

---

14 Constanța is an ancient city in Romania situated on the Black Sea coast.

Transfer to the SS Intelligence Service

moment all archaeologists and geologists to whom, in my opinion, it is probably granted to luxuriate undisturbed day after day in such thoughts and considerations, because for our sort these can only be oasis-like moments of joy in the hubbub of daily life. But our bosses had not sent us on an official trip for all of these things but – as always – the affair was based on a gathering of information, on a collection of political news.

Through the intermediary of the representative of the official "German News Agency" in Jerusalem, Dr. Reichert, a Jewish functionary from the Palestine visited me in Berlin months before our travel. According to the instructions of my superiors, the visitor was declared to be a guest of the Reich Security Service Head Office, and I received the order to take care of him. We ate together in the "Traube" at the Zoo and conversed, for each wished to get from the other that information which he lacked in his own case. My interest was in the Zionist life in Palestine. The end of the story was an invitation from the guest to me to visit him in Palestine.

I obtained an order to accept this invitation. That was how the trip came about which my immediate superior departmental head of that time joined. I travelled as "editor of the *Berliner Tageblatt*" and my superior as "student of the international studies faculty of the University of Berlin", whose dean was our mutual next higher superior at that time. We could indeed have, when all is said and done, travelled at that time as members of the Security Service Head Office, for the person inviting me indeed knew who I was and had recently anyway announced to the English secret service from what nest these two birds were; exactly as, among us, a member of the Secret Service or one of the $2^{\text{ème}}$ Bureau,[15] when they came to Germany, were also as a rule known very quickly. We did nothing against one another, we were very polite to one another, only we did not assist the colleague from the other side, or if we did, then there was a special reason for it that lay in reciprocity. But it was after all peacetime.

We were in Haifa for about six hours and then travelled according to our programme on our Romanian steamer to Alexandria and wished to start our actual Palestine visit within the next fortnight or three weeks. But then the English regretted that they were not in a position to issue a visa for this purpose. Good, then the mountain must come

---

15   The Deuxième Bureau de l'État-major général (Second Office of the General Staff) was France's external military intelligence agency from 1871 to 1940.

False Gods

to Mohammed. Dr. Reichert and the Jewish functionary were invited by us to Egypt. The representative of the German News Agency[16] in Cairo joined us so that we five men made up a rather good news team. We boarded in the Mena Hotel, near the pyramids of Giza and the "Nuremberg Laws" were far from us.

However I myself did not get my money's worth with this official trip to the "Near East" - when I consider the official aspect – because through the English prohibition I did not get to see Jewish life in Palestine. Privately and personally I had experienced a fine enrichment through an abundance of experiences. My travel companion, who was my superior, originally coming from the newspaper establishment, was able to record more success for himself from an official point of view, for the economic and political announcements which he obtained first-hand insofar as they concerned the Near East were satisfactory for him.

Now, after this stay of many weeks in the sunny lands, we returned to the late autumn, almost winter landscape of our "fortress Germany". They say that if anybody undertakes a trip then he can converse, but he can also posit comparisons. We returned to Berlin through Italy and Switzerland. I saw much tolerance, much liberalism, and that was what struck me most. I knew it from my long Austrian period, from my parental house, from the school, in short, all of life in Austria had been a big tolerance commission as Emperor Joseph II may have dreamed of, if I consider the period until about 1932. But in my case, it was already lightly covered over by the more than five years in between of totalitarianism that I had lived through. Not obliterated; on the contrary, the travel experiences removed once again a large part of the whitewashing. All at once I saw the *Stürmer* again more clearly – even though it was neither valued nor read in the SD Head Office; I saw its wallowing in pornography; in the confused mediaeval mysticism of the worst type. I saw the Reich Ministry of the Interior in its industrious fabrication of laws and ordinances, the Secret State Police in its arrest orders, the Propaganda Ministry in its publication of the prohibition of the Jews from using the "benches in the park", the Reich Foreign Ministry in its activity of excluding the Jews from economic life, and the Foreign Office in its obstructive work with regard to the emigration of Jews, even though that was in itself wished for. But the Reich or its leadership wanted it – so I have always

---

16 The Deutsche Nachrichtenbüro was the official press agency of National Socialist Germany.

Transfer to the SS Intelligence Service

German Foreign Minister Joachim von Ribbentrop

supposed – and the majority of the Jews considering the hardening of life hoped to strive for the same goal. And the Security Head Office obtained news and fabricated reports. All that seemed to me like a cat that bites its own tail.

For example, an international conference took place in Evian and the British ambassador in Berlin discussed with the German Reich Foreign Minister von Ribbentrop whether the Reich government was ready to work together with the other interested states in the solution of the question of emigrants, especially in the promotion of the emigration of Jews of German citizenship, because no country was ready to accept the emigrating German Jews if they were without means - whether therefore the Reich government was ready to cooperate in the transfer of capital into Jewish hands. Since the Reich government did not fundamentally place any obstacles to the promotion of emigration one would have had to suppose that such an inquiry on the part of the official British offices would have found joyful agreement.

Not so in the case of Ribbentrop. He informed the British ambassador that he would have to refuse all cooperation with other interested states since the emigration of Jews was an internal German problem. Even the question whether Germany could facilitate a transfer of capital

False Gods

into Jewish hands had to be answered in the negative. So the question of a cooperation with the powers meeting in Evian did not arise for Germany. The Secretary of State, Weiszäcker, sent this opinion on 8 July 1938 to ten relevant German embassies and consulates for their acknowledgement. So, instead of an alleviation of emigration there remained a handicap and a hardening. Instead of that, there was issued a call of the Foreign Office to all diplomatic and professional consular representations abroad to send reports for the establishment of a card-index on all government members, members of parliament, economists, scientists, high officers and journalists, insofar as they were Jewish, of Jewish origin, or Freemasons. In a telegram of Kennedy's[17] to the Secretary of State in Washington of December 1938 Ribbentrop, in his loud and most undiplomatic verbal abuses against Jewry, comes off as anything but good.

At the beginning of 1938 we departmental heads in the SD Head Office received from our departmental chief an instruction to collect materials for a memorandum in which it was to be explained that the Jewish question is not to be solved at present, on account of financial difficulties, etc., and that one must work to find a foreign political solution such as was already negotiated between Poland and France. At that time I wrote the following:

1. "Wait for the results of the census."

2. "With the conditions remaining the same, in 10 years there will be in Germany only around 60,000 Jews."

3. "When the poorer Jews have emigrated, the richer Jews will then be de-capitalised with the help of State Police measures."

That was the situation. In this way was it carried out. It was the cat which, curling up in a circle, always bites its own tail.

At that time I was also involved in a battle against the economic restrictions that were set up against the Jews among which counted the foreign exchange requirements. I held the view that the "poor" Jew wishes to emigrate as gladly and quickly as the "rich" Jew. For both of them the quicker it was, the better it was to go abroad, and even

---

17   Joseph Kennedy (1888-1969), the father of President John F. Kennedy, was United States Ambassador to the United Kingdom, under President Roosevelt, from 1938 to 1940.

the Reich government wished for that. Whether it was out of envy or niggardliness, out of stupidity or lack of understanding, or out of blind hatred, most of these offices did *not* promote this emigration but, consciously and unconsciously, restricted it.

Why did the Reich have to take away money from the rich Jew and incorporate it into the Reich treasury instead of financing the emigration with part of his money? Naturally – so I thought – the "rich" Jew should receive more since it was indeed his money, but he should make a part of his money available for the purpose of financing Jewish religious communities and for the financing of Jews without wealth. For emigration was expensive. Travel costs, minimum financial requirements for visas, etc. Instead of a ten-year long drifting, an emigration could, in my view, be arranged quickly and briskly and the Jews could go to a new country in this way in possession of their health and physical strength. The immigrant countries anyway hardly accepted anyone who had grown ill through a gruelling wait lasting for years. No, insofar as this was practised at that time, it did not work; and Ribbentrop made a serious mistake here although he was the Reich Foreign Minister and should have known that. He could have informed himself through any travel agency proprietor better than through his legation counsellors and under-secretaries of state.

Besides, I suggested in this proposed solution, as its last point, monthly discussions between all offices involved in this matter so that the constricting strife between the authorities would stop and, finally, ownership of their own land for the Jews and added in brackets there: "Madagascar". But all this was hopeless with the obstinacy of the German bureaucracy. I do not wish to say *German* bureaucracy, *every* bureaucracy is equally bad, equally stubborn. Only the information services of all countries tend rather to action; it lies in the nature of their task. Even the SD Head Office was at that time nowhere near as bureaucratised as it was to become. Naturally every bureaucratic work demands its measure of orderliness, that is clear; but it should not at all become a goal in itself.

Transfer to Vienna

A short while after the "Reunification of Austria with the German Reich" I was transferred to Vienna, to direct the emigration of Jews as departmental head of the "Danube" SS primary command. It was spring 1938. But what I saw when I went to Vienna was a destroyed

False Gods

Jewish organisational structure. Locked and sealed by the Secret State Police. The Jewish functionaries were in prison. The Jews wanted to emigrate but nobody worried about them. They were sent from official to official. They stood in queues for half a day or more and then had to hear that this office was, from the previous day, no longer responsible for their case. No system, no order; the result was annoyance, anger and resentment on both sides, if not worse.

At first I held talks for the assessors and governmental counsellors on how they prevented any emigration. On that there was not much more to be said other than by following the "current trend". Then I outlined to them my plan which had been approved by my superiors. Release of the Jewish functionaries, re-opening of all those Jewish organisations insofar as they were serviceable for the emigration. Further, the approval of a Jewish newspaper in which could be read everything worth knowing about emigration and the things connected to it. The raising of Reichsmark sums for the initial financing of the Jewish organisations, the establishment of helpers and the institution of Jewish welfare offices for the purpose of the care of the sick and the old.

When I had activated the Jewish organisational life in this way and visited the Secret State Police in Vienna for agreement with regard to the "new line" I applied there for a position that had become free, of departmental head at the SD sub-division in Linz on the Danube. My parents lived in this city and I had grown up there. I now wanted to go back there. Of course it was the lowest position within the structure of the Security Service but I wanted to be back home and, who knows, perhaps I would have one day obtained permission to leave my service on taking over the parental business.

Fate. I always say that nobody can jump over his own shadow. For my boss, Prof. Six, received information about my preference and so he wrote on 16 May 1938 to my then superior, SS Oberführer[18] Naumann in Vienna that I was in no way to go away from Vienna, since, in case I did not wish to remain in Vienna, he would have me transferred back to Berlin, if necessary through the Chief of the SD Head Office.

Yes, that was how it was already in 1938, in peacetime. I was no longer master of my liberty, I had to obey and do that which I was ordered to do. Later I often said to my sons, "See that you never become officers,

---

18   Senior leader

Transfer to Vienna

for then you will never again be free". In the meantime I had been promoted to officer and my bond to the gods had become even more binding than before.

So, according to orders, I had to remain in Vienna. The restrictions to which the Jews were subjected were increasingly palpable. The Office of the Reich Commissioner for the Reunification of Austria with the German Reich was busily active in bringing out ordinance after ordinance, even in the "Jewish" sector. The authorities treated the Jews roughly and unprofessionally, to put it mildly, according to the instructions issued from higher places, so that a person wishing to make his emigration papers complete never got anywhere. For, a part of the documents, such as, for example, the "tax clearance certificate", had a validity of only six weeks, after which they became invalid and the standing in queues to obtain a new certificate had to begin again. In the meantime, however, other papers then became invalid so that it was like an eternal screw.

The Jewish political functionaries complained of their distress to me. Dr. Löwenherz, Dr. Rottenberg and commercial counsellor Storfer had new issues daily that they brought to me. The complaint against me said that the documents would indeed prove that mine was the responsible office for everything, in the truest meaning of the word, related to the Jewish question in Vienna. Although it was not accurate, as I shall soon show, I cannot quite disagree with the complaint so clearly. For, one only needs to take into account the abundance of file notes prepared by Dr. Löwenherz for the director of the Jewish Religious Community in Vienna on the regular consultations with me at that time – insofar as one deals with those that were drawn up *at that time* and not after 1945. He came to me with literally each and every thing.

Now, it is far from me to want to make myself out to be better than I was. But why then would Löwenherz, Rottenberg, Storfer and others, high Jewish political functionaries, have come to me of all people? At that time I was of the rank of a lieutenant, later senior lieutenant and then captain; there were positions of far greater significance. My official position was only that of a departmental head in an SD primary division, and not even in the executive but only in the information service.

My language at that time was hard, or so the witnesses of 1960 and 1961 say. In fact I must confess that my tone was of a barracks sort.

False Gods

And yet I know that it was free from the insulting tone, free from the bullying, free from the shouting, in short, free from all the background music that the common civilian too gladly attributes to all "barracks speech".

How then would it have been possible that one can read even today in a Löwenherz memorandum how he came to me with complaints and informs me dolefully that the Jews were treated *"roughly"* in the housing office of the city of Vienna? This presupposes that the Jews were treated *roughly neither* by me *nor* by my officers, junior officers and men who were subordinated to me at that time. And in every case where I could not perceive that I had any responsibility, and moreover not even the Police were responsible, I made a telephone call or visited the authority in charge in order to request, even then in my "barracks tone", a remedy for that which Löwenherz pressed upon me. I did not always succeed in it, but I tried. But the Jewish functionaries must finally have got along with the barracks man in a civilised manner, for even they could speak openly with me without having to consider their words ten times beforehand for fear of losing their teeth. And one could not do this at that time everywhere without running into trouble - that the functionaries already knew.

The Reich pressed for emigration. The Jews wanted to emigrate, and I did all to achieve this. Where I was responsible for a case this was anyway clear. Where I was not responsible, I complained and tried to deal with it. So it came about that people pestered me and demonstrated to me the sources of a lame red-tape system that could not function any more on account of its sheer pedantry. And a centralisation of the official work was proposed to me by the Jews. Well, this was precisely where one always got on the wrong side of the authorities, no matter in which country of the world.

Something like that which now went through my barracks brain had never yet been, even in the history of Prussian German administration.

I thought to myself, everything that had to do bureaucratically with the issuing of papers to emigrating Jews would run under a single roof and under the direction of the SD. Then it must be possible for such a damned passport to be ready in a good 48 hours instead of in 10 or 12 weeks or even longer.

No sooner thought than done. I reported all this to my boss, the inspector of the Security Police and SD, who at the same time

Transfer to Vienna

jointly directed the "Danube" SD primary division. He cleared the necessary paths, conducted the necessary discussions with the Reich Commissioner Bürckel, and through official ordinances a "Central Office for Jewish Emigration in Vienna" was created to which all the authorities concerned had to assign their consultants.

The leader of the "Danube" SD primary division was the director. I was entrusted by him with the execution of the task as the order indicated in the terminology of that time.

In fact passports were now ready in two, at most three, days. One hundred and thirty thousand or one hundred and forty thousand such passports could be issued within the period of roughly a year.

Now, if the prosecution in the trial against me maintains that it was a forced emigration with all its bad accompanying conditions it is indeed right in that. I also cannot describe it any other way. But this should also be taken into consideration: I did not order the forced emigration, even though I considered it under the given circumstances as the best alternative and even as the best possibility of a solution considering the position that had been adopted by the Reich government with regard to the Jews. The Jewish political functionaries with whom I constantly discussed this matter were of the same opinion considering the tendency with regard to the Jews.

I did not think the matter up myself. I must have drawn the inspiration from somewhere. I could not have drawn this from the Reich offices; for that I need only to point to Ribbentrop's official position. And if one says further, 'Yes, at that time there was no trace at all of an annihilation of the Jews and nevertheless Eichmann set up here an emigration tempo that was horrifying', I must simply say that the result alone counts. And no "ifs" and "buts".

The issuing of passports and the necessary paperwork processes now ran within an uncomplicated machinery. Emigration costs much money - a lot of money. And from where should one obtain this with the general impoverishment of the Jewish masses. They were indeed excluded from the entire economic and commercial life, let us say, in short, simply from all fields of life. There was the necessary financial requirement in foreign exchange, the travel costs. Funds had to be raised by the Religious Community in Vienna for the most urgent aid cases through their welfare office; the officers and employees of this Jewish religious community, of some 500 and more, had to be paid.

False Gods

No Reich office helped, they were not bothered about anything. These offices only ordered, "Out with the Jews".

Löwenherz came to me. Indeed I could have said, what did I care about all this. I could have said this even earlier. Perhaps I would have stood in a better position today, for I would not have actually allowed myself to get so deep into these matters. I wished to tolerate Löwenherz and Rottenberg and Storfer and they wished to do the same doubtless with me. So we got to know one another increasingly more closely. And so they discharged everything onto me. Literally everything. They had found in me a man who listened to them for hours without losing patience. Not as they were accustomed to with other officials, and in addition it so happened that what was arranged with me actually worked. So now there was financial distress.

I myself had no money; personally I had always been poor, and remained so. I had no bookkeeping strengths; account books and such had always been a torture to me. And it was a matter of indifference to me if I had one hundred or a hundred and fifty marks in my pocket. I had no personal interest in money. In my house my wife administered and economised; I was glad of that and in this way I did not have to worry about these things.

And now suddenly I had begun with this torturous matter. But I must say that when things are the way they are, one also deals with things that one does not understand. And in my ignorance of finance I did not imagine the matter to be so difficult. For only such a person could, in his innocence with regard to such things, accomplish something like that which I now initiated. The Jewish functionaries merely had to travel abroad - for that I obtained for them the approval –, request the Jewish aid organisations for dollars and return to Vienna thereafter. Then the religious community sold a part of these dollar amounts to the Jews who still had much money at a several times higher value than the official exchange rate and with these monetary proceeds they paid wages for their employees, aid, travel costs for the poor Jews, and gave them as a loan that sum of dollars that they needed as an emigration financial requirement. Many of the immigrant countries then sensed a business in this and they constantly raised the immigration fees. Everything went well, but I did not think of the fact that we stood under the strictest foreign exchange controls. Even this I could only finally deal with by applying pressure, since I had invited to Vienna the Reichsbank counsellor Wolf from Berlin - he was working in the Reich Ministry of Economics in the foreign exchange department. We

Transfer to Vienna

Josef Löwenherz, in the parish hall of the Jewish Community of Vienna, 1938.

already knew each other from Berlin. I explained my plan to him. He then discussed this matter with his state secretary, who approved it. This was good, for people already complained to me that my practice must lead to a theoretical undervaluation of the Reichsmark since the dollar would to a certain extent be officially flogged to black market prices in Mark values. Thereby and - as one can further gather from the Löwenherz file memos - by means of other financial businesses, the financial part of this affair was accomplished.

On 10 November 1938, after the shooting of a German embassy counsellor in Paris the Reich's political leadership, called for immediate retaliation. The official reports at that time reveals that, with a few exceptions, the offices of the Secret State Police and the SD, were notified of this only when the synagogues and the houses of the Israeli Religious Community were already burning. Jewish shops were smashed and Jews were locked up in their thousands.

The gods had clearly transformed themselves into false idols. These orders were not only nonsensical, they were criminal. But this time the consequences of the "orders for the Reich Night of Broken Glass" had an effect in their stupidity even on me. For what I had rebuilt with difficulty in Austria, that is, a functioning Jewish organisation with the mutual goal of Jewish emigration, was all shattered in one night. Office equipment, file cards, files, foreign correspondence, in short everything, fell victim to the flames. In addition, there was the arrest of Jewish functionaries. I did what I could, to save what could be saved, but it was not much. Eventually I managed to have the functionaries released. I shall spare myself the presentation of details since it would seem to be too much like self-adulation. I had however to act, and to rebuild all again.

These orders for destruction led to even sharper measures against the Jews. Even in financial terms. An ordinance of the foreign exchange office in Vienna declared that Jews could only withdraw four hundred Reichsmarks per month from their bank accounts. This would have been a devastating blow to the Jewish Religious Community, if this ordinance had been extended to them. But they were excepted and could withdraw any amount from their accounts according to their needs. The Central Office for Jewish Emigration always gave its endorsement in the case of withdrawals of higher sums.

In the case of younger Jews, proof of training in a practical occupation was often the prerequisite for the issuing of an emigration approval. So such offices had to be created and here application had to be made to the regional state and party offices for approval for that. Naturally, given the uncoordinated mandates of the diverse office bearers, such efforts finally remained incumbent on me.

For example, in one of the memos of Dr. Löwenherz, it says, on his consultation with me on 9 March 1939: "The leader of the Palestine Office received a commission to report on the possibility of the establishment of an agricultural Hachshara (training) on the Markhof property, and to indicate which state and party offices were for and against the establishment of this Hachshara."

In the same file note of Dr. Löwenherz and Dr. Rottenberg it says then further: "SS Hauptsturmführer[19] Eichmann declared that he was ready to grant the removal of the mortal remains of Herzl to Palestine, though under the precondition that through this inducement the controlling Jewish organisations would create new immigration possibilities for 8,000 persons from Austria, and he commissioned those readied for this to conduct the necessary negotiations regarding their stay abroad."

---

19   SS captain

Transfer to Vienna

Naturally I could not by myself grant approval here. As everybody knows, many paths to the authorities responsible for it are necessary for such an approval of exhumation, and at that time, "after the Reich Night of Broken Glass", I also had great difficulties with the most diverse authorities in all things that dealt with Jews.

In retrospect it is always very easy to represent someone – I speak now of myself – as being endowed with full dictatorial powers and to manipulate this representation in such a way that this man is made completely responsible for everything. It is more interesting, easier to read and is under circumstances also not at all inopportune. Only – again referring to myself – it is not accurate and is therefore not true.

When, 22 years later, I consider the documents of those times, I must ask myself how a reasonable man can attribute to me of all people hatred and a will to annihilate. On the contrary, I must have certainly been well-disposed towards the Jewish-political functionaries; naturally without any personal hatred, for one can speak almost of a mutual officially conditioned trust that is to be discerned without difficulty from and between the lines of those documents.

Once, one morning, there came to me the jurist from the Israeli Religious Community in Vienna, who, with other Jewish officials of this institution, was attached to the Central Office for Jewish Emigration. I have forgotten his name, so I shall refer to him as 'Dr X'.

During the night the State Police had made arrests. We discussed the event and Dr X then said: "An insolent Jewish lout attacks the harmless German lion", and in the same breath he said that he was aware, however, of to whom he could say such a thing.

I said to him that he was indeed right in his perception but if he uttered such a thing elsewhere he would perhaps have to say to himself afterwards in a police cell, "If you had kept your mouth shut you would have been a wise man"; this translation was given to me by one of my Latin teachers for "*Si tacuisses philosophus mansisses*". On the other hand, my engineering professor once, on the occasion of a statistics test, said to me, "With the brain shut out, the nose runs along without sensation". And I said to the jurist that I would indeed not want him to have to make such complaints to himself one day since that would not serve either of us, for it would "never be forgotten" and I would have to act on his behalf.

False Gods

But my task is not to point to these passages in detail; whether professionals do this one day or leave it aside is a matter of indifference to me. I was besides formally something like a complaints office to which people could come with all concerns and I certainly maintained an objective correctness with regard to Jews and non-Jews; and quite certainly they did not come to me full of personal fear.

Of course it cannot be denied that later, with the increasing war-events, the ordinances and orders even of my superiors which I had to forward to the offices concerned became steadily sharper and more radical.

But it had not yet gone so far in Vienna. Though the increasing pressure of the state and party leadership in Austria for an accelerated dejudaisation became increasingly palpable.

If I had really been the "hater", the "bloodhound", the "bad arrow", as many contemporaries represent me after 1945, one would doubtlessly be able to read this somehow between the lines of the Löwenherz file memoranda, but it really seems to me that the opposite was true.

Naturally I speak here of the documents that were drawn up *before* the end of the war. And, moreover, Dr. Löwenherz' style, for example, is to be described as completely dry and objective.

The bureaucratic Germany of that time, and at its head the Foreign Office, created an "endless screw", a "cat biting its own tail", and it had, as the end of its wisdom, no other orders to issue than such as those that led to the Reich Night of Broken Glass. Other powers, of which the British ambassador in Berlin made himself the spokesman, declared, "No Jews without capital", In God's name, what other possibilities could there have been. I have already regretted it often that at that time I did *not* stick my hands in my pockets and taken the position of many others. I would really have turned out better today. *Bueno*, but I did not stick my hands in my pockets as one can see. But others can examine whether the majority of Jews could have then emigrated from Austria. At that time in Vienna I took the middle way between those two extremes, that is, of the obstruction of emigration on the one hand, linked to the sharpened legislative pressure through the bureaucratic German offices, and of the declaration of the foreigners, on the other hand, that they did not wish to accept any Jews without money.

Hitler Gives His Warning

During my trial, Hitler's speech to the German parliament on January 30, 1939, was mentioned:

"Today I wish to be a prophet once again. If the international financial Jews within and outside Europe should succeed in plunging the nations once again into a world war, then the result will be not the Bolshevisation of the earth and therewith the victory of Jewry, but the annihilation of the Jewish race in Europe".

Naturally, international finance is in major part to blame, indeed responsible for the distress of the nations, for the misery and the suffering as a result of the war which it manufactured. But it is foolish to wish to speak here of a *Jewish* international financial bloc. So far as it concerns Jews here, who also sat in powerful financial cartels, it was doubtless a question of Jews to whom their Jewishness meant as little or as much as the Catholic or Protestant financial magnates may have worried about their Catholicism or Protestantism. The predominant characteristic of precisely these Jews was their assimilationist attitude. Not always to the satisfaction of the really religious Jew. No, international high finance was, and is, the greatest of all evils, there's no doubt about that. But to place the stress here on the word "Jew" indicates an ignorance of the state of affairs. And Hitler was ignorant of this state of affairs; as he was so often, so disastrously often.

I wish to explain more precisely what I just said. It may have been 1936 and 1937; one department of the SD Head Office relating to the subject of "International financial Jewry" kept track of the international *Jewish* high finance. I personally did not have anything to do with it professionally since the focus here was on "economic research". But I read many files that arose in connection with this research. I also had the opportunity of speaking at that time now and then with one or another of the departmental heads responsible for it on this question. I still remember that particularly the result of the investigation of "Unilever company" was brought forward; it was a huge margarine and soap cartel, further large enterprises were affiliated to it. Its connections were really international. Its shareholders, if I am not mistaken, and even parts of its chairmen of the governing board, were partly Jews, who were well known, and with international names. Indeed, one spoke of parts of the Unilever company as a family structure. It is also true that name bearers within this economic structure had active connections, for instance, to the

False Gods

Hitler addresses the Reichstag, German parliament in Berlin 1939.

"Anti-Defamation League", the "Anti-Nazi League", to the leader of the boycott movement against Germany, Samuel Untermayer, and also to many other political and economic centres, as the business of the multi-millionaires in high finance is naturally constituted.

Now, I have described my attitude to the Jewish boycott movement. In spite of enthusiastic research – the lever of this intermediary activity was located at that time in Holland and extended to a large series of countries including the USA – nothing more was discovered and determined than could have been determined in connection with any common businessman who had joined this boycott movement. Certainly their financial support was greater than those of these lesser rich men. But for that reason the consideration of their economic enterprise placed on them an incomparably higher amount of caution and restraint than the little men necessarily had to observe In other words, nothing incriminating resulted that was worth trumpeting loudly throughout the world. And the SD Head Office was at that time very well connected – as one used to say professionally – with the Unilever company. If something had really been ascertained, this would have been announced with the citation of all details, (at the time of the occupation of Holland at the latest), to the international press and certainly also to the diplomatic corps in Berlin through the mediation of Goebbels, as this was so commonly done. But that nothing happened up to 1945 is a confirmation of the accuracy of my description.

Hitler Gives His Warning

Naturally, international "financial Jewry" was a commonplace term. But if one just takes the sum of all multimillionaires on a dollar basis, then one sees how high the number of Jewish and how high the number of non-Jewish multimillionaires is in relation to the dollar amounts represented by them. One may do the same with the chairmen of the boards of directors of enterprises, companies and corporate associations. Of course, the status of a multimillionaire is not definitely and necessarily to be attributed to board directors, members of the executive committee and chairmen of such corporations, though, on the other hand, their economic influence can be great.

What does one see? Certainly nothing but what we also saw in the SD Head Office at that time. The number of Jews was very small in comparison with the number of non-Jews. The individual company, the individual Jewish financial magnate, the individual non-Jewish chairman of a board of directors or multimillionaire could not undertake anything more against the Reich than a pinprick on the skin of an elephant. Only through their agglomeration, through the unity of the major part of the international high finance for the accomplishment of their goal does this power become sinister and dangerous. But, from this point on, the *Jew as such* has nothing more to do with it; he is still only one percent in a hundred, a percentage that is far from a majority.

So was it, in any case, in those years about which I speak. And if such was made clear to me as a small departmental head, how much more must it have been to the top leadership. For this information research was conducted for them and the reports were sent to them.

When I say that we departmental heads in the Reich Security Service Head Office believed, in the case of such a speech of Hitler's, only in the attainment of a propagandistic effect, this may be correct. On 30 January 1939, in my opinion, *nobody* in all of Germany seriously thought of an annihilation of Jewry. The idea itself would have also been too absurd and I dare to maintain this in spite of all the really very harsh measures that had up to then been applied against the Jews. For, that all politics in every country was a great lie and a great deception was known to every person in every country even then - if he was able to read a newspaper.

The Jew was used – as so often in his history – even by the highest leadership of the Reich as a catalyst on whom all their failures and all their coming difficulties and inconveniences were to be

False Gods

blamed. Nothing changed in this basic attitude, and so there arose at that time the propaganda of the "Protocols of the Elders of Zion", and the "Jewish ritual murder" image. This is by no means my attitude to these matters only since the time I have been a prisoner here in an Israeli prison. I basically owe this awareness to the knowledge of my teacher in this field, Baron von Mildenstein. He saw things dispassionately and soberly, as they actually were. Free from mysticism, free of the "Stürmer" conception and free of propaganda delusions. I was able to find the correctness of my opinion confirmed over long years with the help of official documents.

That the individual Jewish financial magnate was exactly as bad or as good as the non-Jewish financial magnate, and all taken together would be even more so, is a totally clear matter but it does not have anything to do with Jewry.

One may argue that it is undeniable that, in comparison with the entire population in Germany, the Jews hold a relatively disproportionately higher share in banking and the stock-exchange, in art, literature, film and theatre - all belonged to the Jews; also in trade in general, in certain professional sectors such as doctors, etc., in the field of the law and education and things of the like. Of course, I must say to this that it is correct. And that was indeed also the mesh into which the National Socialist propaganda cut into constantly. This was perhaps so - with certain historical exceptions in one or another form - for centuries and more. And this fact repeatedly led to pogroms and economic pressure on the Jews.

Many exploited this fact to their own advantage; the provincial princes for the welfare of their private treasuries and the politicians for the acquisition of votes that they required to obtain key positions. All used this opportunity, which was welcome for their personal ambitions, in order to achieve - through the imaginative capitalisation of awakened instincts of envy - their goals, which they otherwise would have hardly, or with much greater difficulty, been able to achieve, lacking intellectual talents of their own.

There are two causes to which the Jews had to attribute their fate. The exiles, lasting for thousands of years, to which the Jews were led long before the Christian era, to Babylon and to Egypt. Certain branches of professions were allowed to them here, others forbidden.

Hitler Gives His Warning

It was often this way even in the Middle Ages. And when one observes what was at that time permitted to them to conduct, it was, in the majority of cases, those professions in which the Jews of the modern age had a *larger* share than was proportionate to the percentage of their population within the total population. It was quite clear, they had become specialised in these through compulsion. As for the other cause, what was responsible for it was the fact that the possibility of statehood was denied to them.

And now that every nationalism is latent egoism, at first the problem had to be solved in Germany through emigration. This was not new, this had innumerable precedents in history; I recall only the Jewish expulsions by Isabella the Catholic. The external declarations of motives changed in the course of the ages. The motive itself remained always the same. I personally *constantly* and *emphatically* pointed out then that *only* statehood would solve the problem. But I was officially outnumbered as well as in the battle against lies and propaganda. And I maintain today that the story of human cohabitation, is *one big* and *loud* symphony of lies. Bernard Shaw, the expert in human nature and a satirist, narrates a nice story to us:

> "As soon as a lie has become popular, and that do all fairy-tales become, it is impossible to keep pace with it if it has a head start. Of Lord Melbourne, the mentor of Queen Victoria, it is narrated that, when she ascended the throne, he had, during a meeting with his ministerial colleagues, blocked the door of the council chamber and called out to them: "It is of no importance to me what kind of damn lie we have to tell but not one of you will leave this room until we have agreed on the same damn lie."

The German tanks rattled through Prague. The golden city on the Vltava. "Slata Praha", as the Czech says of his capital, the architecturally most beautiful of all Central European capitals, if not more than that. One who stands on the Vltava and allows his gaze to be led over the stone saints of Karl's Bridge, up to the Hradčany and St. Vitus' cathedral, and does not fall contemplatively under the spell of the centuries cannot be alive any more.

I knew Prague already from a time of deep peace. I knew Prague when it still belonged to the Imperial and Royal Austro-Hungarian monarchy and I became acquainted with these charming festivities on the Vltava with understanding and love in the years from 1931 to 1933. From the dream-like alleys of the Old City and the Hradčany there wafted a breath of the Middle Ages suggestive of enterprise and architecture. And thousands of old sagas murmured to the attentive ear. And hundreds of towers and domes gleamed golden in the last rays of the setting sun. Oh, how I loved Prague!

It was doubly homely to me, this city - as an urban architectural gem and, moreover, my beloved in those years, my future wife, was settled in Czechoslovakia. In a few days it will have been thirty years since that time when I began to love Prague.

Assignment to Prague

In the middle of 1939 I received the order to travel to Prague and to report to the commander of the Security Police and SD there. It was apparently set up as a mirror-image of the "Central Office for Jewish Emigration in Vienna". It was on 28 July 1939 that the central office in Prague began to operate. Until then there had not yet been any organised emigration. Any Jews who wished to emigrate had to obtain the necessary official documents by himself. For that he had to go to the visa office of the Secret State Police which decided if emigration was granted to the person concerned or not. After the establishment of this "Central Office for Jewish Emigration in Prague", the Jewish religious community was given the responsibility of seeing to it that the emigrating Jews fulfilled the legal requirements.

The visa which permitted the leaving of the "Protectorate territory" was from now on issued by this same central office. A large number of documents was necessary at that time to be able to emigrate abroad and I am hardly mistaken when I say that this number was very much the same for Jews and non-Jews. These included:

1. Proof of residence from the police authorities

2. Police criminal record certificate

3. Issuance of a visa from the senior district administrator of Prague

4. Application for the issuance of a passport to the police authorities in Prague and the senior district administrator's office in Prague

5. An official form for an emigration visa from the police authorities in Prague

Assignment to Prague

Jews queue in Prague for tax and other documents required for Visas.

6. Confirmation from the municipal authorities in Prague regarding the payment of municipal taxes
7. Application to Group VII/Economics of the Reichsprotector
8. Application and questionnaire to the tax administration for the purpose of obtaining a "tax clearance certificate".
9. A filled out questionnaire of the federal tax office
10. Application to the audit department of the Finance Ministry and the national bank for taking along moved property
11. Registration of the moved property at the audit department of the Finance Ministry
12. Declaration of wealth for the DSK[20] of the Customs Investigation Office
13. Confirmation of the payment of the emigration tax, taxes related to the moved property, etc. according to the government ordinance No.287/1939, and much more.

As one sees, it was not only in Prague, difficult just to fulfil these manifold conditions. For the individual often a torture. The creation of a central office had already much in its favour, though it also

---

20   Devisenschutzkommando, an SS commando that collected the gold of Jewish emigrants.

had disadvantages. And those may judge between advantage and disadvantage who were faced with the necessity of obtaining such certificates. They will know.

I said those who were faced with the necessity. Yes, and it passes through my mind that:

I joined the National Socialist German Workers' Party because it fought against the injustice of Versailles, against the dictate, against occupation, against national ignominy, against landgrab. And what did we bring about? injustice, dictates, occupation, national ignominy, landgrab. It is true, we brought about precisely that!

Precisely all that rattled on the heels of our tanks, against which we once rose up and revolted. All this and more we dictated to other nations. It is true: one injustice does not remove another from the world. And our leadership at that time should have known that. They were the politicians with the responsibility. It was this attitude that made me persist as a servant in the dance around the gods. Of course it was at that time difficult, very difficult to break out of these ranks, even when one wished to. But I must admit that at that time I no longer thought of and did not begin to think again of a disengagement from my service.

On 27 September 1941, Heydrich was appointed Deputy Reich Protector of Bohemia and Moravia. The desire of this ambitious and very power-hungry man had been fulfilled: his leap into larger political events.

Once, on some occasion, I heard him say that it was a satisfaction for him to be moved from the "negative" of police "activity" into a "positive constructive job". But this declaration seems to have had no consequence any more, for he continued to retain his position as chief of the Security Police and SD in a joint office. In addition, he was SS Obergruppenführer[21] and Police General, member of the German parliament, acting chairman of the "International Criminal Police Commission", to name but a few of his most important functions and titles. But his secret goal was the expulsion of Ribbentrop, and to see himself as Reich Foreign Minister. His spring-board into politics as the Reich Protector for Bohemia and Moravia was to serve him to this end.

---

21   SS lieutenant general

Assignment to Prague

He had formed for himself, as its "architect", the structure of a Reich Security Head Office which he built up, through tenacious painstaking work, from meagre beginnings into that mighty institution and as whose chief and master he became as a person absolutely untouchable.

Courage and determination, coupled with bravado, could never be denied to him, especially when it was a question of indulging his ambition and his vanity. He wanted to come into possession of bravery decorations. To this end, in his scarce leisure time, he assumed the uniform of an air force major and cultivated himself as a "Messerschmitt"[22] fighter. And then he actually participated as a fighter pilot in battles over the Channel, shot down some enemy planes, and received frontline flying-clasps and an Iron Cross. After that, Himmler forbade him any further flying whatsoever.

So he had fulfilled this wish too. At a press conference in Prague, Heydrich had in his impulsive way allowed himself to be carried away into naming an impossibly short deadline for the "Dejudaisation of Bohemia and Moravia".

To comply with his words to some extent, Theresienstadt was in the following period cleared by the German troops that were garrisoned there and the Czech civil population was resettled by the responsible ministry of the Protectorate government.

A document that I have before me describes the discussion with Heydrich in which I too participated. I have not seen the original. The document that I have at my disposal - a photocopy - shows neither a letterhead nor a diary number, neither a sign nor a signature, so that I cannot perceive who made these notes, by which office they were made, in short, this document cannot be considered as official so long as I have not seen the original. In addition, there is the fact that I have a different recollection of the matter, even though I do not wish to maintain that, after such a long time - twenty years have with all their turbulence passed in the meantime -, my recollection is infallible.

At that time Heydrich - now that he had been confirmed as Reich Protector - asked me for my opinion on how I imagined the solution to myself. He asked dozens of persons and offices. I told him he could make available a city with a sufficient hinterland. The Jews of

---

22   Messerschmitt was a German aircraft manufacturing company famous for its fighter planes.

False Gods

Bohemia and Moravia could be settled in this city, the hinterland had the necessary agricultural products to supply. The current emigration would then solve the problem by itself in the course of the years. And so did it happen then, though without a hinterland. The few hundred hectares of land were too little and, in the meantime, emigration too had been forbidden. Moreover, in the following period, all possible party and state offices of the Reich territory, in their eagerness to be free of their Jews, pestered Himmler to be able to send Jews from their side to Theresienstadt. And then again Himmler one day ordered that Theresienstadt should be transformed into a model old-age ghetto to show foreign countries how the German Reich solved its Jewish problem. This was one of the camouflages ordered by Himmler.

Theresienstadt

Theresienstadt was under the Commanding Officer of the Security Police and SD in Prague. The commanding officer in turn was, on the one hand, for matters of the Protectorate region, under the Senior SS and Police Chief of Bohemia and Moravia as the plenipotentiary representative of Himmler, the SS Reichsführer and Chief of the German Police; on the other hand, under the same person in his capacity as state secretary for the security system in Bohemia and Moravia. This was the SS Gruppenführer and lieutenant general of the Police and the Waffen SS, K.H. Frank.[23] Thirdly, the Commander of the Security Police in Prague had to observe the orders of the Reich Security Head Office insofar as a national scope was allotted to it, and Frank had no veto.

Until the day when the bombs were thrown at Heydrich from whose splinter injuries he died on 5 June 1942, Heydrich too, as Chief of the Security Police and Reich Protector, directly gave orders to his Commander of the Security Police in Prague. It was a complicated situation, just in view of the paths of command and the possibilities of control conditioned by them.

From time to time the offices of the Security Police approached the Reich Security Head Office under pressure from their regional

---

23 Karl Hermann Frank (1898-1946) was appointed Secretary of State for the Reich Protectorate of Bohemia and Moravia in 1939 under Reich Protector Konstantin von Neurath. On the assassination of Heydrich in May 1942, Frank and the deputy protector Karl Daluege undertook the retaliatory destruction of the Bohemian villages of Lidice and Ležáky.

Theresienstadt

Jewish children at Theresienstadt during an inspection by the Red Cross 1944.

superiors or the party authorities to deport to the east a proposed number of Jews for the purpose of relieving the density of settlers in Theresienstadt as the emigration of Jews to European or extra-European countries had been forbidden by Himmler with effect from 10 October 1941. Only Himmler could personally decide on such applications and so they were forwarded to Himmler, undersigned either by the Chief of Office IV of the Reich Security Head Office, SS Gruppenführer and lieutenant general of the Police, Müller, who had in the meantime become my immediate superior, or by Heydrich's successor, SS Obergruppenführer and general of the Police and Waffen SS, Dr. Kaltenbrunner as Chief of the Security Police and SD. He either approved or rejected.

I said that the establishment and operation of the Theresienstadt ghetto was ordered by Himmler as a camouflage. So all applications that the offices of the Red Cross made at the responsible Reich offices such as the Foreign Office, insofar as they had to do with the International Red Cross or at the Führer's Chancellery or the Reich Chancellery, insofar as the application emanated from the German Red Cross, went through Himmler, who, as the final authority, permitted or forbade. In this way, in June 1943, Theresienstadt was visited by the general secretary of the German Red Cross, Hartmann,[24] as representative of

---

24 Walther Georg Hartmann was head of the foreign department of the German

False Gods

the Duke of Coburg, and, on 5 April 1944, by a Commission of the International Red Cross itself.

I too took part in this visit according to orders. Naturally it is easy to say today, "Well, could you not have told the Commission at that time that it is all a fraud, all a camouflage of Himmler's, who wished to mislead international public opinion". Apart from the fact that I stood under an oath, apart from the fact that the Jewish killings were incontestably known also abroad in June 1943 and that all the sparrows chirped it out from the roof in April 1944, apart from the fact, further, that I would have been placed against the nearest wall and shot, apart from all this, how would it have helped the matter? Indeed, I could not stop anything just as I could not start anything.

In the entire Jewish matter too many commanders were put in place. Starting with Hitler, through Himmler, Heydrich and Kaltenbrunner, through Krüger, the Senior SS and Police chief in the Generalgouvernement, the Oberdienstleiter[25] Brack[26] in the Chancellery of the Führer; the SS general Pohl, the senior SS and Police chiefs in the Reich territory and the Occupied territories, the Gauleiters and Reich governors, the Reichsleiters,[27] the Reich Minister of Foreign Affairs, the Reich Propaganda Minister and the Reich Minister of Justice, the chief of the Army High Command, and many others. What could a man with the rank of a lieutenant-colonel do here? Nothing!

The constant double and triple possibility of checks, by the superiors to whom every recipient of orders, without any exception, was subjected within the structure of the Security Police ensured also a party-loyal maintenance of the course prescribed by the leadership.

This control mechanism not only within the Security Police, enabled the gods to become false idols. For reasons of a better overview I have

---

Red Cross. His report on the visit concluded that conditions in Theresienstadt were "grausam" (terrible). As a result, the ICRC decided to undertake a visit of its own, the arrangement of which Eichmann deferred until the spring of 1944.

25 Senior head of service

26 Viktor Brack (1904-48) was the organiser of the euthanasia programme T4. He was sentenced to death in 1947 and hanged the following year.

27 The "National leaders" formed the elite of the NSDAP and included Bormann, Himmler, Rosenberg, Goebbels, Darré and von Schirach, among others.

gone ahead of the chronology with my observations, insofar as they deal with Bohemia and Moravia. I must therefore retreat somewhat to add the observations on what had happened in the meantime outside the Protectorate territory.

Invasion of Poland

On 1 September 1939, at five in the morning, the German divisions moved in the direction of Poland. Dive bomber squadrons engaged the Polish standby positions. The totality of the German, English and French stupidity in the Polish question allowed it to come to war against this country. Tragic destiny had allowed the Polish Marshal Pilsudski to die too early. Under his state leadership it would never have come to a war against this country.

The fury of this war raged through Poland and, after a few weeks, there stood opposite each other at the demarcation line Soviet Russian officials of the Ministry of the Interior, German Secret State Police offices, Siberian infantry regiments and German grenadier units, in a border area almost like that of peacetime.

On 21 September 1939, Heydrich had called together his office chiefs and Einsatz Group chiefs operating in Poland to Berlin for a meeting. I am also mentioned in the attendance list of a protocol but I was at that time not at all in Berlin and as little was I an Einsatz Group chief. (This document moreover bears neither a signature nor a seal. Of course, not the original but only a photocopy was given to me.) It must be a mistake; I did not take part in this meeting. My former superior, Dr. Six, who participated in this meeting, was questioned about this as a witness, in Germany, in 1961. He declared that I did not take part in meetings of office chiefs at all. My predecessor in Berlin, a government councillor Lischka, signed on 16 October of the same year a letter of his department concerning the Reich Central Office for Jewish Emigration. Dr. Löwenherz confirms for the first time in his file note of 17 December 1939 that I informed him that I had to from then on deal with the Reich Central Office matters. So I had nothing to do officially in Berlin before that. I was working in Vienna and Prague in the central emigration offices.

Heydrich had at the meeting ordered the ghettoization of the Jews in the Generalgouvernement.

False Gods

On 6 October, Hitler announced the nationalising of the eastern provinces that had just come to the Reich and commissioned Himmler with its implementation through his appointment as Reich Commissioner for the Consolidation of German Nationality. As chief of the German Police and as the SS Reichsführer, he needed, in organisational terms, apart from an asset holding institution, no other new institution related to this for the implementation of the additional task allotted to him by Hitler. The government offices of the Generalgouvernement, as the German occupied part of Poland was called from now on, were already being built. The Trust Office East established at that time acted as asset holder of the entire wealth – moveable and immoveable – of those to be deported following the nationalisation. The deportations to the Generalgouvernement took place. On 30 October Himmler issued the following order:

"In November and December 1939, as well as January and February 1940, the following resettlements are to be undertaken:

1. From the former Polish, now Reich German provinces and territories, all Jews.

2. From the Danzig-West Prussian province all "Congress" Poles.[28]

3. From the provinces of Posen, South and East Prussia and eastern Upper Silesia, a number of especially hostile Polish people who will be specified.

4. The senior SS and Police Chief of the East (Generalgouvernement) will announce the acceptance capacities of the Gouvernement for those to be resettled and that according to district offices and bigger cities.

5. The senior SS and Police chiefs of Weichsel, Warthe, North-East, South-East and East or the inspectors and commanders of the Security Police will together determine the resettlement plan.

6. The senior SS and Police chief is responsible within his territory for the decampment and transport; for the accommodation in the new living area the Polish administration or self-government is responsible."

---

28 Poles belonging to the Kingdom of Poland created in 1815 by the Congress of Vienna which was joined to and, in 1867, made part of the Russian Empire. It included the regions of Kalisz, Lublin, Łódź, Masovia and Świętokrzyskie.

Invasion of Poland

This was the first deportation order. Dozens would follow it. Following this order, the SS and Police generals assembled at the Generalgouverneur's in Krakow on 8 November 1939 for their first briefing. The main points of their meeting were the accommodation and resettlement ordered by Himmler of the ethnic Germans from the Baltic lands and Volhynia[29] who were to be brought into the Reich, as well as the deportation of Jews and Poles.

The senior SS and Police chief general Krüger, of the East (Generalgouvernement), took the chair, the major general of the Police, SS Brigadeführer Streckenbach, who was commander of the Security Police in the Generalgouvernement, was charged with the central planning of the settlement and deportation in the eastern territory. He also had, according to the instructions issued to him, to undertake the negotiations with the Reich Railways for the purpose of making transport trains available. Following this meeting, around 1 million Jews and Poles were to be deported from the new eastern provinces to the Generalgouvernement by the end of February 1940. A figure which, in practice, as a result of the difficulties arising, could not be adhered to even approximately within that time period.

As Chief of the Security Police and SD, Heydrich involved himself personally in this matter, and subdivided the total plan into many short-term plans. He determined in detail the responsibilities related to deportation and final destinations. The inspector of the Security Police responsible, on behalf of senior SS and Police chief, had to determine from which places the deportation would take place. He likewise determined, on the basis of the proposal of the provincial counsellors, when and how many persons would be deported from the individual districts. The commander of the Security Police in Krakow had to announce the destination stations for the transports.

Ambition, craving for recognition, and hunger for power celebrated their triumphs in these weeks and months. Every one of the regional public authorities had decided to throw their utmost authority into the meeting and to derive dictatorial rights from it. And now it began. Everything rushed into activity. It was too slow for everybody. The responsibilities often overlapped and the difficulties resulting from this were not observed, for every public authority was filled only with provincial egoism. The result was a hopeless confusion.

---

29 A historic region straddling the current states of Poland, Ukraine and Belarus.

False Gods

German troops parade through Warsaw, September 1939.

Wrong destination stations. Overcrowding of trains. Deficient communication of news between the senders and transport receivers. Scattiness everywhere. The entire travel-plan became disorderly. Those who suffered were those who were in any case the most affected by the deportation.

Assignment to Gestapo Office IV

In December 1939, I received orders to report for service to the Chief of Office IV of the Reich Security Head Office, Müller in Berlin. My request to be excepted from official employment in Berlin - pointing out the fact that my family lived in Vienna and were preparing for a move to Prague, and that Berlin was inconvenient for me - was declined. If one was drafted for troop service one had to comply without flinching, but in the case of an official service I thought I would be able to make such a request. However, their reminder of the war situation allowed me no further possibilities of appeal.

In Berlin, already for some months, a Reich Central Office for Jewish Emigration had been founded "on paper". Its director was, according to the ordinance of the Reich Marshal Göring, in his capacity as Commissioner for the Four-Year Plan, Heydrich. As his manager Heydrich appointed his Chief of Office IV, Müller.

Assignment to Gestapo Office IV

Further, in accordance with Göring's instructions, some senior officials of the Ministry of the Interior, the Foreign Office, and the Office of the Commissioner for the Four-Year Plan had to be active on the committee of this Reich central office.

I received the commission to conduct this office practically from now on so that it would function on a regular basis, as well as to conduct the office business following the instructions of the manager. Further, I was entrusted with the coordination of the deportation transports.

The relevant ordinance was issued by the Chief of the Security Police on 21 December 1939. My office designation was "Special consultant of IV R", that is, special consultant for evacuation in Office IV of the Reich Security Head Office. The designation "special consultant" is explained by the fact that it was a new department within Office IV of the Reich Security Head Office, thus of the Secret State Police, and the next annual assignment of official positions was due only in February 1940.

So from this time on I was, according to the official positions, consultant of IV D4 in Office IV of the Reich Security Head Office. I therefore had, from the beginning, no other powers than those which each of the other 100 to 150 consultants of the Reich Security Head Office also had. After an interruption of about 1½ years I was working once again in Berlin. Pity, I would rather have remained in the provinces, and best of all in the smallest provincial city possible. But my wishes were not consulted, I had to obey. But who already thought at Christmas time in 1939 that the war would continue. Everybody counted on a settlement between Germany, France and England. At that time I read Kant's *Critique of Practical Reason*. The things that surrounded me I found impractical and I could not trace much reason in them.

I spent the Christmas holidays with my family members. My wife was annoyed with the transfer to Berlin and declared to me very decidedly that she was not in any way thinking of moving to Berlin; and she enforced her will and did not move to the Reich capital. Of course, neither my wife nor I had the least against Berlin and the Berliners, on the contrary we spent, from 1935 to 1938, three full happy years within the walls of the Reich capital and learnt to love it and, with it, the Berliners. But the animosity of both of us to large cities surely arose from our innate penchant for provincial life, for

False Gods

we both grew up in it, my wife as the daughter of a farmer more even than I, although a thousand cords pulled me away from stone piles of the cities where one's glance could not roam freely, where it constantly encountered hundreds upon hundreds of corners, where the earthly smell of dew never arose with the first rays of the rising sun, where bird chirping concerts never took place, where one was reminded only by the daily schedule that it would be sunset in 15 minutes and that one should then get into the car and drive 10 minutes to one's usual observation place and then to be able to enjoy, for 5 minutes, the spectacle of the glowing red setting of the giver of life. Only five minutes; peace; silent enjoyment. That was how it was, even in Vienna.

Winter or summer, whether it was fine weather or streams rained down from the heavens, I just could not bring forward the strength to place myself behind a desk without first going to the Kahlenberg early in the morning to watch the approaching day. I know my comrades from that time considered it a strange quirk of mine, but they got used to it.

When I was still a sergeant and could not have any weapons at my disposal, when I had to take the tram of line 21 from Berlin-Britz to the Anhalt station for half an hour every morning at precisely half past seven, I used to set out early enough from my house to walk a few kilometres. Not for the sake of the walk, but because a spruce had grown there at a sawmill and it was this spruce in the midst of a sea of houses which attracted me. In it I saw the Bohemian woods, the woods of the Mühlviertel country; silent, dark green, rustling and murmuring. And after I had, like a simpleton, held my daily morning conversation with this spruce I became happy and inwardly cheerful and free. I gladly sacrificed my morning time to it. For three years I spoke to it, and it knew my concern, it knew my joy and also my sorrow, but mostly it was joy. Once again my comrades from that time got used to the fact that I got onto the tram only when it was en route, they got used to this loner's custom.

In my trial here in Jerusalem one of the judges asked me during a cross-examination if I had *lived* according to the Kantian imperative. I could freely say, of course I at least tried to direct my life according to the Kantian imperative, or to live according to it. I at least tried to live always in such a way that the guiding principles of my will could always serve at the same time as the principle of a universal legislation.

Assignment to Gestapo Office IV

In any case, I had recognised at a definite point in time that I could no longer act according to the moral law intuitively innate in me as I was no longer master of my actions to be able to do so. I *should* have acted according to it. That is right. It is in theory also quite easy and fine to say that. But in real life circumstances can arise that prevent one from doing so. An unlimited possibility of practical action is possible to the recipient of orders in wartime only in the rarest cases. And only in the rarest cases do orders in the war correspond to the principle of a universal legislation, to the moral law innate in me. And then one may discuss ethics with one's superior SS general in this context. He would give you a kick in the pants! But not only in the SS. That is how practical life is. You are proscribed as an alien fool, and treated according to the court martial ordinances because the enemy too does not advance singing psalms and hosannas. In the best case one is reminded of the oath of allegiance and the national emergency and brought into order. So, when the recipient of orders lacks commanding authority, one cannot speak any more of practical action, that is something different from his own inner attitude to events which he recognises as being contrary to the Kantian imperative. But this is without any outward results.

During my 1½ years of absence from Berlin, that is, from spring 1938 to late autumn 1939, the organisational structure of the Security Police and SD had essentially changed. The two head offices of the Security Police and SD had been united into one central office.

From now on the Reich Security Head Office consisted of seven offices, that is, the "Personnel" office; "Administration"; "Observation of the enemy with regard to the living space"; "Combating the enemy with regard to world-view and living space", called in short Secret State Police Office; "Combating criminals", or the Reich Criminal Police Office; "Espionage and Counter-Espionage – foreign countries", called Defence; and "Scientific research against the enemy". The chief of the Head Office was Heydrich; my immediate superior was the director of the Secret State Police, or Office IV, SS Gruppenführer and lieutenant general of the Police, Müller.

The subordinate authorities of the Reich Security Head Office were in the Reich territory, the inspectors of the Security Police and SD, as well as the state police offices and the SD departments; the commanding officers of the Security Police and SD and the commandants of the Sipo and SD were in the occupied territories.

False Gods

I therefore had to deal with two task fields, the emigration and also the coordination matters related to the transports for the evacuation of the new German eastern provinces that had been ordered. An activity that I began practically on 2 January 1940.

For me personally there began now, very much against my will, a period of separation from the family which found its end only in 1952, in Argentina. Naturally I was until 1945 very often together with my family at the weekends, but what does this amount to.

On New Year's Eve 1939, I left Vienna, took a stop for greetings at my parents' house in Linz, the same at my stepmother's in her farm in south Bohemia, and thought of dashing through in my 3.4 Mercedes Benz in a long drive to the highway near Dresden and then it would be only a short sprint of about 140 kilometres to Berlin. But for some reason, which I do not clearly recall today, I think the snow chains were responsible, I came only to a place on the ridge of the mountains behind Aussig.[30] I have no map here. It must have been part of the Erzgebirge if I am not mistaken. Thick winter, and stomach upset. I should have rather celebrated New Year's Eve together with my wife and my child, especially since our hours together would be very limited.

I thought to myself, hopefully the damn war will end soon, and I cursed the order which bound me now to Berlin. I looked for a decent guest-house, the car was taken care of, and then nothing like the "Turkish blood" to flush down the stomach-upset. "Turkish blood" was my favourite drink on occasion. Half champagne, half red wine, the stuff is gladly knocked down. The New Year's Eve holiday had created some business in this guest-house. Winter sportsmen, locals and an SS captain. At that time there was still everything that one desired to eat that the kitchen could offer. Dozing off, I philosophised to myself, sticking my nose deep into the glass; I allowed the gentle year-end bustle to rebound onto me without my taking part in it, not even feeling anything. Exhaustion then hurled me onto the mattress.

There is hardly a more beautiful picture among winter images than a hoar-frost morning in the mountains. Bushes and trees, little houses and villages become sugar-coated. The oblique morning rays allow the myriad diamonds of ice to gleam, from dark violet through the deepest blue and red that you ever saw to the brightest yellow and

---

30 Now Ústí nad Labem in Bohemia

Assignment to Gestapo Office IV

you wish only to gaze on and never be satiated. The endless purity of Nature tells you in every glistening crystal how bad its creation, man, has indeed become in his activity. Not that I mean thereby anything special about the work of man; or that I wish thereby to characterise myself particularly; I was, and am, neither better nor worse than the great mass of average people. But when I think of the general actions and desires of men – including myself – and see the untouched purity of Nature, I am often overcome by an ardent and yearning desire for the living beings that stand before me in endless diversity. The thousands upon thousands of deaths that we organic life-forms have to pass through are not worse than the thousands upon thousands of births that each of us still await expectantly.

My belief in the gods was sore afflicted at that time. The flames ordered by them on 10 November 1938 made me hesitate. Of course I did not have anything to do with the executive action, but now I was in the middle of it.

When something goes against the grain for a man for a long time then he becomes insolent, and the sudden extraction from my circle of the familiar went against my will. Of course, the same was true of hundreds of thousands of others at that time, for the country was at war and nobody was asked if it suited him or not. I had only to obey, but the service in the Secret State Police was sufficiently irksome. Up to now we in the Security Service had looked down upon the members of the Security Police, we considered ourselves better than they, and now I was one of them. To be sure, even the hundreds of thousands, and later the millions, were not asked where and with whom they wished to serve. They were ordered and had to obediently carry on with their service.

One of the first official questions from Müller was the matter of my transfer to a bureaucratic appointment. Now, I have nothing against officials or against the bureaucracy in general, but how can I express it without stepping on somebody's toes. One must know that my superior was a so-called "pure bureaucrat". The Director of the Reich Criminal Police. So one could not well say, "You know, I have no interest in a transfer to the bureaucracy". One should not annoy a tiger, for precaution is a virtue. And god knows I had often enough been lacking in this virtue. So I said that I did not wish to give up my official connection to the brigade, especially now during wartime. In any case this sounded good and gave me the hope to be able one day to leave, when the circumstances were favourable, the bureaucratic atmosphere bound to a writing-desk. The transfer to Berlin was very much against the grain for me.

False Gods

To my joy, it was not possible to free me from my military service. The reasons for this were that I had not been released from the personnel department of the Security Service. In this way is to be understood the fact that I never made use of my executive right as consultant with regard to any official authorities but always got instructions for myself, a right that I had and which I henceforth claimed. Thus I myself could never make a mistake, and in this way also I myself bore no responsibility, and I also did not arouse the envy of every official who had already been serving for a long time who should long ago have become a consultant.

The emigration now followed its normal course. In terms of numbers, on account of the war, it became ever smaller. Regardless of that, I made use of every possibility to promote emigration within the scope of the existing ordinances and decrees. The deportation issues had become a great chaos which nobody could understand any more. There were only complaints: from all corners and quarters.

In a word, I encountered the most wretched conditions. Everybody seemed to have his own deportation plan, as it were, once he felt that he had to be the first to make an implementation report according to the "order of the Führer" in his district. The provincial heads of the new German eastern territories worried that such a procedure would lead to deadlocks and difficulties in the Generalgouvernement and that the German railways could, on account of this confusion, no longer maintain its travel plan. Most of all those who were deported according to the orders from the highest office had a right to complain about it, and justifiably. So my task was to remedy through a coordination of the transports these defects that had arisen.

They were remedied too, as far as that was possible at all. The *implementation of the transports* was not to be equated with the *implementation of the deportation*. Other offices were commissioned with this according to the orders of Himmler and Heydrich. Even the *planning* did not rest with my department, as little as the *conduct* of the deportation as well as the *selection* of the persons to be deported, their *concentration* and their *treatment*. The fact that I was entrusted with the coordination of the transports does not demonstrate any special powers that were transferred to me but proves that I was working on the express higher order of Heydrich and subordinate to the Chief of Office IV of the Reich Security Head Office.

Assignment to Gestapo Office IV

If somebody wishes to coordinate something, he must as a rule first bring all those involved in the dealings "under one hat" in order to give them a working direction, and this I did.

On 8 January 1940, all the representatives of the offices involved in the transports were summoned to Berlin for a meeting. Nothing could be changed in the essential existing order, but through the new instructions that I now had to issue with regard to transports, no office could in future set a train in motion *without* prior approval through my department. Naturally, Berlin was far away and when I say that nobody could carry out a transport without permission this was also a rule that was, in spite of everything, confirmed by repeated exceptions here and there. For, the regional Gauleiters and Reich governors or the provincial governors were not subject to the orders of the Reich Security Head Office. On the contrary, these offices were, according to decree, entitled to issue to the State Police offices or other offices of the Security Police and SD operating within the field of their jurisdiction or command instructions that the latter had to comply with. Very often this remarkable ruling was a source of anger and the basis of numerous disagreements. But that was part of the functioning of the system of double and triple checks.

On the basis of all these considerations Heydrich issued a summons to a central conference on 30 January 1940 to which the regional office chiefs and unit chiefs were invited. He outlined to them the biggest population migration of the modern age and conveyed Himmler's order, which Himmler gave in his capacity as Reich Commissioner for the Consolidation of the German Nationality. He repeated the figures and groups of people already ordered, supplemented these with 30,000 gypsies and ordered first the deportation of some 10,000 Jews from the territory of the Old Reich from Stettin to the Generalgouvernement. He gave precisely 14 days' time, by this date the deportation should be completed. The reason for this was that the regional offices of which I spoke earlier wanted to see this deportation carried out for, through it, they thought to resolve the local housing shortage emergency and had therefore promised this deportation with the agreement of Himmler.

The direction of all these offices were in offices above my department. I only had to work out with the Transport Ministry the travel planning and whatever was connected with it after the necessary documents were sent to me both from the deportation authorities and from the receiving offices of the Generalgouvernement. This is of course just one sentence, but what an abundance of difficulties, work and persuasion, promises and counsels of patience, appeals to reason, and also sharp crackdowns for the remedy of problems this activity demanded, all that this single sentence does not reveal. Each of the regional people responsible wanted to see his deportation work ended first - without any considerations. It was a harsh winter, nevertheless the deportations had to be carried out. None of the commanding officers would announce that this plan would be postponed to the start of spring, to a season which, just through its better climatic conditions, would put an end to a large part of many difficulties.

Today it is easy to say, "Eichmann carried out the deportations. He is the one responsible." In retrospect it is always easy to open one's mouth wide and to fill it with opinions. This has been so at all times in history. And if we had won, even those who today do not wish to know anything about executive responsibility would have trumpeted their credit in "the implementation of the order of the Führer" more audibly to the whole world than they did this at that time. So a new "line" had to be discovered and this, for 1½ decades, was called "Eichmann".

One can see the result in the literature, in short in the publicity up to the beginning of the cross-examination which I was subjected to. There for the first time I could kick the lying masters in the pants just as they deserved to be kicked, but it would be a miracle if my defence would bear results. Nevertheless: it is a deep consolation, for "dogs always bite the last person". I can only recommend to these ignorant people that they should try standing up, having the rank of a captain, against a dozen generals and a further dozen provincial public authorities and high officials. Then they will experience their miracle. More so at a time when they had got used to the tempo of the *blitzkrieg*.[31], more so in my position as a consultant without any special powers, merely as a consultant, as the name itself signifies, and all this with a conscious decentralisation by Himmler of the basic orders.

If I had at that time been Himmler's consultant, I would of course have been able to present another proposal. I was not one of Himmler's 12-14 Head Office chiefs but of an office chief who in turn was subordinate to a Head Office chief. The documents prove this clearly.

---

31 "lightning war" was the term used for quick military strikes against an enemy supported by the air-force.

Assignment to Gestapo Office IV

Poles expelled from Reichsgau Wartheland in 1939.

Naturally, after 1945, the regional offices and the central authorities which eagerly sought out responsibilities and defended these like lions at a hundred meetings did not wish to know anything more about such things. Today I write in 1961 and I have only one inward consolation: dogs *always* bite the last person. On the scope of the decentralisation of the executive activity there is a telegram that I had to address on 30 March 1940 to the Inspector of the Security Police and SD in Posen which is eloquent testimony:

"Re: technical procedure in the resettlement of the Volhynian Germans. Expulsion of some 120,000 Poles.

File number: None.

I request that the technical procedure and the planned handling of the settlement of the Volhynian Germans in the Warthegau[32] be communicated in detail in a report."

This resettlement was ordered by Himmler. I had to manage the travel-plan with the Transport Ministry, but I was not aware of a single detail, and that was in March 1940. So, after the receipt of a memo relating to this from the Reich Transport Ministry, it was decided that the Reich Railways in Posen should make the necessary trains available in 48 hours.

---

32 A district of the Reich formed within Polish territory that was, in the nineteenth century, called first South Prussia and then the Duchy of Posen. Its capital was Posen (Poznań)

False Gods

In March 1940, a functional and personnel reorganisation of the Reich Security Head Office was once again undertaken. From this time on I had to take over the department within the Secret State Police Office that dealt with Jewish matters, that is, it was incorporated into my department. Not that I thereby became responsible for *all* Jewish matters of the Reich Security Head Office but just for those of Office IV. There were similar responsibilities for Jewish matters even in Office II, in Office IV and also in Office VII of the same Reich Security Head Office. Indeed even Offices V and VI dealt with them inasmuch as their range of work marginally included them.

I considered the No.1 problem to be the absence of a Jewish independent state. I am not so presumptuous as to maintain thereby that this knowledge of mine had suddenly discovered the root of the problem and had therewith set the philosopher's stone in motion. No, this was urgent and known already from the eighth *decade* of our era[33] and manifest every two hundred years.

In more than a thousand dealings with the Jewish functionaries I repeatedly heard the wailing for their own land. Whether one believes me or not does not bother me and is a matter of indifference to me, but I was glad and eager to act when, after the Polish campaign, I was able to observe in my superiors an agreement with my plan of freeing to the Jews one of the four new districts into which the Generalgouvernement was subdivided for a Jewish settlement territory. I imagined a protectorate status similar to that which Slovakia had, not to that of Bohemia and Moravia.

It was clear to me that such a thing does not happen overnight, it must develop and needs time. Besides, all peacetime organisational life was destroyed in Poland and, in addition, there was the confusion of Himmler's population migration from east to west and from west to east, which increased in chaos through the ambition of regional power-holders.

My superior at that time, the commanding officer of the Sipo and SD in Prague, had been commissioned by Heydrich with the plan created by me along with Jewish political functionaries like Dr. Löwenherz, Storfer and Edelstein. Nisko on the San was the temporary springboard. The first two thousand should, like pioneers, create,

---

33 The Roman Emperor Titus conquered and sacked Jerusalem, which had been besieged by the Jews from A.D.66, to A.D.70.

according to the preconceived plan, accommodation possibilities here for their descendants.

When the first trains were unloaded, men and materials, labourers and doctors, construction teams and administrative people, "Polish Frank", who had in the meantime been appointed Generalgouverneur, struck a blow and shattered everything with one order. He had run to Hitler with his counter-proposal and Hitler from then on took him into his confidence. Therewith this hope disappeared, for Frank's political goal was the dejudaisation of his area of command.

The commanding officer of the Sipo and SD in Krakow at that time whose area of responsibility was the Generalgouvernement informed me that Frank had given an order to arrest me on entry into the Generalgouvernement. Apart from the absurdity of such an instruction, for no regional commanding officer of the Security Police could arrest a consultant of the Reich Security Head Office unless he had the order for that from Müller, the Chief of Office IV, from Heydrich, the Chief of the Security Police and SD, from Himmler the SS Reichsführer and Chief of the German Police, from the responsible military commander, or from Hitler, the leader of the state and the Reich chancellor. Nevertheless, Frank was the "sole dictator" in his Generalgouvernement.

Resurgence of the Madagascar Plan

Hardly had the ink on the cease-fire treaty in Compiègne between Germany and France dried[34] than I unearthed again, after the fiasco of Nisko on the San, the old "Madagascar plan". Now there was a possibility of its realisation. In any case I worked on the plan. Heydrich's ambition came in handy here. It is possible that he already saw himself as the governor of this island. Obviously with the retention of his previous powerful position.

I myself could not bring forward this project to Himmler or Heydrich, and Heydrich's wish to stick his finger into foreign political matters was widely known. Even here I imagined a protectorate. Its initial status was rather of no consequence to me! I had also no influence in

---

34   The armistice of Compiègne was signed between Germany and France on 22 June 1940 after Germany's decisive victory in the Battle of France. According to this treaty, northern France would be occupied by Germany while the south would remain under the French government.

False Gods

this regard. Only time could create a plan and something final. But now that Hitler granted his approval to Madagascar the race of the other offices of the Reich began. Everybody claimed departmental authority and priority in the handling of this novel case, and before I could prepare for it I had to deal with twenty or more consultants. Each of them had his "if's" and "buts" according to his superiors' orders. A cooperative work materialised that was *not* in accordance with the intention of the initial idea.

My concern regarding this was not great, for I thought to direct matters personally on location. I had already obtained the approval of my superiors for that. It would certainly not have become a concentration camp, and seven million cows on this island were a comforting treasure; with an agricultural basis with which alone one could achieve much. I worked on its realisation up to late 1941.

The further course of the war and the political radicalisation put an end to the plan through Hitler's order. Even today, as then, I am filled with an ungovernable anger when I think of the damned rashness, wrong-headedness and stupidity of our own power-holders of that time.

Naturally, my plans of that time do not sound good to all Poles and Frenchmen. But one may imagine a boiler which is heated beyond the permitted atmospheric pressure through foolish heating methods. It is stoked further; the boiler will break if I do not take care of the valve. I had nothing to do with the heating. Even the boiler did not stand under my charge. Every ministry had its own "boiler inspectors" and nobody who would have said then that it could not go on like this. I had no possibility of doing so, for I did not belong to the board of "inspectors". I tried to work with the valve, to find a possibility of holding on. Whether it was good or bad I had no way of deciding. For me it was a matter of preventing an explosion. Then later people more professional than me might occupy themselves with a final normalisation. A provisional measure, this was the most that I could plan and conceive. Apart from the Jewish functionaries of that time, I had not a single one of the present-day bawlers and equivocators helping me in that.

But what am I saying, "helping"; they prepared difficulties and inconveniences for me. Yes, I do not shrink from calling a spade a spade; for that was the fact!

Already at the beginning of 1941 Department IE of the Reich Ministry of the Interior convened an important meeting. All the authorities of the Reich interested in it were invited to it. Basically it was a matter of classifying personal statuses of those newly come into the Reich according to the Reich citizenship laws. Hitler had rejected an initial plan of the Reich Ministry of the Interior relating to this. This department had sketched a new, sharper one. This regulation draft then came into force on 25 October as regulation 11 of the Reich citizenship laws.

It announced the deprival of citizenship of all Jews on crossing the Reich borders, and the confiscation of their assets in favour of the Reich.

In the same year there followed a further radical step, namely the identification of Jews. Having to wear in a visible manner a star of yellow material. Frank, the state secretary for the security system in Bohemia and Moravia made the request, the Reich chancellery and the Ministry of the Interior were referred to and Goebbels, as Reich Minister for Public Enlightenment and Propaganda, obtained from Hitler the order for the identification of Jews in the Reich territories and in Bohemia and Moravia. On 15 September 1941, this ordinance came into force. Two years earlier, on 23 November, Frank had already ordered it for the Generalgouvernement.

The Attack on the USSR

On 21 August 1939, Ribbentrop travelled to Moscow to sign, on Hitler's orders, the non-aggression pact with the Soviet Union. But, on 22 June 1941, German divisions set out from their deployment positions, moving in an attack on the Soviets. Exactly that which Hitler had in his book criticised as a mistake of the political leadership of the Reich during the first world-war he himself now did. And therewith he destroyed himself and the Reich. Even Bismarck's doctrines in this regard were of no consequence to him. I remember even today how at that time I celebrated the pact with Russia with my comrades; with beer and wine, that was the custom.

I still remember the feeling that filled me when I heard of the preparations for the war against the Soviets. Even in the SS there were two *personal* orientations that were never outwardly manifested. One that was politically left-wing and another attitude tending to the extreme right. My personal political feelings lay towards the left, at least emphasising the socialistic aspect as much as the nationalistic.

Our opinion at that time was that National Socialism and the Communism of the Soviet Republic were sort of "siblings". And it may also be that this attitude was peculiar especially to an Austrian SS member. For his enemies at that time were not Social Democracy and Communism; these were combated by the Austrian aristocracy as much as he himself was; the former at that time occupied the leading positions in the "Home Guards"[35] and their challenge was to the National Socialists, Social Democrats and Communists equally.

Indeed, there were times when the followers of these two orientations were united through party truce and mutual help and support in the battle against their chief opponent. In no way however did they betray each other and in the worst case be "prepared for battle", as one used to say. It may be that this attitude of a left-wing tendency began at this time. However it may have been, it was in any case present, and 22 June 1941 saw us sullen and discontented, but we obeyed as the oath ordered us to.

Hitler's Order for Physical Annihilation

In late autumn 1941[36], my office chief informed me that, according to Heydrich's order, I had to report to him. If one were summoned to Heydrich then one could bet a thousand to one, that one would be faced with an hour-long wait in his antechamber. A delay in the schedule of the appointments book was part of the normal routine of a very busy man. A similar thing occurred to me too with the frequent meetings with my office chief, even if the wait time here was not nearly as long as that in the case of the Chief of the Security Police himself. It was clear, more high-ranking persons always came first, however late they may have come and however long the officially more subordinate person may have waited. It was exactly the same when visitors from

---

35   Heimwehr

36   By late Autumn 1941 the attack on Moscow had stalled, and in December 1941 Germany declared war on the USA, and Hitler ordered German forces on the Russian Eastern Front to move from an attack, to a defensive strategy, and with it he probably recognised the possibility of losing the war. On January 20, 1942, at Wannsee, Berlin high-ranking Nazi Party and German government leaders gathered to discuss the practical implementation of Hitler's order for the killing of the Jews.

Hitler's Order for Physical Annihilation

abroad suddenly appeared. Now all this was understandable, and following the motto, "The soldier waits half his life uselessly", one surrendered with equanimity to one's destined waiting.

Since my relationship with the adjutant was a comradely-friendly one, a glass of wine or Armagnac helped me through the boredom of the waiting room, and homely gossip with the adjutant shortened the time. But everything has an end. I reported to the office most obediently, as ordered.

"*The Führer has ordered the physical annihilation of the Jews.* Globocnik has received his instructions from the Führer. According to these he should use the tank-ditches for this purpose. I would like to know what he is doing and how far he has progressed. Go to him and report to me on what you have seen and heard." Therewith I was dismissed.

I had first to allow the concept "*physical annihilation*" to go through my mind in an orderly manner to be able to measure its total significance. I had to digest something that was unknown, new, unusual, and hitherto unheard of. But Heydrich spoke calmly, not in the customary nervous and loud manner that otherwise characterised him. I only said, "Gosh, this is extreme!" And with these thoughts I went one floor higher in order to report to Müller.

I informed Müller of the order received but he seemed to know it already, for his efforts were directed to the signing of my marching orders which his adjutant had already prepared for me. I left, with bad images in my head of what I would have to witness. The only consolation was my military flask, which I had filled with a litre of red wine. It was covered with brown felt as military flasks are indeed wont to be and only from its weight did I notice that I had to refill it in one of the places through which I travelled with my driver. In this way I arrived in Lublin.

On the next day I drove with an adjutant of Globocnik's to the office which I had to report. At that time Globocnik was SS Brigadeführer[37] and major general of the Police. His position was that of an SS and Police chief of the Lublin district in the Generalgouvernement. He was under the senior SS and Police chief in the Generalgouvernement and state secretary for the security system, in the government of the

---

37   SS brigadier general

Generalgouverneur in Krakow, SS Gruppenführer[38] and general of the Police, Krüger.[39] He and therewith his four SS and Police chiefs were immediately under Himmler. So much about the personnel.

After about two hours' travel, it could also have been an hour and a half, we came to a wood clearing in which on the right side of the road there stood a little farmhouse. There the car stopped.

We were received by a regular policeman in rolled up shirtsleeves, obviously working manually. The style of his boots and the cut of his riding trousers indicated an officer. During the introduction I learnt that I was dealing with a captain of the regular police. The name slipped my mind a long time ago in the post-war years. Only through the post-war literature did I recall it. His name was Wirth. My imaginary pictures had been nightmarish and the effect manifested itself in internal and certainly also external trepidation.

The Gassing of Jews at Lublin

In the last days I felt the way I remembered from my schoolboy days when I had to carry home a bad report. The longer the walk home the better. So I went home at a slow pace, in slow-motion, and to pass the time I studied all the shop-windows of the shops with doubled thoroughness to postpone the moment of the delivery of my report as much as possible. Of course, I could not apply my schoolboy methods now. I could not tell my driver that he should drive only at a tractor's pace. He raced on good roads at eighty kilometres per hour and sometimes even more, and on the bad routes in a correspondingly curbed manner. As on the previous day, on this day too I tried red wine and distracting conversation. The said Wirth thus drove us to a small forest path on the left side of the road and there stood under deciduous trees two small farmhouses. I can no longer remember with certainty if, at the moment of our visit, work was going on there, but Wirth explained his commission to us.

According to it, he had to close all the windows and doors hermetically. After the completion of the work, Jews would come into the rooms who would be killed through the exhaust gas of a Russian submarine

---

38   SS major general

39   Friedrich-Wilhelm Krüger (1894-1945) was Senior SS and Police chief in the Generalgouvernement from 1939 to 1943.

The Gassing of Jews at Lublin

motor that would be introduced into these rooms. That was all that he had to say.

There was nothing to be seen of tank-ditches, and I saw neither Jews nor corpses. I must say that I felt very relieved, for hearing and speaking is always different from doing or seeing. I remember even today that, on the return journey, the red wine and cigarettes were especially beneficial to me in relaxing my nerves. For, when I considered it retrospectively at that time, so many things had already been ordered over the years and then revoked. I just did not take the gassing seriously. I returned to Berlin, and made my reports to Heydrich and Müller. They were acknowledged without any comments.

Heydrich's nervous manner and his curt military behaviour to subordinates, his high rank and great position permitted no personal issues. It was different with Müller. In his Bavarian and more casual manner it was permissible to bring forward personal matters, questions and wishes at all times which he also listened to from beginning to end and never interrupted. But seldom did one obtain a response to it. The rule was a sudden switch to some official matters, as if wishes or personal matters had never been the object of the talk. One never knew where one stood. The only thing that could be expected was communicated in a "yes, yes", coupled with a thin, fatherly smile. Exactly as if he wished to say, Yes, my dear man, I understand all this, but we cannot do anything about it.

Müller himself, in all the years that I had to work under him, moved away from his desk only very seldom, that is, he took no holidays, was almost never sick, and seldom went on an official trip. He worked until late in the evening and even then his chauffeur carried briefcases full of work materials into the car which he worked on in his private residence.

Among the documents of the Israeli prosecution there are, among others, two telegrams that Müller himself signed at a late hour on "Christmas Eve". He worked without rest on Sundays and holidays. Not only I but also other witnesses can state that he took a personal interest in literally all matters, of even only little significance, and even concerning individual cases, giving instructions, as soon as they came into his official responsibility. I myself was every week at least twice with him for consultations. Either summoned or else I sought him out for that purpose. In the course of time, these days became such a routine that one could without exaggerating speak of fixed days and hours. And if I took with me every time only 25 files to get my chief's instructions – mostly however it was more – then I can calculate roughly that in the course of a year there were around 10,000 to 15,000 procedures on which he himself gave instructions or orders about what was to be done and submitted the rest to his boss for obtaining instructions.

Müller himself was not of a specially decisive nature. Rather, he was the cautious, anxious bureaucrat, and he demanded also from his consultants the stubborn maintenance of bureaucratic prescriptions. All this will be confirmed also by the man who must have known him better than many others, that SS Standartenführer and government director who was for a while, towards the end of the war, Müller's official representative who recorded his statements in this regard in a testimony.

One thing is clear, Müller was one of those men who was always well informed on all events. He had not only the function of Chief of the Secret State Police Office, but also that of the general border inspector.

Eichmann Witnesses the Murders

It must have been January 1942 that Müller gave me the order to go to Kulm[40] near Posen and to make a report to him on the killings of Jews being implemented there. I must say that my anxieties about seeing frightful things were not so severe as in the previous autumn. Even though I had in the meanwhile read in the reports that circulated as secret communication within the Reich Security Head Office much, and constantly, about shootings in the east. But I had not ordered that and I did not have to work on it, I could also not influence or stop it, I could not even imagine it very correctly as a reality since I had also never seen it. I had not spoken to any eye witness. So, once I arrived in the Warthegau, I was conducted to Kulm by an official of the State Police Office, but what I saw there was horror itself, and my idea that I could get away as well from it as last autumn in Lublin was transformed by the most dreadful reality that I had ever seen.

I saw naked Jews and Jewesses get into a closed van without windows. The doors were locked and the engine started. The exhaust gas however did not flow into the open air but into the interior of the vehicle. A

---

40   Kulm is the German name for Chelmno.

Eichmann Witnesses the Murders

doctor in a white gown pointed out to me a peep-hole near the driver's seat through which one could see into the interior of the vehicle and asked me to observe the process.

I could not do it any longer. I also lacked the words to express my reaction to these things for it was all too unreal. I think that, at that moment, I did not have conscious control of myself any more. I had also not been able to carry out Müller's order to halt the timing of the killing. I had forgotten it, and would not also have been physically capable of it. Then this bus started. I myself was driven to a sort of forest meadow and when I arrived there, this bus too turned in, it drove to an excavated pit, the door was opened, and corpses tumbled out into the pit. One on top of the other. That was a gruesome inferno. No, it was a super-inferno. I had just seen them alive. Now they were all dead. Then a civilian jumped into the pit and checked the mouths and removed the gold-teeth with a pair of pliers.

I still remember that I had to pinch the skin of the back of my hand to make sure that I was awake, that what I had seen was real, and that I was not just dreaming.

I can remember when, on that May evening in Buenos Aires, I was attacked thirty metres from my house, my feet and hands were tied and I was brought to a country house in a car, put in pyjamas and tied by the feet to a bed after my eyes had been bound, I likewise pinched the back of my hand to determine what this really was, am I dreaming, or has something that I imagined actually come about.

The same thing happened to me at that time. I myself had nothing to do with the things. The task ordered to me was to see at first hand and to report on it. I do not know if, when one has to do with such things as a person ordering or a person implementing, such sorts of signs of paralysis or delusions take hold, but my consciousness of reality was somehow fully changed. There occurred something like a climbing out from the realm of the still thinkable to the unreal, a displaced world in which I saw only waves on which everything moved.

Then it suddenly struck me, You must check if all this is true; the pain of the pinch then confirmed it. It is remarkable and surprising into what situations one can enter, and frightful complexes of the imagination ruled my waking and did not leave me even in sleep. During my trial I was asked by one of the judges whether lack of moral courage was one of the reasons that one could go along with

False Gods

The destroyed "Gas Van" at Kulm (Chelmno), Poland.

all this. This is correct, and accurate too, and I said to him, "The German officer corps did not know anything about moral courage. That is true, and the term itself signifies it in its form".

Duty, fulfilment of orders; obedience and fidelity! But moral courage never appeared anywhere in the official regulations. It is really regrettable, I must say.

I drove to Berlin. I had to report to Müller. After the report, I said to him, "If only I had another appointment; I am not the right man for this. Just in terms of nerves I cannot bear such a thing; that is not a political solution!" This time he replied to me: "The soldier at the front too cannot choose where he would like to fight. But he has to do his duty where he is placed."

If up to now doubts often occurred to me whether the actions of the gods themselves were, even making the greatest allowances, to be characterised as divine actions, I could always say as the final wisdom that, with the exception of the flames of 10 November 1938, *I* have still not seen anything of all the horror. They are all reports. Partly they were hearsay reports, partly of course official reports, but there was a great difference between letters and images, especially when one – like me – is not at all officially concerned with it. Even Müller did not

Eichmann Witnesses the Murders

order it; even he would not have been able to stop it. But now I served false idols; this became clear to me.

Everything that I could really become enthusiastic about, looking for and finding a solution to the problem on a political basis and being able to work on that for the welfare of both parties, had now been broken. Of the gruesome matter I do not at all wish to speak again, for my sensitive nature is revolted by the sight of corpses and blood. It would have been an easy thing, even child's play, in comparison with the violent solution now ordered, to create at least a temporary arrangement of a political solution; it did not indeed need to be anything final. During a war everybody often satisfies himself with only a partial solution of a problem when nothing else works. Peace would automatically bring something clear, firm. How I had broken my head looking for alternatives from my standpoint. But I had truthfully not contributed anything to such a violent solution and I could, like Pontius Pilate, wash my hands off it. But whom would even this serve? One who rides the tiger cannot get off it.

My fatherland was in distress. The war against Russia and England in full swing, and, on 11 December 1941, Germany had declared war against the USA. Everything unimaginable. Müller's order: I have to do my duty where I am placed, there is no choice for the soldier. No exit: already long ago I had become obliged to war service for the duration of the war, like the other members of the Security Service. One was not asked; it was an order from above! Perhaps if I had received orders to kill or to order killings I might have been able to say: No, nobody can order me to kill civilians when these have not actively proceeded against the laws of war. But I never received such orders. One who was in the Einsatz Commando and received orders to kill would have had the possibility; whether with success or not remains undecided.

A few cases are demonstrable where the person making a request succeeded in releasing himself from the implementation of an order. I do not know under what circumstances, for I myself heard about it for the first time in Israel. But be that as it may, I sat in Berlin at the writing desk and did not have anything to order in this regard. I did not have the necessary support for making a request for a transfer with a hope of success.

Outwardly I could not of course rebel against it by showing lack of discipline. Inwardly I stood *against* compulsion and pressure and, not exceeding the limits of the enforced subordination, I took up a position against it in words. Clearly without success; for my immediate superior to whom I proposed such a thing himself stood under compulsion and pressure. Indeed, more even than I myself. For, the extent of his knowledge of secret procedures was certainly incomparably greater than mine. To the degree that I recognised the futility of a personal opposition to this pressure I attached myself to this compulsion following the principle of the rubber ball and recognised it finally as a sort of legality from which I could not withdraw. I lived in a situation in which one oriented oneself with difficulty to that which was new, for the results of the education I had enjoyed battled in me against the totalitarian claim of the recently freely elected Führer. Of course, at the moment of this election, I had had no idea of its comprehensive demands on my entire person; on my physical and psychological personality. I could finally be glad if I still preserved for myself on the whole a moderate civil manner and form which would present itself in my activity like a sediment, for I lived in an environment in which the aesthetics of tolerance disappeared like the snow under the March sun.

I had inwardly resolved not to need to make decisions even in my daily office work handling files. In every detailed case the way to my office chief always stood open. I could thereby avoid personal inner strains. I adopted this path ever since my transfer, which had been ordered *against* my will. My custom regarding this was known to the entire department and beyond it. If my chief had decided my will, obviously I took the ordered Security Police precautionary measures. I was obligated to that by oath. As gladly as I worked in the information service so burdensome was the executive part of the police service to me. As much as I, concerned for the Reich, viewed the orders of the German Reich government with an increasingly pessimistic standpoint, whether it was a matter of the series of declarations of war that seemed to me unnecessary or of orders with regard to the Jewish question, nothing more remained to me - in view of my service rank as SS senior lieutenant and my official position as a consultant, thus as a recipient of orders - than to obey. The responsible political leadership offices and the regional and technical commanding officers of these high national offices had to bear the responsibility.

I was roped in and could not move legally in any another way; like one thousand other senior lieutenants. If the others wanted to do what they believed, I could not prevent them; I also did not have to answer for that. It was my duty to be faithful to my oath of allegiance and, as I had repeatedly heard, do my duty where the orders placed me.

Eichmann Witnesses the Murders

But one thing I recognised fully clearly, that the "obligation to act" according to a moral law innate in man became hard, if not impossible, for me, conditioned by the laws of war to which I was subjected and which bound my will, against my inner understanding, and made me unfree.

Of course I recognised this already from the time of my transfer to the Secret State Police in late autumn 1939 but not with the present frightening clarity. For, up to 1941, I lived in the delusion of the possibility of a political solution. From now on I had to recognise that this had been a delusional idea of mine. I recognised also that the then chiefs of the Reich did not worry about moral demands; not at all about the Kantian conceptions of things. They did not give a damn about it. Their attitude was only for the present moment, and even then they failed lacking plan or idea, and in the senseless bustle they lost every active initiative in the realm of war leadership.

But even on the other side, on the part of the leadership of the different hostile nations, one cannot in any way claim that they employed a purely ethical will. Politics is and remains a rather common whore. Not that I would today mourn the lost war. For a long time I have stood *beyond* my post-war attitude with regard to this.

My only desire for the future would be to make war and its inevitable consequences impossible. But when I describe the matters of that time I must be present in them through memory. I must relive and re-experience them again so that I can recount them here.

Even today I am of the point of view that the war was originally forced upon the German nation. Economic and competitive envy were behind it, but I am not sure that it would have been inevitable if our own government had presented a different attitude. I am only sure that the war experienced an enlargement through folly and a disregard of all realities on the part of *our* own leadership; this is in addition to everything else. And so the German nation was divided gradually into several groups in addition to those which already existed:

- Those whose orientation and attitude were conditioned purely through instinct, their way of looking at problems was simple and uncomplicated.
- Those who went along outwardly and, loyal to the oath, obeyed orders but inwardly kept a distance for reasons that I have just described.

False Gods

- And thirdly, those who from now on distanced themselves inwardly as well as outwardly, indeed sabotaged.

The consequence of this lack of uniformity among the recipients of orders finally found its visible mark in a lower endurance capacity. That was not changed either by keeping the civil population in the centres of the bomb-battlefields or by the courage to sacrifice individual divisions and armies, neither was it changed by the stubborn attitude of loyalty to the oath of allegiance of the war marines and air squadrons. There gradually gained ground everywhere a deconcentration and distraction as a true mirror-image of the conduct of the leadership of the Reich. In their arrogance they believed that they could implement measures in times of war that would have been impossible under normal circumstances and did not think of – *ignoring everything else here* – the inevitable psychological consequences.

I did not belong to the group which finally led to a "20 July 1944"; I did not belong to the coarsest group whose inward and outward attitude remained the same. I was part of those who obeyed outwardly, did nothing that brought them into conflict with the oath that they had undertaken, and served honestly and uprightly and fulfilled the duty that was ordered. However, through this inner attitude there came about a personality split, a condition that obstructed. A condition that had to kill all impetus and drive. A condition under which the individual suffered more than he ever wished to admit or admitted, and he numbed himself with "duty", "oath", "loyalty" and "honour".

But, apart from that, it makes no difference what type of state it is: traitors and those who refuse to obey their order, saboteurs and those who wound themselves, undergo during wartime that treatment from the state that relates to the breach of an oath of allegiance. I have also not learnt that anything has changed in that even after 1945, and the crimes against humanity, war crimes and other atrocities that have occurred after this year are legion. This in spite of the Magna Carta, the UNO, and other security regulations. Human insufficiency today and yesterday, wherever one looks. Nothing has changed.

I do not wish to gloss over the actions of our power-holders of that time. In the present work I serve nobody and I gloss over nothing. Just as I have, through my experience, lost all respect for authority.

Indeed I write for nobody's praise and it is a matter of indifference to me whether my work is read, and a matter of indifference whether

Eichmann Witnesses the Murders

it is praised or damned. I only wish to warn, and warning words are neither milk or honey. They are thin and dry like the thorn bushes of the pampas, or like bleaching bones in the desert. The people themselves whom I saw at the places of killing or with preparatory work for this had been made available through the involvement of the "Chancellery of the Führer".[41]

The Oberdienstleiter[42] Brack from this chancellery, whose name also appears in some documents during my trial, had regulated this matter with Himmler himself. He had had to carry out the killings of the mentally ill and, after the completion of his activity, presented to Himmler the personnel that he had available, at which time Brack made available this Globocnik. Wirth was originally an official of middle rank in a criminal police office in the south-west of the Reich. I saw him in the uniform of an officer of the regular police and, during the trial, my defence counsel showed me a photograph which represented him as an SS Sturmbannführer. Wirth conducted the killings through gassing in Globocnik's jurisdiction.

In Kulm also the Gauleiter and Reich Governor was personally connected to this matter. He corresponded on this with Himmler. Bothmann, the director of the Kulm gassing centre, likewise came from the euthanasia staff of Brack, from the "Chancellery of the Führer", just like Wirth. Even the Reich Security Head Office was directly involved in the killings through exhaust gas, as the documents presented during the trial have unobjectionably proven. But it was not Office IV that had its finger in it, but Office II. An entire bundle of written correspondence is available. These buses were transformed for the envisaged purpose by Office II and then sent to the Einsatz Groups in the east. The documents demonstrate this fully clearly.

I shall never understand why Müller sent me at that time with stubborn regularity from one place to another of the killings even though he knew my attitude at the time after my return from reporting. Even though he knew that, the request for a transfer came with equal stubbornness on my part although I knew also that it would not be agreed to in the same automatic manner. Müller certainly had

---

41 The Chanceller of the Führer was headed by Philipp Bouhler from 1934 to 1945, although from 1942 his powers were taken over in large part by Martin Bormann, who headed the Party Chancellery from 1941, after the flight of his chief, Rudolf Hess, to Britain.

42 Senior service director

nothing personally to do with the gas vehicles. And if a temporary *formal* intermediate superior in the official channel between me and Müller named Hartel said in Nuremberg after 1945 that Müller had sent him to the east to become "hard" and explained to him, when he could not take over command for shootings for personal reasons or nerves, that he should really be called not "Hartel"[43] but "Weichel"[44] I find it difficult to believe this. In close connection with this testimony, the state attorney general asked me in the cross-examination if Müller did not, on the basis of my report, also describe me as "Weichmann" instead of "Eichmann"; I had to answer this question in the negative.

Müller had not given the killing orders to these Einsatz Groups; this giving of orders was undertaken by Heydrich, as emerges very clearly from the statements of the unit chief. Müller never gave me any orders to the commands that he ordered me to visit. I was asked to travel for nothing but for his personal information. As mentioned earlier, it will always remain a riddle to me why he chose me when there were dozens of people of a more robust nature than mine.

I do not wish either to exonerate or to incriminate my former superior in things about which I do not know anything precise. Anyway an exoneration is not possible with the responsibilities that he had and incrimination I leave to the documents, for there everything is written more accurately, more accurately than it is now possible for me to represent the matters, after nearly 20 years having passed in the meantime. It is also useless to think back today on such things. What has happened cannot be undone. I received the order and had to carry out the report trips. So I shall prepare myself for the description of my next deployment to Minsk.

The Killings in Minsk

It was around the same time, around January 1942, that I received the instruction to report on the proceedings in the above-mentioned city. It was bitter cold and I wore a long padded coat and took the necessary alcohol provisions with me, for I could carry out these orders only through constant pondering on things. But the alcohol produced some numbing. It was clear that the degree had to be not high enough

---

43 from "hart" meaning "hard"

44 from "weich" meaning "weak"

The Killings in Minsk

for drunkenness, for I indeed drove in uniform with a chauffeur in a police vehicle. But it is amazing what amounts a man needs in case of nerves that have been lashed in order to hold them in order to some degree. Of course, spirits would have been better than red wine but I drank spirits only when red wine was not available. I arrived in the evening, and on the next day I was delayed. The hour mentioned to me had long passed, so I came to the place only when the last group were being shot.

When I approached the place of execution, the shots crackled in unbroken continuous fire in a pit that was as big as many large rooms. They shot with machine guns. On arrival I saw a Jewish woman with a small child in her arms in the pit. I wanted to pull the child out, but then a shot struck the head of the child. My chauffeur wiped away from my coat small pieces of brain. I got into my vehicle.

Berlin, I said to my chauffeur, but I drank schnaps like water. I had to drink. I had to numb myself, and I thought of my own children - at that time I had two. I thought of the meaninglessness of life, and I found no more order in the will and desire of Providence. It was indescribably difficult in this chaos to still believe in anything. I imagined that that which the Christian faith characterises as Hell was not something in the future with which it warns men but it could only be that we are, all together, already in this "Hell". That was the only explanation.

Belief and love, ethics, aesthetics, education, one's parents, placed all care and hope in them. The thinking brain then made its own effort to form ideas within the scope of an appropriate possibility. It found bridges and helps, among other things, in Kant. How could I adjust and bring into harmony all this with what I had seen? It was hopeless. But the ponderings continued.

The reason of my inward attachment to the party was injustice. It was the Versailles dictate, but now we brought injustice ourselves in manifold forms. The leader of the state personally ordered it.

My own judges and the highest judge of the SS and Police jurisdiction ordered all this, and they ordered me too. Here one may try to create order and to bring all these many diverging components to an inwardly satisfying consequence, but it is an impossibility.

The Reich leadership of that time brought one into such an internal jungle. In retrospect it is always easy for a third party to speak. But

False Gods

what would *they themselves* have done in such a situation? If the engine has been started and the energy has been harnessed, the wheels must run, regardless whether the tube, the core of the tyre, bursts, regardless whether the tyre itself tears, they must run, even if only on smashed rims until the driver decides otherwise or until the vehicle goes to hell. I too am comparable to such a wheel, many are. Such a wheel cannot jump out through its own force even when it notices that everything can no longer be all right with the driver.

This is the fate of the recipient of orders. Now that I could not change it, I did the only thing that I could. I carried out the orders issued to me obediently. If it had been peacetime, it would have been easier for me to change my situation compared to the totalitarian claim that the state makes on a person during wartime, no matter what it orders. But I must once again go back in time somewhat and once again shine a light on 1941.

The deportations ordered by Himmler extended, apart from temporary interruptions, even into this year. From East Prussia, and especially from that district newly added to this province, the Warthegau, and even from Vienna.

I have a telegram before me, which went out on 13 February 1941 to all state police offices outside Vienna and was signed by me. Among other things it says: "Re: the evacuation of the Jews from Vienna to the Generalgouvernement.

In view of the especially cramped situation in Vienna, the Führer had ordered the evacuation of the Jews settled in Vienna. The state police office in Vienna had already issued an ordinance on 1 February 1941 according to which Jews who have their permanent residence in Vienna should not leave the Gau territory of Vienna."

This order from Hitler was issued following a statement of Baldur von Schirach, the former Gauleiter of Vienna, during a meeting that he had with Hitler. For that reason too the state police office in Vienna – Gauleiters and Reich governors had a right to issue instructions to their regional offices – could issue a prohibition order for their area of responsibility even before the Reich Security Head Office was involved in it.

On 15 March all evacuation transports from the incorporated German eastern territories, or Vienna, to the Generalgouvernement had to be stopped. The operations department of the German general staff

The Killings in Minsk

wished to have a free hand for their marching plans against Russia in the deployment areas and not be disturbed by any other transport movements. Müller signed the corresponding circular decree of a stoppage.

In July 1941, Göring, in his capacity as Reich Marshal, Commissioner for the Four-Year Plan, and Chairman of the Ministerial Council for National Defence, sent to Heydrich a commission document which empowered him to make all required preparations in organisational, technical and material terms for a total solution of the Jewish question in the German sphere of influence in Europe. In this regard he wished to be presented soon with a total plan.

Heydrich's efforts to maintain the European commission had difficulties insofar as his rival in this regard, the German Reich Foreign Minister, could doubtless manifest his undeniably authoritative powers in this area. There had anyway already been enough mistrust between Heydrich and Ribbentrop ever since the Madagascar plan became current once again.

Even though I am aware from personal experience how much the central authorities were concerned to retain in their hands all powers in their area in the case of a realisation of the Madagascar plan, I have never heard that the Chief of the "Chancellery of the Führer", Philip Bouhler, had been proposed as governor of this island, or that anybody from the Chancellery of the Führer had wishes or hopes regarding this. This was exclusively a struggle between Heydrich and Ribbentrop. The different representation of Oberdienstleiter Brack of the "Chancellery of the Führer", which he submitted in Nuremberg in 1947, was certainly provided for defence reasons. On the contrary I know, with certainty, that it was especially the "Chancellery of the Führer" that constantly wanted to see tightening points incorporated and that it was this which turned my original Madagascar idea inside out. Bouhler committed suicide in May 1945 in Zell am See in Salzburger Austria and Brack was executed in 1948 in Landsberg.

In any case, Heydrich sought to acquire his rights of authority for this Madagascar solution through a written assurance of the Reich chief responsible for this, Göring, and he obtained them.

From Heydrich's idea relating to this up to the completed signature there transpired months. It is wrong to suppose that such powers were achieved as it were in a quick process overnight. Heydrich had to first prepare his ground here. Only weeks later was the Madagascar plan laid to rest by the German ambassador in Paris, Abetz, who made new proposals. But I should speak of that later when I come to speak of France.

But this formulation of Göring's accorded also with the new Paris plan so that it did not have to undergo any changes. Officially the Madagascar Plan was filed away only at the beginning of 1942.

In autumn 1941, more precisely in October, the deportation programme that had to be interrupted by the military operational preparations for the campaign against Russia was stimulated once again from above and the start of the task was once again ordered.

The first wave consisted of altogether 20,000 Jews from Berlin, Vienna, Prague, Cologne, Hamburg, Frankfurt, Düsseldorf and Luxembourg.

My department received the deportation sites, the numbers of the Jews to be deported from these areas, and the destination. It was determined by orders who had to be deported and which categories of persons could not be deported. Himmler himself ordered the extent of the permissible luggage. The receiving areas were occupied Russian territories or Lodz - a concession to the authorities responsible for the travel-plan technicalities, thus to the Reich Transport Ministry. This was the first and also the last time that such a possibility was permitted. In the future only a single final station was always ordered.

Then the following occurred: Shortly before the order for the preparation for this first large deportation of Jews, (if the deportation from Stettin at the beginning of 1940 may be ignored), was issued.

In Lublin. I saw there the preparations for the killing of Jews. I had also read about the shootings in the occupied Russian territories. Even though I had supposed that the same fate was not planned for the Jews of the Reich – I thought I could conclude this from the content of the ordered guidelines – I however knew certainly that in the large ghetto of Lodz up to now there had been no talk of such things at all. So the travel-plans for the Lodz final station were prepared accordingly and issued by the Reich Transport Ministry. But before that the agreement statement of the responsible public authorities in Lodz had to be obtained. I dealt with the man responsible at the district president's office, Übelhör. With what small tricks I obtained his half or three-quarters agreement I no longer remember today. It is true

The Killings in Minsk

that I did not personally request the district president who was alone responsible for it, since his negative attitude to the acceptance of Jews was well known.

The travel-plan was ready; perhaps a train had already arrived at the ghetto – I no longer remember this either. Then Übelhör wrote a sharply-worded telegram to the Reich Ministry of the Interior and other central authorities, complained about me that I had acted with "horse-trading and gypsy methods" and he demanded a stoppage of the transports and my punishment.

The matter went up to Himmler after the district president had involved also the army high command since it was apparently worried about the armaments industry which had been set up in the ghetto; they demanded that the Jews should be transported to Warsaw. Himmler wrote to the high command that it would remain so and Heydrich informed the district president that the Jews would come to Lodz and, further, that a punishment of myself would not considered since I had orders. But as mentioned, in the future the choice between certain final stations was never granted to me but these as well as other matters were determined in the terse military form.

Already at the end of October there followed a second similar order, namely to get 50,000 Jews from the territory of the Greater German Reich including the Protectorate of Bohemia and Moravia into the region of Minsk and Riga. The operation had to be finished by the end of November. But for one thing it began with a delay, and the number amounted to 30,000. So here, along with the number, deportation regions and the date before which the deportation had to be carried out, the receiving place also was ordered in a most precise way. This was the second largest wave of evacuations from the actual Reich territory.

This occasion leads me to speak of a remarkable document. The so-called "Wetzel letter". Dr. Wetzel was a district court judge. From 1941 to 1942 he worked in the Rosenberg Eastern Ministry in a juridical department. There is a document which appears in the following way:

1. A handwritten draft
2. A typed clean copy
3. A typed draft
4. A typed letter to an office of the Eastern Ministry

False Gods

None of the above documents bear a seal or signature. The letter draft and clean copy derive from the handwritten draft. According to this, Dr. Wetzel seems to have dealt with Oberdienstleiter Brack from the "Chancellery of the Führer" regarding the gassing of Jews. It is not so clear in the writing, but that is its unmistakable significance. Some missing words have been left blank, some parts of words can only be suggested.

I do not know what the original of this draft looks like, I had only a copy before me that was not very clear. But under a magnifying glass it is not difficult to recognise that my name and rank as well as office are never written, whereas the clean copy then suddenly records them. I presented this to the court as an indisputable falsification, at least insofar as it concerns me, and I suggested that the original or the copy be investigated by an expert. The fact is, I have never dealt with such things.

The literature in the last 1½ decades has supposed the matter in this manner and then one could read things like "Eichmann's proposal for the gassing of Jews, among other things" In this way thus do fairy tales come about. In all fairness, the Israeli police presented to me this handwritten draft as well; without this I would not have had any possibility of invalidating the letters - which had not been sealed or signed, and which only represent typed drafts - insofar as they dealt with me. It cannot be otherwise than that somebody, long before the Israelis possessed these documents - I suppose in the first of the post-war years, undertook such a remarkable action.

Heydrich had the commission from Göring to make all required preparations for a total solution of the Jewish question in the German sphere of influence in Europe. As a start, he planned a meeting with all the secretaries of state of the central authority offices concerned.

Himmler had indeed already had the physical annihilation of the Jews initiated some months ago in the occupied Russian territories according to Hitler's order, which I received from Heydrich's mouth, and a special commando in the Warthegau had already begun with it. Globocnik too prepared the annihilation of the Jews in the Generalgouvernement according to the orders of Hitler and Himmler.

The Wannsee Conference

The Madagascar Plan was dead, and on 20 January 1942 the meeting which had been delayed many times, took place under Heydrich's chairmanship in the building of the "International Criminal Police Commission" in Großer Wannsee near Berlin. I had to compose the protocol[45] with a typist after I had already weeks before obtained from Heydrich the material required for his speech.

The state secretary of the Reich Ministry of the Interior, Dr. Stuckart, the otherwise so cautious and careful official, got to work very forcefully on this forenoon declaring very concisely and not standing on formalities, that "forced sterilisation" and the regulation that "Mixed marriage partners will be separated", which was still to be legally issued, were the only solution to the problem of mixed marriages and of people of mixed origin. Even Luther from the Foreign Office, Ribbentrop's extremely active under-secretary of state, presented, to Heydrich's surprise, wish-lists from which the unscrupulousness of the Foreign Office in carrying out deportations from the European countries under German influence emerged clearly.

State Secretary Bühler was worried that one might in this matter treat the Generalgouvernement, in which he operated, in a step-motherly fashion and requested that one begin with the Generalgouvernement. For, for one thing, the Jews of his territory were to be designated as bearers of a plague and secondly there were neither work deployment reasons nor transport difficulties that prevented a resettlement.

The chief of the Race and Resettlement Head Office, SS Gruppenführer Hoffmann,[46] Gauleiter Dr. Meyer, the president of the people's court, at that time state secretary for the Reich Justice Ministry, Dr. Freisler, the plenipotentiary representative of the Party Chancellery, and many others also took part. The Police were represented by, apart from Heydrich and Müller as head of Office IV of the Reich Security Head Office, the commanding officers of Security Police and SD, Dr. Schöngarth and Dr. Lange.

---

45 The US government translation of the text of the Wannsee protocol for the Nuremberg trials is reproduced in John Mendelsohn, ed., *The Holocaust: Selected Documents in Eighteen Volumes* Vol. 11: The Protocol and a 1944 Report on Auschwitz by the Office of Strategic Services (New York: Garland, 1982), pp.18-32.

46 Otto Hofmann (1896-1982) was chief of the Race and Settlement Office from 1940 to 1943.

False Gods

If Heydrich thought that he had to operate in a persuasive way through a well-worded speech and comment on all possible doubts and reservations, as experience had showed up to now, at this conference precisely the opposite could be observed. In a rare unanimity and joyful agreement these state secretaries demanded an accelerated crackdown, and it was the experts, authoritative notables who had assembled here to take a decision. Their decisions were final, for they were authorised by their ministers and chiefs not only to declare a binding agreement, but partially also to go beyond that hoped for by Heydrich.

They spoke in an open and blunt way, so when I, as the protocol writer of the meeting of secretaries of state of that time, studied here in Israel for the first time the statements that the different greats who participated in this conference expressed on the same matter after 1945, and when, further, I read the statements of their bosses at that time, I must only say that it is also surprising how little courage these former commanding officers showed. And to such one had sworn obedience unto death.

They were in truth all small, cheap, miserable minds without any character to whom only the tinsel of their high rank or the executive capacity of their position, in the days of their glory, lent the necessary image and posture. But if I had already known all this in autumn 1939, it would have been of as little use to me as it would have been to others. Of course, the civilians in the offices had it easier. The bearer of a uniform had only to obey. The protocol of this conference was long even though I had not had even the essential parts written down. Heydrich worked with his pencil and finally authorised only an excerpt; I had to work on it and then, after many further changes by Heydrich, it was dispatched to the participants of the conference as a "Reich Secret".

The declarations made by Stuckart that he would plead for forced divorce and forced sterilisation were new statements that must have surprised Heydrich himself. The manner and method of the bureaucratic procedures with regard to the regulation of details was still unclear. So, on behalf of the conference participants, it was promised that in a short time a meeting of the experts of the responsible central authority offices would take place in the rooms of my department at 116 Kurfürstendammstraße. It could as well have taken place in Office II of the Reich Security Head Office as in the office of the Security Police responsible for legal matters – and

The Wannsee Conference

The house at Wannsee, Berlin, where Nazi officials agreed on the practical implementation of the "Final Solution".

also dealt with Jewish matters, as the documents show – although of course they would have had much less space in Prinz Albrechtstraße.

The Wannsee conference itself was for this reason not held in Heydrich's central office in the Albrechtstraße. Besides, at that time, extensive reconstructions were taking place in the interior of the building. It was indeed a house with a hundred nooks and corners, dating from the old Kaiser era and little suited for a modern bureaucratic organisation. The offices of the office chief, and especially those of the Chief of the Security Police, were formed by interior designers in the style of the modern age. I found it beautiful because it was simple and clean.

These meetings could have taken place as well in the Ministry of the Interior or the Party Chancellery, the Foreign Office, or even again at Wannsee. Why Heydrich determined precisely my office for it I do not know. But he determined it anyway in this way. That I was not professionally involved in it is shown by the first session relating to it on 6 March 1942. Neither I nor any of the members of my department took part in it. The meeting protocol with the list of those present shows this clearly. The divisional head in the Ministry of the Interior responsible for these questions, the councillor Dr. Fledscher, outlined in detail the opinion of his minister with regard to the proposal made on 20 January. It was a matter purely of the jurists of the Ministry of the Interior, the

False Gods

Party Chancellery, the Foreign Office, the Reich Chancellery, the Racial Policy Office of the NSDAP, the Race and Settlement Head Office, Office II of the Reich Security Head Office, the Propaganda Ministry, and the other central authorities.

This meeting ended with the agreement of all present, though decisions were not taken since the participants were only consultants without decision-making powers.

On 27 October, another meeting took place with roughly the same set of participants. This time I too went and, with me, some men of my division. At this meeting too there were only speeches, nothing was solved. The protocols demonstrate that indisputably.

It was, and remained now too, a matter for the jurists. My department had to take care of the bureaucratic stuff of the protocol preparation and the invitations. It is also quite clear that it is not the task of the Police to bring forth ideas or to carry out sterilisation measures, and not also to ponder on the legal text relating to forced divorces. This is the task of the responsible ministries, or the different central authorities and offices, but never a matter for the Police. Even at this conference the results of the planning of the state secretaries were neither altered nor elaborated.

The result of this conference too was not a regulation of the implementation of the planned measures. It never came to that. It somehow petered out. I too was not involved in either the planning or the implementation of the sterilisation measures; no measures for abortion either were established. Besides, the protocol itself does not in any way lead to the conclusion that I had actively taken part in this meeting.

I read in Reitlinger's *Endlösung*, in the seventh chapter, on page 195: "... Actually in this most sacred section of the final solution – where not even the Gestapo had entry without permission – a clash occurred between the civilian authorities and the SS. Gottfried Boley, who represented Hans Lammers and the Reich Chancellery, explained in Nuremberg that some of those present opposed the claim to power of the Gestapo, especially when one of Eichmann's bloodhounds had blurted out that the Gestapo was making lists of half-Jews in order to be able to incriminate them for secret interceptions of enemy radio transmissions and things like that."[47]

---

47   Reitlinger sources: Trial XI No.2419, XI NG2586-J and No.2419, Affidavit

The Wannsee Conference

To that I can only say that considerable unanimity prevailed at the meetings. I do not know this from personal experience as regards the first session, but certainly with regard to the second conference. One can take my word that, if it had come to a clash in my office among the participating authorities, I would have claimed the right of the "host" and certainly restored order immediately. But nothing, absolutely nothing of the sort happened.

As further evidence that Mr. Boley was obviously only a clever narrator: A legation councillor of the Foreign Office wrote to me at the Reich Security Head Office, or to agents in the office, on 17 February 1943, thus 3½ months later, that I might compile a list of foreign citizens of "Jewish race" settled in the German domains. To that I informed him on 24 February by telephone "that it is not possible for me to comply with the presented request of the Foreign Office since the compilation of a list of these persons was not decisive to the war and so I could not assign any personnel for these tasks."

On 26 February, a further letter came from the Foreign Office to my officials in which it said, among other things:

"... The arguments presented by you by telephone do not seem a sufficient basis for the refusal of the presented request from the Foreign Office."

The Foreign Office therefore had, as one can see, the right and the power to make such impositions offhand on the Police; and this is illustrated too by a further letter of the Foreign Office of 27 February 1943 to its office in Brussels: "... The Foreign Office will inform the Reich Security Head Office every time that there are no objections to the application of the general Jewish measures to foreign citizens. This has not yet happened with regard to the Italian Jews. But this is to be reckoned with after 31 March."

I had really planned to deal with this letter from the Foreign Office later but, on account of Boley's statement I presented it now and must therewith discuss another document on which was placed a great significance in view of the fact that I lived in Argentina for ten years. It is a telegram written by me "on orders" on 27 January 1944, issued as a circular, with an instruction to arrest all Jews of Argentinean citizenship and to convey them to the Bergen-Belsen internment camp (not to be confused with the Bergen-Belsen concentration camp).

Gottfried Boley

False Gods

I do not know when Argentina declared war on Germany at that time, it is also quite unimportant, though I do believe that it initiated this measure. I had an order to issue such an instruction, but what is important in this context is that such a thing could not be ordered even by my office chief, or the Chief of the Security Police and SD, but by the Foreign Office, as the presented letter from it of 27 February 1943 confirms indisputably. One sees therefore that it is correct when I said that the Police itself had nothing to "do creatively" but it received its instructions from the ministries.

To return to the Boley statement. So, if such difficulties were prepared for the Foreign Office relative to the compilation of lists of certain categories of Jews, one will well believe me that we certainly could not have had any lists of half-Jews 3½ months earlier, that is, at the time of the autumn conference.

There was indeed much loose talk at that time in Nuremberg that did not correspond to the facts. Legation councillor Dr. Grell confirmed this in 1961 in a witness testimony in Germany. Good, Boley was also not a person who gave orders. Who can blame him for that. At that time there were hardly any documents present, so one could rattle on merrily about such things.

It is correct that, when individual inquiries were ordered, these were also carried out by the Police. And when such were of special "national importance", this investigative activity had to be carried out even by the divisional head of the Reich Security Head Office. I still remember the amount of work I that I had with an investigative activity that had to be maintained fully secret, that is, dealing with the origin of the "Führer's diet-cook". The order read: "with the greatest speed, with the participation of the smallest number of people possible".

The end of the story was that the diet-cook was "two-thirds" a Jewess according to the Nuremberg laws. That was at that time so exciting that my boss demanded of me all the files accumulated in this matter including the incidental files. I never heard anything more about it. Only that Hitler married his "diet-cook" shortly before his death. It was Eva Braun.

While I am offering explanations, let this be added: Reitlinger's remark "... where not even the Gestapo had entry without special permission" derives from the witness testimonies from the time, shortly after the war, where some anxious gentlemen thought to create a sort of alibi

The Wannsee Conference

for themselves with such suggestions. To that I can only remark that if gentlemen like Boley, one of "the participants from eleven ministries and offices" (Reitlinger, *Endlösung*, p.195) had entry, then all the members of the Security Police too must have had it, and beyond that, within the limits of the general opening hours, all possible persons came for meetings and for obtaining orders, no matter if it was the then priest Grüber - the current provost of Berlin, who confirmed this himself as witness for the prosecution during my trial here in Israel, that he was at my office for the purpose of interventions, or the hundreds and hundreds of other persons, Jews and non-Jews. I can easily say it may have been thousands in all those years. Not to mention at all the passport application offices for the purpose of emigration - because this stopped in October 1941 after Himmler had issued the prohibition of Jewish emigration.

But one can inquire in this regard also of the former Evangelical senior church councillor or the "permanent director of the Fulda Bishops' Conference"[48] who called on me often. He was at that time a bishop. Further the business appointment plans that are available reveal, as documents, that from a certain time I was not accommodated alone with my department in the office building in Kurfürstendammstraße but two additional departments were likewise allotted there with which I had nothing to do.

So, as one can see, people talked their heads off and if I wished to clarify everything that the media took in earnest of such rubbish I would need to have a few secretaries at my disposal.

Regarding the state police activities of Office IV, the Reich Security Head Office, but especially concerning my department, I must generally state that the identification of *who* was to be dealt with and *what* was to be undertaken was not determined by Office IV. Insofar as it dealt with nationality or racial questions these were within the Security Police and SD, especially Office III, but under certain circumstances possibly also Office VI, further the Racial Policy Office of the NSDAP, the Race and Settlement Head Office, the Reich Ministry of the Interior, the Foreign Office, the Party Chancellery, the Reich Chancellery, the SS Reichsführer, and many others. Here everything was deliberated, discussed, set up, authorised in an executive manner, adopted by the chiefs of the central authority offices with the participation of all the

---

48 The Fulda Bishops' Conference is the episcopal conference of the bishops of the Roman Catholic Church in Germany.

offices interested in it, and then forwarded as instructions, guidelines and regulations to Office IV of the Reich Security Head Office for police implementation. As in all countries, the police in this matter did not have to determine in a decisive way by themselves but they had their instructions and orders according to which they had to proceed.

Lacking clairvoyance I do not presume to speak for the entire Secret State Police Office; but insofar as it deals with my former activity in this office, and in relation to the sector that I had to deal with, I can do this so much more definitely. Some one thousand six hundred documents which were presented to me in Israel, which I commented on and were in large part introduced in court as exhibits, both on the part of the prosecution and on that of the defence, consolidate my statement without any doubt.

In the spring of 1942, I received from my immediate superior, the lieutenant general of the Police, Müller, an order to travel to Auschwitz, and to report to him on the actions of the commandant of the Auschwitz concentration camp against the Jews.

The Gassing of Jews at Auschwitz

Höss, the commandant, told me that he killed people with hydrogen cyanide. Round pieces of felt were soaked in this poisonous liquid and thrown into the rooms where the Jews were gathered. This poison had an immediate fatal effect.

He burnt the corpses on an iron grating in the open-air. He took me to a shallow pit in which a large number of corpses had just been burnt. It was a gruesome picture that was presented to me. Only alleviated by the noise and the huge flames. He used some oil for the burning.

I refrain from describing my thoughts and deliberations at that time, for, on the one hand, I would not like to hear a possible complaint that it would have been reasonable for me to subsequently make constructive attempts for this reason and, on the other hand, my applications for a transfer actually did not have any success, so that it is not easy for me to present evidence in these things. Even though my defence informed me that the witness, Dr. Stöttel in Austria, remembered well that I constantly requested a transfer to the general Police administration. It was so.

The Gassing of Jews at Auschwitz

I do not at this point make any further comments since I shall speak further on the essentials of the matter in another part of my observations.

The untruths that Rudolf Höss stated about me after 1945 are pathetic.[49] But they are easy to be recognised as such, partly through his own statements which he reported in another place differently, if one makes the effort to study his statements using the literature and documents as comparative materials. So, for example, Höss said that I had been with him already in June 1941, shortly after Himmler's visit to Auschwitz, and he learnt of all the killing possibilities from me. He says that I spoke to him about gassing by means of exhaust gas.

When Höss further says that I had conveyed to him details of deportation plans this must then have been at the earliest on 20 March 1942, for, at that time, State Secretary Weizsäcker in the Foreign Office authorised for the first time deportations from France. Of course, the German ambassador in Paris, Abetz, had probed Hitler and Himmler for this reason, but I heard of it too for the first time only in late autumn 1941. The first deportation order from the west, that is from France and Belgium and Holland, dealing with large contingents, which Himmler issued through the chief of Office IV, was presented to my department only shortly before June 1942.

Höss had already made the first trial gassings in Auschwitz on 23 September 1941, as it emerges from his own statements. When I went to Auschwitz for the first time, the gassing was already in process. Höss burnt the corpses on iron gratings and I had to report to Müller on how Höss operated. This was the reason why he gave me the orders to travel to Auschwitz. But according to his own statement Höss had begun with the burnings on iron gratings only in summer 1942. He then mentions further that I had spoken with him about shootings in the east. However, I experienced such a thing for the first time in winter 1941/42. I still remember having seen blooming flowers in the garden in Auschwitz. So it must have been the middle of spring.

Höss has – to mildly put it - erred by one whole year regarding my first visit. Müller had not given me any orders that I had to convey to him, and no other person gave me such or similar instructions.

---

49 See Rudolf Höss, *Commandant of Auschwitz: The Autobiography of Rudolf Höss*, tr. C. FitzGibbon, London: Weidenfeld and Nicolson, 1959.

False Gods

I myself never made a proposal regarding the technical implementation of the gassings; on the contrary, I was delighted that I did not have to hear or see anything regarding such things. I had nothing further to do with these matters than to carry out those wretched orders which my boss issued to me because he wished to be accurately informed on all of these measures.

Höss was not under the Reich Security Head Office but - as the documents demonstrate very precisely – under the SS Administrative and Economic Office. Thus he drew his orders from there. His immediate superiors were the SS Obergruppenführer and general of the Waffen SS, Pohl, and the SS Gruppenführer and lieutenant-general of the Waffen SS, Glücks.

Besides, according to the witness statements, and also the statement of Dr. Sigmund Rascher himself, head of the medical experiments of the air force, Rascher had admitted to an English captain - Payne-Best - that *he* had invented the gas chambers and introduced such a thing in Auschwitz.

If I had made myself noticeable as being involved in some way at that time even in the least, then it would be more than certain that I would have been mentioned by many other persons in this regard in the trials after 1945. It was left to Höss, and partly to Wisliceny, to make use of such untrue statements in this field.

Thereby Höss used, for the sake of greater credibility, interludes from my private life, or statements on my attitudes, character and such. Generally speaking, he tried here to shift the responsibility for the actions of the SS Economic and Administrative Head Office, to which he belonged, to the offices of the Chief of the Security Police and SD and made use of myself in particular.

It is devious to wish to play off one SS head office against the other. Naturally, today I do not have to speak myself, for I need only to refer to the great number of documents that are available. Today one obtains a clearer picture than in the years from 1945 to 1948.

Finally, there arises the question why Müller chose me, one of his divisional heads, for these trips and did not undertake them himself. Now, this may have been due to the fact that Müller hardly left his Berlin office. He sat like a spider in its web and the strength of his position was especially based on the fact that he was best informed on each and everything. For another thing, it would have looked like an

The Gassing of Jews at Auschwitz

Rudolf Hoss, the commandant of Auschwitz.

interference of the Reich Security Head Office in the matters of the SS Economic and Administrative Head Office if he had, as *office chief* of the RSHA, made these trips himself.

The effects of the Wannsee Conference, or the Wannsee State Secretary Meeting as it was called at that time, on the occupied or influenced territories in western, southern and northern Europe are described in the second part of this work.

The deportations from the Reich territory, excluding the Protectorate of Bohemia and Moravia, now had to be carried out according to the orders of Himmler with the greatest speed. In the Generalgouvernement, the regional officials of the government of the Generalgouverneur took care of this.

If difficulties with the Reich Transport Ministry were to be recorded which, as a result of a lack of wagons, could often be managed only hardly, or not at all, then Himmler deployed his field adjutant and Chief of the Personal Staff, the general of the Waffen SS, Wolff, to settle these matters with the state secretary in the Reich Transport Ministry, Dr. Ganzenmüller.

In a letter of Ganzenmüller's to Wolff of 28 July 1942 it says: "With reference to our long-distance telephone conversation of 16 July, I inform you of the following announcement of my directorate general of the eastern railways (Gedob)[50] in Krakow for your kind notification:

From 22 July a train has been running daily, each with 5,000 Jews from Warsaw through Malkimia to Treblinka, and, in addition, a train weekly with 5,000 Jews from Přemysl to Belzek. Gedob is in constant touch with the Security Service in Krakow. The latter is agreed that the transports from Warsaw through Lublin to Sobibor (near Lublin) will be stopped while the reconstruction work on this stretch make the transports impossible (around October 1942).

The trains were coordinated with the Commanding Officer of the Security Police in the Generalgouvernement. SS and Police chief of the Lublin district, SS Brigadeführer Globocnik, has been notified."

To this Wolff replied on 3 August 1942 to Ganzenmüller:

"Thank you kindly – in the name of the Führer - for your letter of 28 July 1942. I have learnt with special gladness from your communication that already for a fortnight one train has been running daily, each with 5,000 members of the Chosen Race, to Treblinka and that we are in this way placed in a position to carry out this population migration at a heightened speed. I have for my part got into contact with the offices involved so that a frictionless implementation of all the measures seems guaranteed. I thank you again for your efforts in this matter, and may request you at the same time to continue to direct your attention to these matters."

In Treblinka and Belzec, Globocnik had set up gassing camps on the orders of Himmler and Krüger. Such and similar documents were of course not immediately at hand in the first period of the post-war trials. Therefore one could confidently speak about me in such a way so as to find excuses. Today such a thing is no longer possible. Both these documents were found in Himmler's own staff command. For Ganzenmüller's is the original letter, while Wolff's reply to it is a copy, signed by him, of his letter to Ganzenmüller.

All the essentials were worked out from high places and, if difficulties emerged even in subordinate work, these were removed by the commanding officers themselves directly, among themselves and individually.

---

50 General Directorate of the Eastern Railways.

The Gassing of Jews at Auschwitz

Only after 1945 were such things shifted strenuously onto the recipients of orders of that time, the former chiefs obviously had nothing to do with such questions, and they generally did not know anything in the least about such things.

In March 1942, the Reich Transport Ministry complained of insalubrious conditions arising through the use of the regional public transport by Jews. It occupied itself with a new regulation concerning the use of public transport by Jews and intended to announce this to the officials of its jurisdiction, with which plan the Chief of the Security Police and SD was in agreement. This signified a further restriction in view of certain decrees already issued. For a uniform adherence to guidelines a general police circular decree had to follow. Here my department had to take into consideration the wishes of the Reich Transport Ministry and the Reich Post Ministry and Heydrich then signed the supplemental decree on 24 March 1942.

Everywhere there prevailed in the German sphere of power of that time, in 1942, a certain rush. In retrospect one could almost be tempted to say that it was as in the case of a farmer who, sensing rough weather, tries to bring in his harvest even more quickly under shelter.

Then came the death of Heydrich at the beginning of June 1942 as the result of a bomb assassination attempt on his life, when the Reich elite was seen in an unprecedented activity in the field of deportations and other final solution measures.

Hitler, Goebbels, Himmler, the Foreign Office, the Gauleiters, the state secretaries for the security organisation, the Party Chancellery, and whatever else the commanding central authorities may have been called, displayed an unprecedented vigour and a fanatical will with detailed regulation and continuous personal control.

On the basis of a decree of Hitler's of 7 October 1942, which was preceded by an instruction of Hitler's of 18 August, the leadership responsible for the combating of partisans in the Generalgouvernement was assigned to Himmler. In the course of the fulfilment of this task Himmler issued the following ordinance:

"The Zamość district commission is declared to be the first German settlement area in the Generalgouvernement.

The area should become the new secured homeland for

False Gods

1. Those resettled from Bosnia.
2. Endangered ethnic Germans from the occupied eastern territories.
3. Ethnic Germans and people of German origin from the rest of the Generalgouvernement who have to be resettled for security police reasons in this area for the removal of their present distress.
4. Other groups that have to be resettled.

The total direction in the implementation of this task lies in the hands of my representatives in the Generalgouvernement, the senior SS and Police Chief in the Generalgouvernement, State Secretary for the security organisation, SS Obergruppenführer and Police general, Krüger, in association with my captains.

My representative in the Generalgouvernement in his capacity as state secretary for the security organisation will carry out the required resettlements of Poles from the area.

On 11 October, the director of the central office for itinerants in Litzmannstadt, which had established a branch office in Zamość according to an order of Himmler's and which was, for the duration of its activity, under the senior SS and Police Chief in the Generalgouvernement, pointed out in a progress report to my representative in my department the classification made by the Race and Settlement Head Office of Poles who were to be deported into evaluation groups.

According to an order of Himmler's of 3 October and another from the beginning of November, it was determined that the Poles classified by the Race and Settlement Head Office under evaluation groups I and II had to go for Germanisation through an external office of this head office in Litzmannstadt. The members of evaluation group III fit for work were taken to Berlin, to relieve the Jews there working in the armaments industry, and the members of evaluation group IV fit for work were sent to the Auschwitz concentration camp. The old-age groups belonging to evaluation groups III and IV between 14 and 60 years and those unfit for work in these groups were accommodated in the Generalgouvernement in so-called "pensioners' villages" and especially in the Warsaw and Radom districts. They received there one house per family and to each family was allotted ½ a hectare of land.

Himmler had first determined the age limit of those to be evacuated at 10 to 60 years but then let himself be convinced by the Chief of Office

The Gassing of Jews at Auschwitz

IV of the Reich Security Head Office, Müller, that the age limit should be raised from 10 to 14 years.

The department led by me had, in the case of these operations, received an order to arrange the travel-plan matters with the Reich Transport Ministry for the Poles who were to be deported to Berlin and to Auschwitz according to the existing instructions. The figures and, therewith, the number of transport trains were issued by the Race and Settlement Head Office-Evaluation Groups III and IV. The determination of the groups of persons to be deported and the destination of the deportation did not lie with my department, and neither did the transport itself or the delivery.

On Heydrich's orders a further 55,000 Jews from the Old Reich and the Protectorate of Bohemia and Moravia as well as from Austria, had to be deported in March 1942. A document of the State Police office in Düsseldorf on a meeting that took place in this connection in my department has survived. I had orders to inform the participants at the meeting that SS Gruppenführer Heydrich had made the directors of the State Police offices personally responsible for the implementation of the guidelines.

Further I had to inform them: "So that individual State Police offices may no longer be subjected to the temptation of deporting to them unsuitable older Jews. Let it be said in reassurance that these Jews remaining in the Old Reich will most probably be deported already during this summer or autumn to Theresienstadt, which is envisaged as an old-age home. This city is now being vacated and for the time being 15-20,000 Jews from the Protectorate could be resettled there. This is taking place in order to preserve our image abroad."

This was one of the camouflage prescriptions ordered by Himmler. If, after 1945, many "witnesses" maintained that it was I who "hoodwinked" them, this document is the most conclusive evidence that I certainly did not do that. I repeated matters without concealment or disguise as they were ordered to me.

The reporting official of the then State Police office in Düsseldorf further informed his chief that "the so-called WS or special account[51]

---

51 A W Sonderkonto (W special account) was established by Friedrich Suhr, a colleague of Eichmann's in IV B4, in December 1941 to finance the deportations of Jews. According to Suhr's circular decree, all Jews had to contribute at least one quarter of all their assets to this account.

False Gods

was at the disposal of the divisional head of IV B of the Reich Security Head Office (that is, my division) since, according to regulation 11 of the Reich Citizenship Law, the Reich Security Head Office no longer had access to the wealth of the Jews. In order to make sufficient money available for this fund it was ordered to force the Jews to make considerable "donations" to the W special account soon."

Now that official, as one says, "got hold of the wrong end of the stick" here. Even I was surprised when I was asked in Israel about a "WS special account" which was supposed to have been maintained by my division. Only the documents emerging in the course of time provided greater clarity here too.

Regulation 11 of the Reich Citizenship Law was issued through the operation of Department I of the Reich Ministry of the Interior in November 1941 and proclaimed the revocation of the state citizenship of the Jews and the confiscation of their assets in favour of the Reich treasury. The confiscation was undertaken by the appropriate regional finance presidents. The Jewish organisations continued to maintain their accounts at their banks for the defrayal of expenses.

After the Jews were now deprived of their assets, the jurists of the Reich Security Head Office or even some "State Police offices" discovered that "donations" for their Jewish organisations were not forbidden by the legislator. So they were appealed to for such "donations". For, if the treasury had the entire wealth, it was hard and time-consuming to again scrape up money by making applications to the relevant financial authorities.

For the purpose of the deposit of such donations the Jewish organisations then opened a special "W account" in their banks from which these organisations could make withdrawals, after the issuance of a clearance by their relevant Secret State Police office.

The money then served for the payment of the Jewish functionaries as well as of the employees and other assistant personnel, support, treatment of the sick, all other actual needs, and even the payment of transport costs for deportation. This last was the real reason that this matter was permitted by the chiefs to the lawyers, who found "legal loopholes" in this way. Neither I personally nor anybody else of my division had anything to do with this "W special account" - as the documents demonstrate indisputably.

The Gassing of Jews at Auschwitz

Security Police operations within the scope of the "preservation of the blood law" were carried out also against the dark-skinned gypsy people who originated from unspecified distant lands. According to orders I had to deal with that part that was assigned to me: travel-plan preparation.

On the occasion of the "Heydrich meeting" of 30 January 1942, Heydrich conveyed to the regional commanding officers who had been invited and were charged with the resettlement or deportation Himmler's order to deport, among others, 30,000 gypsies too to the Generalgouvernement. Neither I nor my division were responsible even here for their concentration or their arrest or their admission into a concentration camp.

Only during the already mentioned first wave of deportations in 1941 when for the first and the last time *two* final stations were available to me for the setting up of a travel-plan did I "send", 20,000 Jews, but also 5,000 gypsies to Litzmannstadt instead of to places where I had heard or read that people were being killed or where preparations for this had been made.

I have already described the complaint of the district president Übelhör against me in this matter. I was responsible neither for the resettlement nor for the arrests. I only carried out, on the orders of the Chief of the Security Police, the travel-plan agendas with regard to the transports of gypsies from the Reich territories.

The former criminal official, Fritz Friedel, says the following in his written declaration in prison in Białystok on 12 June 1949:

> "Already before 1933 a central office for gypsies had been established in Munich. By this central office it was dictated that all gypsies were to be arrested and registered according to lists. The then provincial criminal police offices that had to maintain gypsy card-indexes were charged with this. After 1933 an ordinance was issued by central office for gypsies to control the gypsies more strictly and to send them to concentration camps in case of repeated offences. Then there was issued, as far as I remember, in 1943 by Office V (Reich Criminal Police Office) of the Reich Security Head Office, Berlin, a decree according to which all gypsies were to be arrested and sent as anti-social elements to a concentration camp."

In this report of the criminal official he has clearly erred in the year, for it was not 1943 but, as the documents prove it was in 1940/41.

How closely the highest SS leadership at that time were, personally, involved in the details of issues, is shown by a letter from my chief Müller, to the already mentioned general of the Waffen SS and Chief of the Personal Staff of the SS Reichsführer, of 17 September 1942. The latter had spoken to Müller by telephone on the evacuation of Jews who were employed in a petroleum company in order to avoid an interruption of work in this company and therewith of the coupling of the deportation with the availability of substitute work force. No matter if it was a matter of small individual cases or the preparation of wagons for hundred thousand people, in every case the masters at that time showed an amazing activity – an activity that many did not wish to know anything about after 1945 or that it was brought about by each of them.

I said that I kept to my tasks which it was my ordered duty to implement according to my bureaucratic position and the spheres of responsibility. In all those years, I stubbornly refused everything else that was brought forward in this connection.

Of course, all possible offices came up with the most unusual wishes and requests. Of my office chief of that time I must say that in general – if I disregard the official trips to the fields of death to which he sent me - he spared me from supplementary orders, and besides also took over files which I gave to him during consultations when I did not have personal responsibility for them patiently and always without any complaint, as if they had been misdirected documents. This I must declare objectively and soberly. He had the most complete understanding of bureaucratic necessities, for he was a born bureaucrat, and he had groomed me in a similar way in the course of the years.

The Strasbourg Skeletons

One day, on 16 Nov. 1942, I received in my mail a letter from the "Personal Staff of the SS Reichsführer" concerning the preparation of a collection of skeletons in the Strasbourg Institute of Anatomy. And in it I read the following remarkable matter:

"The SS Reichsführer has ordered that everything necessary be

The Strasbourg Skeletons

made available for his research to the director of the Straßburg institute of anatomy, SS Hauptsturmführer Prof. Hirt,[52] who is at the same time the director of a department of the Institute for Applied Defence Research in the Ahnenerbe Office.[53] On behalf of the SS Reichsführer I request you to make possible the preparation of the planned skeleton collection. Regarding the details SS Obersturmbannführer Sievers[54] will get in touch with you."

A week later the Personal Staff sent a copy of the above-mentioned letter to the above-mentioned Sievers for acknowledgement.

I was not responsible for something like this. In the numerous documents present, no reaction on my part is evident. As so very often people directed to me letter after letter, but there is nowhere a reply or comment on my part. This was remarked also by one of the judges in my trial.

Indeed – lacking responsibility – I could not do anything else but hand over the files to my chief. What he did with it is beyond my ken.

In the Nuremberg trials a diary of Sievers' was also the object of court discussions. There, for 28 April 1943, is written: "Reich Security Head Office IV B, SS Sturmbannführer Günther. Experiments now possible." This was Sievers' record of a telephone conversation with Günther conducted at 10.45 on the same day. So it was six months before Müller finished the matter with Günther. In this connection the witness testimony of the former government director, Huppenkothen, is interesting, who, both shortly after 1945 and in 1961, declared objectively and simply that it was one of Müller's customs to entrust, going over the head of the departmental head, some member of a department with special tasks. The person so entrusted had no obligation to report to his departmental head with regard to such a

---

52 August Hirt (1898-1945) was a chairman of the University of Straßburg who collaborated with Sievers and Beger of the Ahnenerbe institute. He committed suicide before he could be tried for war crimes.

53 The Ahnenerbe (Ancestral Heritage) Institute was founded in 1935 by Himmler along with Herman Wirth and Richard Walther Darré and dedicated to the study of Germanic antiquity.

54 Wolfram Sievers (1905-48) was appointed general secretary of the Ahnenerbe by Himmler in 1935 and in 1943 became director of the Institut für wehrwissenschaftliche Zweckforschung (Institute for military scientific research) which was affiliated to the Ahnenerbe institute. He was sentenced to death in 1947 and hanged the following year.

special task but he was as a rule bound to total silence when such tasks came under "Reich Secrets". Günther belonged to my department.

On 21 June 1943, Sievers wrote to me again. He referred to a letter of my department of 25 September 1942 and repeated personal discussions that took place in the meantime and informed me that the work in the Auschwitz concentration camp had been concluded on 15 June 1943 on account of the danger of an epidemic. An SS Hauptsturmführer Dr. Bruno Beger[55] had carried it out. He writes further:

> "Altogether 115 persons, of whom 79 Jews, 2 Poles, 4 Central Asians, and 30 Jewesses, have been worked on. These inmates were admitted, partially separated into men and women, into the hospitals of the Auschwitz concentration camp and are in quarantine. For further experimentation on the persons chosen an immediate transfer to the Natzweiler concentration camp is now necessary, which must, in view of the epidemic danger in Auschwitz, be carried out with speed. A list of names of the chosen persons is attached. It is requested to issue the necessary instructions."

Even this letter was not answered by me, but, following the existing instructions, handed over to the office chief. I was not responsible, for only the SS Economic and Administrative Head Office had to decide on transfers, and also its office group D, that is, the "Inspection for the concentration camp system" under SS Gruppenführer and lieutenant general of the Waffen SS, Glücks. In the guidelines of this "Inspection" it says among other things: "Transfers to other camps, especially at Level III, are not to be requested from the Reich Security Head Office or Reich Criminal Police Office. Transfers are essentially ordered only from here."

So, a clear and indisputable case of the lack of responsibility on my part, and Müller may, in my opinion, have done the only thing possible and handed over the process to Glücks. It is, in terms of the bureaucracy, not thinkable otherwise. In any case, there was no reaction from me to this letter.

During the trial against Sievers in Nuremberg he declared: "I already said that Himmler visited Wirth in Straßburg. I was not present at this

---

55 Dr. Bruno Beger (1911-2009) was a racial anthropologist who worked for the Ahnenerbe. He accompanied Ernst Schäfer on his expedition to Tibet and was also responsible for the selection of human specimens from concentration camps for August Hirt's skeleton collection in the University of Straßburg. Beger was sentenced to three years' imprisonment in 1974.

The Strasbourg Skeletons

visit. As Wirth then informed me, he had, on Himmler's instructions, to get in touch directly with Glücks and, if necessary, make use of my mediation if he could not himself come to Berlin."

Sievers was then asked by his defence counsel if Himmler's order was known to the Inspection for the Concentration Camp System even before Sievers' discussion with Glücks. To which he replied: "Yes, Himmler's order was with Sievers before I spoke to Glücks at Wirth's request."

He was then further asked why such a letter was still necessary to me if Glücks already knew of this order. This is a totally clear and logical question of the defence counsel. To which Sievers gave a reply that allows us to see clearly that Sievers, who was prosecuted at that time, sought by all means to extract himself from the affair into which he was thrust by his Ahnenerbe story and concretely by his letter. In human terms this is understandable. But it was wrecked on the fact that there was nothing present from me as a result of my refusal to work on it or the submission of the files to my superiors. Müller and Glücks dealt with things directly. Both were office chiefs, both were lieutenants general, the one of the Police, the other of the Waffen SS.

Now, I have begun to describe this matter and wish to describe also the end, for a completion of this sad matter: Sievers wrote on 5 Sep. 1944 to the Personal Staff of the SS Reichsführer through SS Standartenführer Ministerial Councillor Dr. Brand:

"According to the proposal of 9 February 1942 and the agreement there of 23 February 1942, the collection of skeletons lacking up to this time was prepared by SS Sturmbannführer Prof. Wirth. As a result of the scope of the scientific work connected with it, the skeletisation work has not yet been completed. With respect to the required time, Wirth requests some 80 orders, in case one has to reckon with a threat from Straßburg on account of the handling of the collection in the morgue of the Institute of Anatomy.

He can undertake de-fleshing and render them unrecognisable, but then the entire work would be in vain and a great scientific loss for this unique collection because thereafter human casts would no longer be possible. The skeleton collection as such is not striking. Soft parts would be declared as old bodily remains left behind by the French during the takeover of the Institute of Anatomy and consigned to be burnt. Request decision on the following proposals:

1. The collection may be preserved.

2. The collection is to be partially destroyed.

3. The collection is to be totally destroyed.

Sievers,

Standartenführer

I am not a lawyer, and also know too little of the entire process, but Sievers documents one thing here through his own telegram, that the proposal to prepare such a collection of skeletons was made by him or by his office at that time. And I am of the view that, if one proposes such a thing, then one must also have the courage later to admit it and not foist the matter onto "smaller people". But I have perceived that, apart from a few exceptions, the higher the rank the readiness to foist matters off becomes ever greater.

In connection with what has just been described I must deal with another macabre matter.

Burning the Evidence

The Einsatz Groups in the east and the Commandos of the SS and Police Chief in the Generalgouvernement as well as the commando which Himmler had set up with the Reich governor Greiner in the Warthegau left behind numerous mass graves. These now had to be obliterated in view of the advance of the Red Army; that is, the corpses had to be dug up and burnt.

The SS Standartenführer Blobel received the orders for this. He was, until the end of 1941, the chief of a special commando of the Einsatz Group C working under the orders of SS Brigadeführer and major general, Dr. Rasch in the region of the 6th army of Field Marshal General von Reichenau. Then he was, according to his own declaration, transferred for disciplinary reasons to Berlin and "received in autumn 1942 the task, as Müller's appointee, to go to the occupied territories and to obliterate the traces of the mass graves which originated from the executions of the Einsatz Groups. This task he had until the summer of 1944."

Burning the Evidence

This information I have derived from a declaration of Blobel's, under oath, of 6 June 1947, which he made in Nuremberg. There were some 4-6 men in Blobel's commando who came from his earlier Einsatz Commando.

Until May 1941 he was Chief of the SD section for Düsseldorf. Professionally he was an architect. Now, since he was directly under Müller, he had to continuously and directly report to the latter or to report to him personally. In a house near the office, in which my department was accommodated, some free rooms had, according to the orders of the chief of Office IV, to be always kept available on one of the floors for guests passing through. Blobel then lived in such accommodation along with his retinue when he came to Berlin for reporting. For this reason he also had his private mail directed to my official address. One could say that the man from my department who did the house supervision had to look after him economically, and since this man could not look after anybody economically unless he had received orders for that from me or my department, it is correct to say that Blobel was economically taken care of by my department. In order that thereby no false interpretation may creep in, I would like to add: insofar as it was a matter of private personal needs such as an apartment, private post, food stamps. That was all.

Even an attempt of Standartenführer Blobel's to issue orders to the guard of the office building at Kurfürstentraße 116 led to a clash with him and an official complaint from me, for no person from outside the department could give official instructions to the guard. This was a generally valid rule and demonstrates that Standartenführer Blobel did not belong to my office. Obviously, the other departmental heads accommodated in the same house could issue orders to the guard; but Blobel was not that either. If this commando, or even parts of it, had been under me, or if members of my office had belonged to this commando, then Blobel would quite certainly have indicated this at some point during the many interrogations or during his trial. But he was, in his own words, an "appointee of SS Gruppenführer Müller". So he was directly under him and under nobody else.

It was left to the consultant for the Jewish question at the German consulate in Slovakia, SS Hauptsturmführer Wisliceny, to invent, in addition to his numerous untruths, which all were agreed on in Nuremberg, further lies about me, among which was also the statement that Blobel was under me, or that I had issued concrete instructions to him.

False Gods

Blobel himself, for whom such a thing would have certainly had an exonerative effect, chastises Wisliceny for his lies. It is also not worth going into greater detail into Wisliceny's tattle, since it has been exposed in the course of my trial both by my defence counsel and by me with the help of the available official documents of that time.

I find it also not at all worth the effort to waste further words on him in this context since what he proposed in one of his many handwritten plans to the North American occupying force at that time characterises him sufficiently. In it he develops for them his plan regarding how best I could be caught. He had many conjectures regarding where I was staying at that time. Such proposals prepared by Wisliceny of all people somehow have a blemish of a definite sort. In the final analysis he had once been my superior departmental director in Jewish matters in the SD Head Office.

So he proposed a search operation including his involvement and lasting around six weeks. During this time my wife should be interrogated regarding me, my comrades at that time, and in addition, all my relatives and acquaintances, as far as Wisliceny knew about them.

"In the most loyal manner" he offered the North American occupying force his help or cooperation in this regard and "he was happy as a lark", it says in a North American report.

It seems to me to be important to strip down a certain part of the then National Socialistic terminology. Through the ongoing camouflage orders of Himmler, many words and concepts became in the course of time so ambiguous that only the particular office that had to send such transport trains to the final station knew with absolute certainty what really happened to the passengers of a transport train. The orders regarding what actually was to happen went from the commanding officers directly to the implementing office.

Naturally one knew the attitude of the orders in a general way, inasmuch as one was bound to the total work in some way.

I said "one". Therewith is to be understood all the officials of the central offices in Berlin, and all the officials of the middle offices insofar as they were deployed in the deportation and other security police tasks directly or indirectly, cooperating either in an executive or only in a marginal manner.

The Meaning of Special Treatment

What exactly happened or would happen, for instance, with a transport from one place or another, whether those in the transport were killed, whether they remained in a concentration camp, or whether they went to work-deployment in one of the armaments industries, all these things the offices did not know. Even I myself never knew such things at any time. It was also not dependent on me, nor could it be influenced by me in any way. Just as little as I or other offices could have done this with respect to the issuance of deportation orders.

All this was reserved exclusively to the commanding officers.

Camouflage words were, among others:
- "Special treatment"
- "Migration to the east"
- "Transfer to the east for work-deployment"
- "Evacuation to the east"
- "Final solution of the Jewish question", etc.

Nobody outside the central office knew whether the actual meaning of the word was used or whether Himmler or the SS Economic and Administrative Head Office (Inspection for the Concentration Camp System) or the Chief of the Security Police – the last however only in rare cases –, diverging from the given forms of the words, ordered "killing" to the last office.

Himmler ordered the Chief of the Security Police to deport a certain contingent from a certain territory within a certain time-period to a certain destination, and the SS Administrative and Economic Head Office received orders from him regarding *what* was to happen the deportees.

This emerges unequivocally from the documents. Even the term "special treatment", which was generally interpreted as "killing", really had the most diverse definitions or interpretations. So, for example, regarding the deportation of Poles ordered by Hitler and Himmler; here under "special treatment" was understood the following:

The Race and Settlement Head Office recognised who was to be classified in the evaluation groups I to IV set up by this office. Himmler or his appropriate regional representative, the senior SS and Police chief, decided what was to happen with the individual evaluation groups; that is,

1. to work-deployment to the Reich
2. to be deported from the new eastern territories to the Generalgouvernement
3. distribution in pensioners' villages in the Generalgouvernement
4. to the Auschwitz concentration camp, or
5. capable of Germanisation

All this came under the term "special treatment".

Official forms of the Race and Settlement Head Office have survived in which it says:

"Subject: Special treatment – (Name)

Ref: Decree of the SS Reichsführer S IV D 2

… Hereby the above-named has fulfilled the requirements in racial terms that must be set for foreign peoples who are to be Germanised. He is capable of Germanisation."

Another example of a form page:

"Subject: Special treatment – (Name)

Hereby the above named has *not* fulfilled the requirements that must be set for foreign peoples who are to be Germanised. He is not capable of Germanisation."

It emerges without doubt that the term "special treatment" in such cases does not have the least to do with "killing". The term was chosen here without ambiguity, thus without any camouflage intentions, for an extraordinary treatment of a group of persons, who were, according to a command of Himmler's, classified in different categories; no matter if the result was "capable of Germanisation" or not, this examination was characterised as "special treatment". When I write of such things today it is as if I were speaking of events from distant, unreal worlds. Yes, man can, in his foolishness, arrive at quite improbable acts of arrogance.

The Meaning of Special Treatment

Another example, from the guidelines of the Chief of the Security Police and SD according to which war criminals were to be handled. They date from 26 September 1939 and it says there:

"Special treatment" (execution)

… special treatments are dealt with essentially by II A with the exception of cases of special treatment of priests, theologians, and biblical scholars, for whom II B is responsible." So here "special treatment" means indisputably "killing". Such cases were decided – the guidelines indicate this expressly - by Himmler personally.

Two further examples:

"Subject: Special treatment of Jews

Re: Report of 6.5.42 – II B 2

The SS Reichsführer and Chief of the German Police has ordered that the Jews more closely identified in the above report (seven names follow) are to be hanged in the Neuhof ghetto in the presence of their racial comrades."

"Subject: Special treatment of Jews

Re: Report of 27.3.42 - II B 2

On the orders of the SS Reichsführer and Chief of the German Police, the special treatment proposed from there is to be carried out against the Jews (four names follow)."

In both cases they are telegrams of the Reich Security Head Office to a state police office which made a request for special treatment. The Reich Security Head Office was in these cases nothing but the office which had to forward such requests on orders to Himmler and then conveyed his order to the requesting authorities. Even here quite indisputably by "special treatment" is to be understood to mean "killing".

The deportation trains ran under subjects like "Final solution of the Jewish question", "Special treatment", "Evacuation to the east", as it was ordered. New instructions appeared every couple of months relating to this.

False Gods

They went to Auschwitz, the Generalgouvernement, Riga, or the Warthegau. Here "special treatment", "final solution", "evacuation", etc. were not always to be equated with the word "killing", for there followed work-deployment as well as killing.

Himmler himself personally took care of the camouflaging.

A report of the Statistics Inspector, Dr. Korherr, on the numerical situation of the Jewish matters in Europe, on deportations, mortality rates and emigration figures of spring 1945 is approved by Himmler in April of the same year to the Chief of the Security Police with the words that he thinks this report useful for a later time for camouflage reasons; in addition, he wishes that evacuation to the east should be carried out, as far as it was humanly possible. He asks for just two more reports with two figures that are to be presented to him every month: the figure of the Jews deported in the month of the report, and the figure of the Jews still present in the individual countries.

As one of the consequences of the death of Heydrich, who was hit by a bomb hurled at him on 29 May 1942 in a suburb of Prague, the village of Lidice in Bohemia was razed to the ground; its inhabitants were either shot or deported.

Around hundred children from this village were, according to an order of the Senior SS and Police Chief for Bohemia and Moravia, lieutenant general of the Police, K.H.Frank, deported by the Race and Settlement Head Office, Prague branch office to the Central Office for Migrants in Litzmannstadt.

These children had been divided into those fit for Germanisation and those unfit. The former were transferred to the "Brocken" children's home and as regards the children unfit for Germanisation the then director of the Litzmannstadt Central Office for Migrants wrote to all possible offices with a request for instruction regarding what was to be done with them.

My department was not responsible for Czech matters. Nevertheless, Günther, my "regular representative", replied, for a reason that I, lacking any sort of responsibility, cannot understand and cannot explain, to the Central Office for Migrants that the children unfit for Germanisation were to be handed over to the state police office in Litzmannstadt, which would authorise further action.

The Meaning of Special Treatment

The prosecution now accuses me that I had allowed these children to be led to special treatment and that they were killed. It is one of those attacks drawn from thin air against me for I had nothing at all to do with this entire matter. Neither with the deportation nor with any instruction regarding what should happen to the children.

The children were not to be killed and were not killed. According to the information of the then SS Obersturmbannführer Krumey, the director of the Central Office for Migrants in Litzmannstadt, in his witness testimony of 6 June 1961, said that they were to be attached to a transport of Poles to the Generalgouvernement.

According to a declaration of Mrs. Waltraut Elise Freiberg, given under oath, which was made before the notary public Dr. Kurt Merling in Bremen on 21 June 1961, there were still some thirty children from Lidice on 20 January 1945 in a home in Puschkau (former Generalgouvernement). I was blamed by the prosecution, but the prosecution officials were not able to submit any evidence to support their accusation.

Apart from the fact that I obviously tried to save my skin when things were imposed on me with which I had nothing to do, it is a harrowing image and indescribably sad when one sees in this way what harm the spawn of the war brings upon mankind.

Everything, the entire horror of war is shameful in the highest degree, I too am ashamed beyond all measure, no matter whether I had anything to do with it or not. It is gradually coming about that men are now bestowed with a protection against overambitious people lusting for power which makes such an occurrence impossible, for its acute danger is greater than ever in the age of nuclear mass destruction.

Should the present situation continue, the future of mankind is pregnant with disaster, every moment ready to produce a new violent death, new tears and new sorrow, and therewith spread a new graveyard gloom over mankind.

Those who have to bear the sorrow will, as up to now, be and remain precisely those who were not involved and, in the final analysis, were also likewise recipients of orders.

If we of the present were too stupid to bring about a change, then our children should draw a lesson from our stupidity and make the step towards a conformation to human wishes. That would be a step forward; in the field of human cohabitation we old people went, at most, a step back. We obviously lacked the courage for it. The youth of the nations must unite. The organisational pre-requirements will take the form of thousands of youth associations. Come together and become one! Then abolish the idea of statehood with its particularist sovereign rights and the entire political appendage. Instead of that, create a centrally governing body for the benefit and welfare of all the nations of the earth.

To endow such a body with all necessary trans-national governmental powers obviously requires the overcoming of restrictions related to authorities and ideologies. The shifts of responsibilities too will doubtless be bound to certain initial difficulties. But granted that orders for murder and annihilation may be issued by the state leadership with the expenditure of fewer restrictions and difficulties, the question still remains if it were not worth it to hazard even the *greatest* difficulties, no matter of what kind, and to work at their correction if thereby peace, joy and happiness can be brought among men. If the male sex does not produce such a renaissance - this might possibly be true - since it has unfortunately brought only calamity in this field, then women should attempt it. For they are indeed the maintainers and preservers of life. In any case, one can trust their ability in this field more than the obsolete arts of men in this regard.

That is, women allow themselves to be guided by feelings, whereas we men might adopt the standpoint of reason. Apart from the fact that I have anyway not noticed any rationality in this field of politics up to now, I ask myself what one could have against women's emotional nature superseding the irrational viewpoint of the male. It can never become worse; on the other hand, mankind would have the prospect of things very probably becoming better.

Here is another such example of male "reason" before me. It is a letter of the Chief of the SS Economic and Administrative Head Office to Himmler of April 1944.

"Reichsführer!

I am sending a map of the Reich territory of the Generalgouvernement, the eastern countries and the Netherlands in which all concentration and work camps are marked according to the situation as of 31 March 1944.

The Meaning of Special Treatment

There are now:

In the Reich territory	13 concentration camps
In the Generalgouvernement	3
In the eastern countries	3
In the Netherlands	1
Total	20 concentration camps

In addition, the following work camps are maintained:

In the Reich territory	130 work camps
In the Generalgouvernement	3
In the eastern countries	30
In the Netherlands	2
Total	165 work camps

In Eicke's time there were 6 camps in all, now 185!

Heil Hitler!

signed Pohl

SS Obergruppenführer and general of the Waffen SS"

Regarding the Eicke I have mentioned,[56] he was the predecessor of Glücks, the Inspector of the Concentration Camp System. In 1941, the SS Gruppenführer and lieutenant general of the Waffen SS, Eicke, received orders to take over a front unit. After that, in 1941, "Eicke's time" came to an end. From 1941 up to April 1944, a total of 179 concentration and work camps were newly created.

---

56 Theodor Eicke (1892-1943) was appointed inspector of the concentration camp system in 1934, a post which he held until he was assigned to combat duty in 1939, when his post was taken over by Richard Glücks.

False Gods

Ulrich von Hutten,[57] where are your days! Truly, there is no more joy in living. It is incredible to me and appears improbable that I myself stood in the midst of all these events. If only such situations had ceased at least in 1945, but how many concentration camps in the world may there perhaps be today?

I am glad of one thing, that fate has made it possible for me to be able to still speak freely and frankly about all such things, and to record these things, not indeed from hearsay, but from personal experience and from my own point of view.

My words do not issue from any personal bitterness, for I have learnt to understand myself and to the degree to which I understood myself I saw also the mistakes that I made.

Kant set this self-recognition as a precondition of my basic attitude, of my practical consciousness, and Socrates too, that wise man of antiquity, made this self-recognition something primary, a pre-requirement to be posited for my focus on ethical values. But what use is self-recognition to me and all the fine doctrines of dead and living wise men when the current state holds me under its thumb as its ward. Even Socrates was not able to do anything against the *state authority* except through a sacrificial death. Dismissing the possibility of escape obtained by his friends, he pointed to the legal conditions, recommended to them to sacrifice, after his death, a cock to the gods and emptied the bowl. Thus the story as it was handed down to us. I was *not* a Socrates; I was also *not* a Giordano Bruno.[58] And even a mind of the stature of a Plato did not succeed in swaying the tyrant Dionysius from his state political orientation and to practise, instead of this, Platonic ideas of state leadership.[59]

---

57 Ulrich von Hutten (1488-1523) was a critic of Roman Catholicism and supporter of Johannes Reuchlin (1455-1522), the Hebrew scholar who opposed the efforts of the anti-Semitic Jewish Catholic convert, Johannes Pfefferkorn (1469-1523), to confiscate all Hebrew books as a means of ensuring the conversion of the Jews to Christianity.

58 Giordano Bruno (1548-1600) was a Dominican friar and philosopher whose unconventional cosmological and theological views caused him to be charged with heresy and burned at the stake.

59 While in Syracuse, Plato served as instructor to Dion, uncle of Dionysius II. After Plato's return to Athens, Dion persuaded Dionysius to invite Plato to Syracuse once again in order that the philosopher might groom the tyrant into a philosopher-king. Even though Dionysius did invite Plato back, he was not quite amenable to Platonic instruction and Plato was finally forced to flee Syracuse (see Plato, *Seventh Letter*).

The Meaning of Special Treatment

Jewish prisoners at Buchenwald concentration camp.

On the instructions of the German Foreign Minister von Ribbentrop, there took place on the 2nd and 4th of April 1944 in Krummhübel a workshop of Jewish consultants of the German foreign missions in Europe. It was filled with two envoys, ten doctors, some legation councillors, consuls, government councillors and others. Envoy Prof. Six handed over, after the welcome address, the chairmanship to Envoy Schleier. The latter spoke in his opening lecture on the "Tasks and goals of the foreign anti-Jewish operation". This was followed by Dr. Six on "The political structure of world Jewry". There followed a lecture of government councillor Dr. von Thadden: "Jewish political situation in Europe. Overview of the situation of the anti-Jewish executive measures".

Envoy Dr. Six declared that Jewry in Europe had played out its biological and, at the same time, its political role; the physical removal of eastern Jewry has deprived Jewry of its biological reserves. The Jewish question must be resolved not only in Germany but also internationally,.

Legation councillor von Thadden concluded his remarks to the representatives of the foreign missions with a request to suppress every propaganda, even that disguised as anti-Jewish, which tended to restrict or prevent the German measures. Further, to prepare an understanding in all nations of the executive measures against Jewry. In addition, to report constantly on the possibility of implementing,

False Gods

through diplomatic channels, sharpened measures against Jewry in the different countries. And finally to report constantly on evidence of counter-actions of world Jewry so that timely counter-explosives may be laid.

The details propounded by the consultants on the situation of the executive measures in the different countries were not recorded in the protocol since this was to be kept secret.

There followed finally some twenty more talks which were held by the different participants of the conference.

These documents have been presented to me here in Israel along with other documents from that time – I was not a participant in the conference – and were subjects of discussion during the trial.

When I read the witness testimony of Dr. Six which he made in 1961 in Germany and, in addition, the witness testimonies of the former legation councillor von Thadden from the years shortly after the cease-fire of 1945, and, beyond that, some of the documents submitted here in Israel from the correspondence of Dr. Six with the chief of the then Danube senior division of the SD and others, I must indeed say that all this is remarkable, very remarkable.

I had much to do with legation councillor Dr. von Thadden, one could say continuously, in the years until 1945, because he was for a while an adviser in the Foreign Office. An active file communication bound his department with mine through our immediate superiors. Hundreds of such documents are still available now.

Personally Mr. von Thadden was an amiable person, moderate, calm, bureaucratically dry. There is only one thing I do not understand, how he could maintain in Nuremberg that he did not know anything at all about the killings and to say that SS Obdersturmbannführer Eichmann had lied to him albeit very skilfully. At the same time he had such unequivocal things to present on these same matters in April 1944 that these could not be recorded in the protocol of the meeting.

I know that lies arise readily and advantageously when one is interrogated, and that much was questioned after 1945. I also do not hold anything personally against Mr. von Thadden. I only declare that, through such and similar things, an image then formed about me as if I truly had been the driving force responsible for the measures against

The Meaning of Special Treatment

the Jews. An image which however was shattered during my trial and had to be acknowledged with surprise by many of the uninitiated, in short it was an assumption that was ship-wrecked. It was such ideas that were able to spread with the result that I developed into the "*deus ex machina*" among many of those imprisoned at that time in Nuremberg. In their "*miserere*" they suddenly recognised that by foisting everything onto me - since I was indeed not accessible - their own situation at that time could only be improved.

Dr. Six had been my superior in the SD Head Office for a while, if one disregards a departmental director who was placed between me and him and a chief departmental director. Besides, he was at that time the dean of the "International Studies Faculty of the University of Vienna"; but I have already mentioned this once. Dr. Six was extremely astute and intelligent; it was impossible to deceive him. When I consider matters from my post-1945 position, I must say that the "international political" aspect of the Krumhübler Conference confirms that, if one considers his intelligence properly, it could not have been better developed than mine. For, it seems to me that it played a terrible trick on both of us. Of course - in order to avoid all misunderstanding - I had at my disposal only that degree of "household intelligence" that was assigned to me; so to compare myself with a former dean seems frivolous to me - I hurry to add this, and I would have not touched this entire subject of "intelligence" if Dr. Six had not broached this of his own accord in his witness testimony in 1961. But, be that as it may, I think that both of us would have done better to deal with other things than with the "world-view" of that time.

And I do not mean this with regard to the present-day economic status which one must put up with to a certain extent as a consequence – even though I would not at all like to complain regarding my external situation in the last ten years in Argentina, which is so much easier for me in that I personally anyway never had a special connection to money or monetary values –, but, in the comparison between then and now, I am thinking of an ethical gain that one would have been able to obtain for oneself in direct proportion to the age that one had in the meantime reached, if one had not, partly through one's own folly and partly through circumstantial conditions, had to pass through a "spiritual vacuum" lasting for years. But I do not hold anything personally against Dr. Six; I was easily able to tolerate him as a man during the time when he was my superior.

The witness testimony of Dr. Six with regard to his attempt to distance

False Gods

himself from the Einsatz Groups or to free himself from it, pointing out that he himself had succeeded in doing so, caused the attorney-general to refer to it in the proceedings against me.

Even the testimony of Mr. von dem Bach-Zelewski – former general of the Police – that there were possibilities of withdrawing from a commission through application for a transfer misses the point, in my opinion, as far as it concerns me.

I do not know Mr. von dem Bach-Zelewski personally, but I have always heard only good and praiseworthy things about him as a man.

I think that both gentlemen will agree with me when I say that it is a big difference when a general of the Police or an office chief in the Reich Security Head Office wishes to withdraw from something and when one of their advisers goes to them with such a request.

Requests for transfer could of course be made, nobody prevented one from doing so, but I think ...[60] and one does not need to waste words on this because such requests were always decided in the negative.

Especially if the adviser concerned did not belong anyway to any Einsatz Group, did not have to kill anybody, did not have to give any orders for that, and did not even have to issue deportation orders by himself. If such an adviser, for example in the Reich Security Head Office, did his service behind a writing-table – and nevertheless applied for a transfer – or if he was transferred to Hungary as a commanding officer of the Security Police and SD, and therewith was placed under the latter as well as the Senior SS and Police Chief, who was at the same time his judge. Or if an adviser wished to be transferred from a senior division to a lower division, let us say, for example, to Linz am Donau. In this case, when there is a negative result for a request, it is only a matter of "obeying and continuing to serve". For, the answers then ran every time more or less in the following manner: "So what do you want, you have only to fulfil your administrative file work. Nobody demands of you that you should kill or give orders for that. Besides, we are living in the midst of the most violent wars. You too have to fulfil your duty; and indeed where you are positioned. During a war nobody can choose where he would like to fight." This was exactly what one heard at that time.

---

60 Eichmann seems to have lost the thread of his sentence here.

Is that correct, gentlemen? Honestly, I do not wish hereby to gain anything for myself; besides the evidentiary hearings have long since concluded in the trial against me. This should only serve the truth; and to give one or another of the persons of low service rank the possibility of appealing to it. I think in the first place – and nobody can deny me this – of the members of my own department of that time.

I can round out these observations with a declaration that Prof. Six made during his witness testimony in 1961, in which it says, among other things, that finally there was for each of us still the possibility of shooting ourselves in case the request for a transfer was not granted. This is true! I clearly failed to shoot myself at the right time; *bueno*, and in a logical interpretation of this alternative I have to bear the consequences even today.

Dr. Six managed to get away from an Einsatz Group. As mentioned, he, as one of the seven office chiefs of the Reich Security Head Office, had it lighter. He exchanged his position in the security police for that of an envoy in the Foreign Office. But nevertheless he appeared again in April 1944 as one of the persons in charge at the Krummhübler Conference.

He was not the initiator but his Reich Foreign Minister, this is clear, and is revealed by the documents. But he too had to obey as an envoy and to do what was ordered to him. How much more obedience did a consultant have to show.

Himmler and the Demand for Obedience

Himmler gave a speech in Posen in October 1943 before his SS Gruppenführers and his SS generals. Among other topics he dealt with the subject of obedience.

He explained:

"Obedience is demanded and performed in the soldierly life every morning, noon, and evening. The small man always, or mostly, obeys. If he does not obey he is jailed.

More difficult is the question of obedience among the senior dignitaries in the state, party and army, also here and there in the SS. I would like to express something clearly here:

False Gods

That the small man must obey is obvious. More obvious is that all higher SS chiefs, so the entire Gruppenführer corps, are models of unconditional obedience ... But the moment that a superior concerned or the SS Reichsführer – indeed that is possible in most cases for the SS Gruppenführers – or even the Führer has decided or given an order, it is to be carried out not only according to the letter but according to the spirit. One who carries out the order has to do this as a faithful executor, as a faithful representative of the commanding authority. If they first thought that this would be right and that would not be right or even wrong, then there are two possibilities.

If someone thinks that he cannot be responsible for compliance with an order, then he must report it honestly: I cannot be responsible for that, I request to be relieved of it. Then in most cases the order will come: You still have to carry it out. Or people think: he has lost his nerve, he is weak. Then they might say: "Good, go on pension. But orders must be sacred."

Now all that sounds fine. But when one considers that it is a question here of SS generals to whom Himmler issued these words then it looks quite different. With regard to a man of the lower service ranks it means: he has to obey; if not: jail. Yes, that is indeed exactly what I said, our chiefs at that time had it easier in this respect. Besides, it has been old military knowledge for generations: the lower people are in rank, the more ruthlessly are they ridden roughshod over.

Man today, especially the city man has been living, and lives, in haste and is hounded in the daily battle for existence. This work and drudgery to which he was subjected for the maintenance of himself and his relations, often under circumstances that drive his nerves to the edge of the bearable, has become the actual content of his existence. And with the increasing density of the earth's population, this battle for existence becomes increasingly more unscrupulous and brutal. It leaves for him increasingly little time and leisure for the gathering of spiritual values according to which he can orient himself. Indeed, beyond that, it becomes increasingly harder as a result of his worn out condition, in physical *and* psychological terms, to bring forth any interest at all for such an acquisition of values. Thus, instead of such desires, a heightened egoism combined with a pessimistic attitude to matters of existence - and, if he should ever consider this, to matters in general - becomes all powerful.

A state or party propaganda directed to this milieu will always have its

Himmler and the Demand for Obedience

Reichsführer Heinrich Himmler during a camp inspection at Auschwitz.

successes here. In Germany, for example, there vegetated at the time of the development of the "National Socialist German Workers' Party" a million unemployed people more or less.

The diverse political currents with their demagogic appeals were forced upon the individual by means of a psychologically specialised propaganda machinery and finally influenced his moral attitude by diverting it into the thought and action desired by the party or state.

The original diversity of attitudes corresponding to individual characters is standardised, is levelled out, and has to be made uniform. But therewith the precondition of an ethics of individual beliefs is lost and in its place there enters a state or party "mass ethics" of a special character.

The individual can now at best still differentiate and decide *what* is valuable and *what*, according to his beliefs and his feelings, *goes against* the universally valid moral values, but he can no longer give *any* visible expression to the result of his own reasoning or his own feelings if the totalitarian claim has assumed a state-executive character without bringing personal physical danger upon himself; indeed, even such a sacrifice will not bring about *any chang*e of the general situation that has been enforced.

False Gods

Freedom of action can be granted expression only in those paths whose direction and goal are agreeable to the state leadership. And, instead of the driving human instincts for a prosperous cohabitation of men with one another being subjected to moral values, it is precisely the opposite. One of the consequences then is, finally, that, instead of the commanded consideration of the interests and rights of other peoples, a law is established which would benefit one's own people alone, without consideration of the necessities of life and the life of other communities, indeed at their expense. So long as this condition is not changed there will be further merciless catastrophes in the life of nations, as certainly as the 'Amen' at church. And parliamentarianism may not hide behind the consolation that such a thing would be possible only in totalitarian states and that the latter alone are the triggering factors. History gives a quite unequivocal report on this.

The power of destiny placed me in existence, in life; as a man. And I disappear from it just as the journey of a wanderer in the night does. On this track everybody has much that causes pain and even sorrow.

Part II

In the last 15 years when publicists refer to me in speech or writing one can, studying their publications, recognise that it is maintained that: of course, it may perhaps seem wrong to maintain Eichmann's participation in the massacres in the east, but he was the person responsible for the solution of the Jewish question in all the territories in Europe occupied or controlled by Germany.

Now, after I have been placed in the central point of such accounts it is not very easy for me to speak especially on the subject of western, northern, southern and south-eastern Europe without, in the case of absolutely every sentence raised against me, getting into a personal defence. But such a thing would be boring to the reader.

On the other hand, however, it still seems obvious that anybody who was not responsible for something, who was not the mastermind, initiator or the commanding officer but has been made guilty of it, such a person would defend himself against false accusations, for otherwise a false picture would arise. I have therefore found the best and, at the same time, simplest solution in a form that I think is the best for the creation of an objective picture, to let by and large the official documents of that time themselves speak in their own words. Thereby it will be seen that every possible imputation that I approached the description of the materials in a "slippery or duplicitous way" would be made impossible in advance. Such a way of observing things - which I illustrate with personal reminiscences and opinions - seems to me to convey a faithful and clear picture, exactly what the reader wishes to know, namely: what really happened at that time. What is true and what lies. It will be the reader himself who can finally form for himself a clear judgement on the reality regarding the events.

France

On 21 June 1940, the cease-fire between Germany and France was signed in the historic dining-car of the "International sleeping wagon company" in Campiègne. On 3 August 1940, the then Foreign Minister von Ribbentrop informed the chief of the high command of the armed forces in Berlin of the following:

Hitler has named the current envoy Abetz ambassador and assigned to him the following tasks for France:
1. Advising of the military offices on political matters.
2. Constant contact with the Vichy government and their commissioners in the occupied territory.
3. Advising of the Secret Military Police and Secret State Police on the confiscation of politically important documents.
4. Securing and acquisition of public art possessions, further of private and especially Jewish art possessions on the basis of special instructions issued for this purpose.

Further, Hitler has expressly ordered that Ambassador Abetz is exclusively responsible for the handling of all political questions in occupied and unoccupied France.

Further, Ribbentrop informs that the ambassador will receive instructions for the implementation of his tasks from him and is responsible to him alone.

This was an appointment with extraordinary powers: and so it is not a wonder that Abetz suggested in a meeting of 17 August 1940 that the military administration in France should order that no more Jews enter into occupied France. Further he demanded preparations for the removal of all Jews from the occupied territory and finally an investigation into whether the Jewish property in the occupied territory could be expropriated.

The chief of the military administration in occupied France had now to work out these matters from the bureaucratic-administrative side.

At the same time, the Foreign Office in Berlin requested the personal staff of the SS Reichsführer for a comment on Abetz's inquiry regarding the anti-Semitic measures that could serve as the basis to later remove the Jews from unoccupied France as well.

False Gods

Jewish youths in the Drancy concentration camp, 3rd Dec 1942

On 20 September 1940, Heydrich hurried to reply to the inquirer, SA Standartenführer and envoy, Luther, under the letter-head "The SS Reichsführer and Chief of the German Police in the Reich Ministry of the Interior, file memo 5-IVD6-776/40g Rs":

He has no objections against the implementation of the measures planned by Abetz and is also in agreement with its execution by the French authorities. But Abetz went one step further than had happened up to now, for he demanded the obligatory registration of Jews settled in the occupied territory, the identification of Jewish businesses and the appointment of trustees for Jewish assets whose owners had fled.

Heydrich thought a corresponding deployment of the German Security Police stationed in France would be advisable – So on 1 October 1940, there was issued a further proposal from Abetz in 19 copies to the most diverse central authority offices, wherein he wished collective denaturalisation procedures to be implemented in the future for specified Jewish groups in the mentioned territory. He finally maintained that these proposed measures were to be seen only as the first step towards the solution of the entire problem.

France

The French government in Vichy had, in the meanwhile, appointed Xavier Vallat as "Commissioner for the Jewish question". The latter visited the German Embassy in Paris on 3 April 1941. Abetz reported to the Foreign Office the following:

> "In order that in a later stage even "people settled for long" could be apprehended through the same measures as the foreign or newly naturalised Jews, a law is necessary even now that would empower the French Jewish commissioner to declare "long settled" Jews who have infringed the special and national interests of the French nation as 'foreigners'. "

He had advised Xavier Vallat to propose such a law to his government in Vichy.

Already on 4 October 1940, the French government in Vichy issued a Jewish statute in which, among other things, the admittance of Jewish foreigners into special concentration camps was stipulated; and, with the decree IVD6-229/40 of 30 October 1940 of the SS Reichsführer and Chief of the Security Police and SD, the creation of special concentration camps for Jews of German, Austrian, Czechoslovak and Polish citizenship was ordered.

The commissioner of the Chief of the Security Police and SD for Belgium and France communicated this to the Paris office, to Dr. Knochen, chief of the military administration in France, on 28 January 1941.

I have highlighted here, based on documents, a short sketch of the legislative basis that was created for the handling of the Jewish question in France. Neither I nor my department entered yet into the picture. It was handled by other offices. SS Hauptsturmführer Dannecker, who had been working for a short time in my department, was, by an order of my office chief, relieved of his work in the Reich Security Head Office and transferred to Paris as an adviser to the Chief of the Security Police.

In the meantime, according to a directive of Göring's, the emigration of Jews from the territory of the "Greater Reich" was to be carried out with greater force even during the war within the scope of the given possibilities. And since, at that time, adequate emigration possibilities, or more precisely, immigration approvals, were not available, an emigration of Jews from Belgium and France would reduce these possibilities still further. Therefore emigration from these territories was to be prevented. Finally, the doubtless imminent final solution of the Jewish question is referred to. This was communicated on 20 May 1941 to all state police offices, the state authorities in France, the SD offices, as well as to the Foreign Office in Berlin. One of my specialists had drafted this letter according to an order of my office chief of the Reich Security Head Office; I dictated the main points of my chief to the specialist (IV-B4b).

My immediate superior at that time, SS Gruppenführer and lieutenant-general of the Police, Heinrich Müller, must have been sick or officially out of office for some days – a fact that counts among the greatest of rarities – for his representative at that time Schellenberg signed this circular decree, that Schellenberg who was later, after the ousting of Canaris, appointed unrestrained master of German espionage and counter-espionage, which was called in short "defence".

I just introduced the word "final solution of the Jewish question". At that time by this word was still understood, as far as I remember, the "Madagascar Plan" that had already been prepared through my involvement, and which represented this "subject",[1] on which I have reported in greater detail in another section of this work. The lines following now will show how this plan – apart from the later military and political situation by which it was superseded – was torpedoed.

A legation councillor Dr. Zeitschel was appointed in Paris for the support of the diplomats there. Abetz informed the military commanding officer in Paris of this. This Dr. Zeitschel made a report on 22 August 1941 for Ambassador Abetz.

In this it says that the progressing conquest and occupation of the large eastern territories could bring the Jewish problem in the whole of Europe in the shortest time to a final, satisfactory solution. One should demarcate a special territory there for them. The Jews of occupied territories like Holland, Belgium, Luxembourg, Norway, Yugoslavia and Greece could be evacuated in mass transports into the new territory and it could be suggested to the remaining states to follow the example. The Madagascar Plan was of course in itself not bad, but it faced insurmountable transport difficulties since there were more important things than giving cruises to a large number of Jews on the world's seas. Quite apart from the fact that the transport of 1 million Jews to Madagascar would take years.

---

1   i.e. in all official correspondence

France

Dr. Zeitschel then asked Ambassador Abetz to present this matter to the Reich Foreign Minister so that the latter may work together with the Minister for the Eastern Territories, Rosenberg, and the SS Reichsführer Himmler in examining the entire matter as proposed by him.

The transport of the Jews into the eastern territories would have to be carried out even during the war.

He requests further that he might emphasise on this occasion that there are not enough camps for internment available and one must, as a result of this, help with all possible laws and other prescriptions, which however can on the whole be only temporary and not comprehensive measures.

Finally he proposes to Abetz that he bring this problem to the attention also of Reich Marshal Göring, who was now very receptive to the Jewish question, as he could, in his present appointment and given his experiences of the eastern campaign, be a strong support in the implementation of the idea developed.

Now, these must have been joyful sounds in the ears of the Reich Foreign Minister Ribbentrop. Certainly, the deployment of the active Heydrich, with his foreign political ambitions, in an executive manner in the Madagascar case was not a comfortable thought to him: it was already bad enough for Ribbentrop that of all people Heydrich was entrusted with the post of a "Deputy Reich Protector" for Bohemia and Moravia. Heydrich's thirst for power was limitless, and Heydrich was, further, sly, refined, and in his way filled with an architect-like desire for building up, quite in contrast to Ribbentrop. In any case, Abetz must have encountered a willing and joyful reception, for, a short time later, or was it at the same time, the Madagascar Plan collapsed as a total solution.

For France itself Abetz had while he was at the Hauptquartier received Himmler's approval that all the Jews interned in the concentration camps in France could be deported to the east, as soon as the means of transport allowed this.

On 8 October 1941, Dr. Zeitschel informed the commissioner of the Chief of the Security Police and SD for Belgium and France of this result through Dannecker.² As he had succeeded in obtaining in this direction the principal approval of Himmler, he requested that the reins be not slackened and that a report be sent off to Berlin every two weeks and urged that the Jews be deported from occupied France as quickly as possible. With this the order for the deportation of Jews from France was achieved. The police received the corresponding instructions and had to obey. For example, what use would it have been if an individual had rather said, No, I do not want to. The SS and Police jurisdiction would have intervened and in his place another would have had to carry on the work.

The military commanding officer in Paris pushed, the ambassador pushed and this pushing had to be accepted by the commissioner of the Chief of the Security Police and SD, for Himmler had approved.

When would they permit it?

Paris pestered the Reich Security Head Office. My chief, the office chief of Office IV, ordered negotiations with the responsible department of the Reich Transport Ministry. The SS Reichsführer, Himmler, and the Chief of the Security Police and SD, Heydrich, determined the groups of people, the exceptions, the final stations in the east, the baggage kilogram limits, all in agreement with the Foreign Office and other political central authority offices in coordination with the first waves of deportation of Jews from the Old Reich territory, Austria and the Protectorate of Bohemia and Moravia in autumn 1941.

No divisional head in the Reich Transport Ministry could have said, We have no trains, the transport situation does not allow it. Everything put together was a gear-train in which one cog gripped the other.

The driving forces of the main wave were, in the case of France, Dr. Zeitschel, Abetz and Ribbentrop; and, further, Himmler and Heydrich. That is not a theory. The documents prove it. The deportations from France were running.

On 23 October 1941, Himmler, in his capacity as SS Reichsführer and Chief of the German Police, ordered the suspension or, better, the prevention of emigration of Jews with immediate effect. However, the

---

2   Wrongly it says in the document "Obersturmbannführer Dannecker". I can swear that Dannecker never rose above the rank of an SS Hauptsturmführer (captain) and never had the rank of an SS Obersturmbannführer (lieutenant-colonel).

France

deportation was once again postponed at the turn of the year 1941/42 as a result of the Christmas holiday traffic. This was communicated on Christmas Eve 1941, at 11 o'clock, by the Chief of Office IV of the Reich Security Head Office, SS Gruppenführer and lieutenant-general of the Police, Müller, to the commissioner of the Chief of the Security Police for France and Belgium.

On 28 February 1942, I received orders to inform the Paris office regarding their inquiry of 27 February 1942 that one thousand Jews could be deported immediately after the conclusion of a travel-plan meeting that was taking place at the moment.

There were obviously still difficulties, for bureaucracy works in all countries at a bureaucratic tempo. According to orders I had to call a meeting of Jewish advisers in Berlin on 4 March 1942. At this the relevant adviser of the commissioner of the Chief of the Security Police and SD in Paris pointed again to the urgency of an immediate deportation.

According to my orders I had to agree to take delivery in the month of March 1942 and announced that, pending the final decision by Heydrich, negotiations could be entered upon with the French government for the deportation of five thousand Jews to the east. According to the instructions, it was at first to be a matter of male Jews fit for work not over 55 years old. Further, care was to be taken that Jews of French citizenship lost their citizenship before the deportation or, at the latest, on the day of the deportation and the processing of assets had likewise to be taken care of. Here the 11th regulation to the Reich citizenship laws cooked up by the Reich Ministry of the Interior floated in the heads of my superiors. The start of the deportation was scheduled for 23 March 1942 by the Reich Transport Ministry.

After the obligatory identification for Jews in the territory of "the greater German Reich including Bohemia and Moravia" was effected by Hitler through the initiative of the state secretary for the security system in Bohemia and Moravia, Frank (holder of the Knight's Cross) and the Reich Minister for Public Enlightenment and Propaganda, Dr. Goebbels, the offices of the occupied territories too now began to subject Jews to this obligatory identification.

The military commanding officer in France issued the ordinance approved by the Foreign Office, Berlin, on 7 June 1942. At the same time, there followed from the senior SS Police Chief in France,

False Gods

Himmler's representative in this territory, SS Brigadeführer and major general of the Police, Oberg, a prohibition of Jews from entering public institutions and taking part in public events.

According to an order of Hitler's, the senior SS and Police Chief was to take charge, who had not yet been in office for a long time. Yet one expected through this new regulation, both from the side of the military commanding officer and that of the offices of the regional security police, a favourable result with regard to the final solution of the Jewish question.

I already said that the start of the deportation from France was scheduled for 23 March 1942 and was to be adhered to essentially as well. Very instructive in this context is a telegram of the Chief of the German Security Police for France, Dr. Knochen, to my department of 20 March 1942 in which he informs me that the military commanding officer had decisively informed him that he could not supply any guards for the deportation of the first thousand Jews from Campiègne or Drancy. He therefore requested that this matter of the transport escort crew be regulated with the German army high command since the latter had indeed obtained the orders for the internment and deportation of these Jews through the Hitler Hauptquartier. Now, 28 March 1942 was mentioned as the date of departure of the transport.

It emerges from this that, along with Dr. Zeitschel – Ambassador Abetz – Reich Foreign Minister von Ribbentrop, even the army high command was responsible for the start or the initiation of the deportations from France. Of course, in the final analysis, the Foreign Office had to give its agreement to such deportations from abroad; to be sure, it was in this case a purely formal bureaucratic necessity as its chief, that is, Ribbentrop, had personally given his agreement to it.

On 26 January 1942, Himmler informed the inspector for the concentration camp system, the then major-general of the Waffen SS, Glücks, that he had to be prepared to accept 100,000 male and 50,000 female Jews into the concentration camps. His boss, the general of the Waffen SS, Pohl, would instruct him on the details, and on 1 February 1942, Himmler created within the concentration camp system a stricter organisational management. He appointed Pohl as head office chief of the Economic and Administrative Head Office to whom Glücks, as chief of inspection, chief of Office group D, was subordinated.

France

According to orders I had to call a meeting in Berlin once again for 11 June 1942 to which I had to invite the Jewish consultants from Paris, Brussels and the Hague through the official channels. In the meantime, Glücks had undertaken preparations for acceptance in Auschwitz, and Himmler ordered the deportation of 100,000 Jews from France, 15,000 from the Netherlands, and 10,000 from Belgium.

According to Himmler's instruction it was an essential condition that the Jews be between 16 and 40 years old, and in this he tolerated 10% non-working Jews. These transports should run from 13 July 1942 and three of them weekly.

When Himmler issued this order to his Chief of the Security Police and SD, the latter was still alive. But on 29 May 1942 he was wounded by a bomb. Seven days later he succumbed to his injuries. Heydrich was dead. Himmler himself took over the direction of his Reich Security Head Office and was to maintain it until the beginning of January 1943. Only at this time was Dr. Kaltenbrunner introduced into his office as Heydrich's successor.

Heydrich's death triggered even more drastic operations against the Jews. Now Himmler ordered, deviating from his original order, that *all* Jews, regardless of age or sex, were to be deported as quickly as possible; both from the occupied and from the unoccupied part of France. I myself had to go to Paris on the orders of my office chief, Müller, to convey this Himmler order.

The comment among the notes dictated by Dannecker on 1 July1942 in Paris shows a number of bureaucratic impossibilities and deficiencies, for example the "letter-head" (there was no RSHA=Reich Security Head Office, IV B 4, in regards to "Paris"). The comment is neither certified nor sealed. There is neither my signature nor Dannecker's. However, I declare it to be rather correctly reproduced.

Already a long time ago Dr. Knochen had in Paris been promoted to SS Standartenführer and colonel of the police and his position was that of a commanding officer of the Security Police and SD in France. After the Himmler order to deport *all* Jews from France, contacts with the French offices were established, especially with the French police chief Darquier de Pellepoix and his representative Laguay, with the chief of the Jewish file in the Paris prefecture, the director Tulard, and, in addition, with the representative of the Seine prefecture, the director Garnier, the director of the anti-Jewish Police in Schweblin,

False Gods

etc. After such a sharp order from the highest office, the inevitable set in. The deportations began in grand style.

On 10 July 1942, Paris informed my department that there would be 4,000 Jewish children as part of the wave of arrests and demanded an urgent written decision on whether the children of the stateless Jews to be deported, from the 10th transport onwards, could be deported along with the latter. Eleven days later I received from my superior an order to inform Paris that, as soon as the deportation to the Generalgouvernement was once again possible, these children had to be transported. I myself had, at that time, three small children. I would not like to say more here.

Once again I had to have invitations issued to the Jewish specialists abroad to a workshop on 28 August 1942. The reason for this was Himmler's order to complete the deportation of the stateless Jews by the end of 1942 and he had ordered June 1943 as the deadline for the deportation of the remaining Jews.

In this context, one of the infamous Rademacher handwritten notes on such an invitation letter - which letters were to be forwarded through the Foreign Office to SS Hauptsturmführer Richter in Bucharest is noteworthy. He writes here that the meeting dealt with technical questions and consisted almost exclusively of two visits to camps.

The imaginative invention of legation councillor Rademacher from the Foreign Office is confirmed most clearly by a note that an SS Untersturmführer Ahnert prepared for his superiors in Paris in which he describes the meeting points precisely. The note dates from 1 September 1942. The only passage that could have anything to do with "camps" is that point in which it says I requested the participants in the meeting to undertake immediately "the acquisition of the barracks obtained by the commanding officer of the Security Police in the Hague. The camp should be set up in Russia. The transport of the barracks could be undertaken in such a way that with every transport train 3-5 barracks are transported". I have reproduced here an order of my superiors. Obviously Rademacher heard something and made up a note of his own sort.

Himmler wrote to my office chief Müller in December 1942: "I order that from the Jews present now in France, as well as from the Hungarian and Romanian Jews, all those who have influential relatives in America are to be gathered together in a special camp. There they

France

should of course work but under such conditions that they may be in good health and remain alive. These sorts of Jews are valuable hostages for us. I imagine here a figure of around 10,000."

That was the procedure up to this point in France. Everybody pushed and everybody in the different central authority offices, insofar as he had a somewhat influential position, wanted to give evidence of his "integrity as a National Socialist office holder" through stimuli and proposals with respect to the "solution of the Jewish question".

The police then had to bear the pressure which then came from above. They were just overwhelmed; deadlines were set to them. Things went too slowly for everybody, the intricate police bureaucracy was tedious in every case. The police had to carry out the entire rubbish that was brewed in the central authority offices. But that was how it was and that is how it will perhaps always remain. So I say that police service, especially service in the political police, is the worst that fate can punish one with. As long as there are *orders*, in connection with the ruling system in the coexistence of nations, there will also be political police. In spite of charters, or the UN, in spite of death and the devil.

Now I wish to continue to describe how things fared further. First this: If I had been, instead of a recipient of orders, a giver of orders, if I had been, instead of Adolf Eichmann, let us say, Dr. Zeitschel, I would not be in a position to report even a line about the entire gruesome happenings; for, at every word, I would have to hear the accusation: "You are the guilty person", and my pen would hesitate at every word. But I have not made such proposals, so I can report that which happened. This occurred to me incidentally, as it were, and if such thoughts really belong to another chapter of this work, I still did not take the effort, with careful appraisal, to set it down in its proper place since I think that one who wishes to read all this will anyway come of his own accord to this passage.

A note of the officials of the office of the commanding officer of the Security Police and SD in Paris, dated 9 September1942, has survived. In this we read: "According to the plan announced confidentially by the SS Reichsführer, the territories occupied by Germany should be already free of Jews by the middle of 1943."

And the then under-secretary of state in the Foreign Office in Berlin, Luther, informed his secretary of state, von Weizsäcker, on 24 September1942 that the Reich Foreign Minister had just given him the following instructions by telephone that the evacuations of the Jews from the different countries of Europe should be accelerated as much as possible. Luther had made a presentation to Ribbentrop in brief on the Jewish deportations in progress from Slovakia, Croatia, Romania and the occupied territories.

The Reich Foreign Minister – so Luther continues in his official note – had ordered that the Foreign Office should now approach the Bulgarian, Hungarian and the Danish governments with the aim of beginning the Jewish deportations from these countries.

Only with regard to Italy had the Reich Foreign Minister reserved *the right* to take further action; for this question had to be appropriately discussed between Hitler and Mussolini or between the foreign ministers of Germany and Italy.

In the meantime, not only had the position of France with regard to the further Jewish deportations hardened, but also, and especially, Italy placed the greatest obstacles to the wishes of the German Reich government in this regard.

On the complete dejudaisation of all occupied territories by the middle of 1943 ordered by Himmler his eastern representative in France, the senior SS and Police chief, sent a telegram to Himmler in which he described the special difficulties of the Laval government and of Pétain's attitude particularly with regard to a deportation of Jews with French citizenship. Italy's position was, as it were, the beacon for the French government. Himmler agreed with the opinion represented by Oberg[3] - at least outwardly – and added that, *for the moment*, no Jews of French citizenship should be arrested. Therewith a further deportation on a large scale was temporarily not possible.

Himmler had apparently revoked his own "dejudaisation" order; but, as I said, only apparently.

At that time, it was September 1942, he still had the directorship of his Reich Security Head Office in his hands and he feared a spread of a hardened attitude on the Jewish question in the other European countries, insofar as they were under German control.

---

3   Carl Oberg (1897-1965) was the Senior SS- and Police Chief in France from 1942 to 1944.

France

He therefore sent the highest-ranked military officer that he had under him, SS Obergruppenführer and colonel-general of the Police, Daluege, to Paris and Marseilles for clarification of the situation. He would be able to get information on location about a new note of the Italian government to Laval, the prime minister of the Vichy government, in which the Italians informed the French that they would not make any objections to measures from the French side in the territories occupied by Italy concerning the Jews of French citizenship, but that they would have to keep their hands off the Jews of foreign citizenship.

This would naturally have brought Laval into great difficulties. He brought this officially to the attention of the German offices and requested them for appropriate support.

Daluege's report is not available; but its contents are not difficult to guess at. Moreover the next pages will reveal in sufficient detail the activity that now followed.

Along with this information-gathering trip of Colonel-General Daluege, the commanding officer of the Security Police and SD in Paris wrote on 13 January 1943 to my office chief, Müller, and requested that he inform Himmler in the most comprehensive manner of this tactic of the Italians and he concluded with the statement that in the current state of affairs one could not be sure that Jews of French citizenship could be transferred in the near future.

In this way had matters hardened since the letter of the senior SS and Police Chief in France to Himmler of 26 September 1942. Even Envoy Schleier[4] serving in the German embassy under Ambassador Abetz reported on 23 January 1943 to the Foreign Office that a fundamental settlement of the Jewish question could only be carried out if one succeeded in bringing the Italians in line with the German anti-Jewish measures and he requested telegraphic instructions on further handling of the matter.

The centre of gravity of German Security Police affairs in this respect, and even that of the Foreign Office, was now temporarily transferred to Rome.

---

4   Rudolf Schleier (1899-1959) was consul in the German embassy in Paris from 1941 to 1943.

False Gods

A secret report of the French prefect in Nice which the latter had directed to his prime minister in Vichy came to the notice of the German security police in Paris, and Dr. Knochen sent it likewise to Müller with a request for immediate presentation to Himmler since it was extraordinarily informative on the position of the Italians regarding the Jewish question.

In this context it is interesting to hear the then official version of the Italian position. The commanding officer of the Italian IV army had informed the relevant French offices that "the Italian government does not permit persons who might dedicate themselves to anti-Italian or anti-German propaganda to be freed of its supervision". The commanding officer of the Security Police, Dr. Knochen, conveyed this on 3 February 1943 to the German senior commander of the west, through the military commander in France. He remarked that a removal of all Jews from all border and coastal départements of the newly occupied territory must be insisted on for urgent security police reasons and requested an intervention with the Italian senior commanding officer in southern France. In the meantime, the German embassy in Paris was mobilised by the Foreign Office and initiated its first official contact with the Italian Foreign Ministry.

I was ordered to Paris by my office chief, Heinrich Müller, to convey to Knochen, the commanding officer of the Security Police, the instruction that, regardless of all the difficulties, the deportation of all Jews of French citizenship should be carried out. I conveyed this according to the orders of my superiors. Nothing shows more clearly my role as a conveyer of information than the letter addressed by Dr. Knochen to Müller on 12 February 1943 immediately after the completion of my commission. He refers to my communication and refers further to his several reports on this matter, then enters into the complications that may possibly arise in political terms and informs that, if the deportations should be ordered, one should reckon with the fact that the French state leader Pétain would set himself against them and forbid them. In order to carry out the measures for all of France, the precondition is that the measures be carried out also in the Italian occupied territory.

Then there followed some thrilling hours, both in the Reich Security Head Office and in the Foreign Office. Ribbentrop himself, who had reserved to himself the regulation of the question in Italy, came alive. On the morning of 24 February 1943, he informed the chief adjutant of SS Reichsführer Himmler, the general of the Waffen SS, Wolff, that

France

the SS national leadership might soon inform him of all their wishes concerning the Jewish question in Italy and in the territories occupied by Italy. These would be discussed in Rome. He wished to have all the details communicated to him so that in a comprehensive discussion with Mussolini a clear and concrete regulation could be obtained. It was further requested that care be taken that this reply "reach us in Rome on 24 February in the forenoon". Envoy Sonnleithner wrote this from Ribbentrop's special train, "Westphalia", which was already on its way to Rome.

Already on the same day the special wishes were sent to the special train by telegram. I had not worked on it, so it must have been given by Müller to the Foreign Office; besides, it seems according to the documents as though a part of the wishes were transmitted directly from Himmler. For example, "Jewish measures in Italy same as in Germany". Further, that "Jewish measures in the newly occupied France and in Greece should not be sabotaged any further by the Italian military commanders in these territories".

Moreover, after this first reaction, the Reich Security Head Office was requested to concretise its wishes and to convey these to the Foreign Office on 25 February. Up to now all this was played out within the domains of my superiors, but in the Foreign Office the then specialist, legation councillor von Hahn, was "pressured" by his superiors to finally conjure up the damned "concretising" which Ribbentrop was waiting for in Rome. Now, one could not pressure Himmler, one did not want also to excessively rush my immediate superior, the lieutenant general of the Police, but there was Obersturmbannführer Eichmann in the Reich Security Head Office whom one could pressure. "According to instructions I inform you", wrote Hahn to me in an express letter on 25 February delivered by couriers, "that Mr. Foreign Minister has this morning again inquired about the status of the concretising suggested by you of the wishes of the SS national leadership regarding the Jewish question in Italy and the territories occupied by the Italians. Envoy Bergmann has agreed to communicate this information this evening."

I had to wait for the "concretising" that my superiors brewed together, and I could not do anything further than reassure the Foreign Office about the agreed deadlines.

Finally I received this with an order to prepare a clean copy and present it to Müller for his signature: It consisted of an old letter of Himmler's to Ribbentrop of 29 January 1943; here he wrote among

False Gods

other things that the remaining of the Jews in the Italian power sphere was the pretext for many circles in France, and in all of Europe, for dealing with the Jewish question more lightly because it would be pointed out that not even our Axis partner Italy was going along in the Jewish question.

Further, following Envoy Bergmann's request, some of the most important cases in this matter were pointed out. So, for example, a communication of the commissioner of the French police chief, Bosquet, to the commanding officer of the security police in Paris containing the note that the Italian government had handed over to the French prime minister Laval.

I now received an order with reference to the telegram of Dr. Knochen to Müller of 13 January 1943 in which he reported that the colonel-general of the police, Daluege, in Paris and Marseilles was informed that he should inform the commanding officer of the security police in Paris that the contents of his telegram were communicated to the Foreign Office and that Ribbentrop would discuss Italy's attitude to the Jewish question.

The German ambassador von Mackensen in Rome received, in the further course of things, an order to convey to Mussolini on 18 March 1943 a note from Ribbentrop, and two days later it was communicated to him on behalf of Mussolini that the police inspector Lospinoso "recognised by the Duce personally as very energetic" had received orders to clear the present difficulties out of the way.

More precise information on the activity of this new man is conveyed in a telegram of 2 April 1943 from my then chief Müller to Knochen in Paris. In it he gives a report and instructions as follows: "During my stay in Rome on 27 March 1943 I discussed the Jewish question in the newly occupied French territory on behalf of the SS Reichsführer both with the German ambassador and with the chief of the Italian police. The Italian police has, on the basis of a clear energetic instruction of the Duce, dispatched the inspector general of the Italian police, Lospinoso, and, as his representative, Vice-quaestor Luceri, along with some colleagues, to the Italian occupied territory in order to regulate the Jewish problems - especially as they have emerged at present - in a German way.

Inspector general Lospinoso has been in France for some days already. I inform you of this along with a request to get into touch immediately

France

with Lospinoso and to investigate what orders he has been given. I request a communication."

Now begins the search for the inspector general of the Italian police.

Knochen had to transmit negative reports to Müller and the latter found himself obliged once again to personally intervene by having the police attaché at the German embassy in Rome get the Italian police chief to see to it that either Lospinoso came to Berlin or got personally in touch with the commanding officer of the security police in Paris.

I was also involved in the Lospinoso search operation in that I received orders to convey the wishes of my chief to the relevant adviser in the Foreign Office, Dr. von Thadden. These included the possibility of even the Foreign Office involving itself in the search operation. Mackensen, the German ambassador in Rome, was again prodded; he proposed that the responsible Italian police chief meet with the responsible German police chief. As a meeting date he gave 18 May, in the office of the commanding officer of the Security Police and SD in Paris, 72 Avenue Foch.

On 24 May the commanding officer had to report to the chief of Office IV of the Reich Security Head Office that even the Italian embassy in Paris was not in a position to give information either about Lospinoso or about his planned trip; and he requested once again that inquiries be made with the Italian government if one could still count on the visit at all. The matter was resolved on 1 June 1943, during a visit of Mackensen to the Italian Foreign Ministry, when the Italian offices "considered such a meeting as inappropriate at the moment".

In the meantime, something different happened in France. Laval, as well as the Justice Minister Cabolde, had signed a draft of a law, according to which all Jews naturalised since 10 August1927 were declared to be stateless. This law was discussed with the Italian officials and on 30 June 1943 it was agreed with the French police chief how the Jews concerned were to be arrested promptly on the day of the announcement of the law.

Dr. Knochen demanded from Müller the assignment for a period of 10 days of at least 250 additional security police who had to master the French language to a certain extent.

Müller replied by return mail; the renewed start of the operation was indeed gratifying especially since Himmler had recently demanded a speeding up of activities but he must unfortunately inform that he would be in a position to assign in addition only 4 men, but he indicated that the police force was at the disposal of the senior SS and Police chief in France out of which he could form contingents.

On the other hand, on the same day, that is, 2 July 1943, the senior SS and Police Chief, Gruppenführer and lieutenant general of the police, Oberg, was able to inform Kaltenbrunner and Himmler that the French police chief, Bousquet, in Vichy had received a visit from Lospinoso, who had informed him that he was occupied at the time with the concentration of 60,000 Jews of foreign citizenship in the Italian field of operation. According to Bousquet, Lospinoso had told him that the Germans were very hard in the implementation of the measures against the Jews, the French harder than the Italians, whereas Italy was striving for a humane solution. Himmler ordered that this report of the senior SS and Police chief be conveyed to the Reich Foreign Minister.

On the instructions of his superiors, the legation councillor in the Foreign Office, Dr. von Thadden, called on my chief, SS Gruppenführer Müller on 16 October 1943 on account of the technical implementation of the Jewish question in the newly occupied territories and explained that the Foreign Office had, especially after the experience in Denmark, a special interest in seeing that Jewish operations were carried out in other territories with sufficient means and sufficient preparation so that difficult political complications might be avoided as far as possible. Müller said to that that even the Reich Security Head Office had learnt much from the experience in Denmark. However, the time when sufficient police forces would be available to carry out the Jewish operations required in the occupied territories promptly would perhaps never come as long as the war lasted. Therefore one could only extract with the means available the best that was possible in this operation in order to implement the ordered operations. Regarding the territory of France up to now occupied by Italian troops, he thought that the speeded up implementation of an operation was a security police problem of the first order whose solution, in spite of the limited forces available, must be tackled immediately. Hitler had, on Rosenberg's proposal, ordered that, in the occupied territories, libraries, lodges, and other world-view and cultural institutions should be searched and secured for their materials. Likewise cultural assets which "in the possession of, or the property of, Jews were without an owner or were not of unobjectionable origin".

Holland

The Reichsleiter Rosenberg Task Force[5] was commissioned with the implementation of this task and, following this acquisition, even the furniture and other moveable objects from Jewish houses were likewise secured and these moved to the occupied eastern territories for use there. At Reichsleiter Rosenberg's request, Hitler had given his approval to this in a letter of the Reich Minister and Chief of the Reich Chancellery of 31 December 1941.

Holland

It began with 400 Jews who were deported to the Mauthausen concentration camp which was situated in Upper Austria. The general commissioner for security for the occupied Netherlands territories had issued the ordinance. This was the senior SS and Police chief at the office of the Reich commissioner for the occupied Netherlands territories; his rank and name was SS Gruppenführer and lieutenant-general of the police, Rauter. The Reich commissioner at that time was Dr. Seyss Inquart, the former Austrian government leader at the time of the reunification of Austria with the German Reich in 1938. The representative of the Foreign Office at the office of the Reich Commissioner, an envoy Bene, informed his Berlin central office that the deportation was ordered on account of the striking down of an SA man, and the consular councillor Mohr added to this announcement of his boss on the day after, 26 February 1941, that a German patrol in the Amsterdam Jewish quarter had been splattered with poison. The consequence of this deportation was a sympathetic strike of several public institutions in Amsterdam.

In June of the same year, however, some 260 more Jews were sent to a concentration camp from Holland. On 5 November 1941, legation councillor Rademacher wanted from the Foreign Office a response of the Reich Security Head Office to the question of the further treatment of the Jews still interned in German concentration camps. He wanted it for an application on behalf of the exiled people submitted by the Swedish embassy as representative of the Dutch protecting power.

The chief reason here was that the Jewish council in Amsterdam had been informed that more than 400 inmates had died. So Rademacher

---

5   The Einsatzstab Reichsleiter Rosenberg was the National Socialist organisation headed by Alfred Rosenberg that was in charge of the appropriation of cultural property from all over German-occupied Europe between 1940 and 1945..

Emigrating Dutch Jews leaving Amsterdam in 1941.

wrote to Müller that the Foreign Office was of course basically of the same viewpoint as the Reich Security Head Office and endorsed the retaliatory measures against Jews as initiators of unrest but care might be taken to see that, as far as possible, the impression did not arise in the announcement of deaths that the deaths always occurred on certain days.

In June 1942, the identification of Jews was ordered, and was directly followed by further restrictive conditions such as night-time curfew, prohibition from using public transport, professional restrictions, etc.

The representative of the Foreign Office at the office of the Reich Commissioner for the occupied Dutch territories made a submission to his Berlin central authority office with the proposal to revoke the citizenship of all Dutch Jews. On the other hand, on 20 July 1942, the Foreign Office considered it desirable to align the Dutch Jewish legislation with that of the Reich through an ordinance of the Reich Commissioner in such a way that, with immediate effect, all Dutch Jews living abroad or were moving their place of residence to foreign countries would, analogous to the 11th ordinance to the Reich Citizenship Law of 25 November 1941, lose their citizenship. Whereby

Holland

it was inconsequential if the Jew in question had left the country of his own accord or was deported. This was presented by Under-Secretary of State Luther on 10 August 1942 to the state secretary in the Foreign Office, von Weizsäcker, with a request for instructions, and authorised by the latter.

On 29 July, the representative of the Foreign Office in the Hague, Envoy Bene, announced that the first two deportation transports had left without any difficulties and the senior SS and Police chief (Rauter) intended to promote this plan in such a way that weekly up to 4,000 Jews should be deported.

On 24 September, the first big progress report of SS Gruppenführer and lieutenant-general of the Police, Rauter, was issued in the form of a personal letter to the SS Reichsführer and Chief of the German Police, Heinrich Himmler. He wrote, among other things:

"Up to now we have ordered, along with the Jews deported to Mauthausen for punishment, altogether 20,000 Jews to Auschwitz. In all of Holland about 120,000 Jews have been deported. But in agreement with the Reich Commissioner I shall deport also all Jewish partners of mixed marriages as long as there have been no children from these mixed marriages. There will be around 6,000 such cases. I shall try to maintain, instead of two trains per week, three. 30,000 Jews will be deported from 1 October. I hope that we will have these Jews too removed by Christmas so that in all 50,000 Jews, that is half of them, will be removed from Holland.

By 15 October 1942, the Jews were outlawed in Holland. Every Jew who was found anywhere in Holland was sent to the large Jewish camps. So no Jew who was not privileged could be seen any longer in Holland. At the same time Aryans who keep Jews in hiding or have moved Jews over the border or have forged identification papers would have their assets confiscated and the perpetrators be transferred to a concentration camp, all this in order to prevent the escape of Jews, which has begun in a major way. The Westerbork Jewish camp is already fully ready, the Vught Jewish camp will be complete on 10-15 October.

Heil Hitler, Your most obedient servant, Rauter."

Himmler wrote on the first page of this secret report, "very good".

False Gods

In April of the following year, government councillor Zöpf (adviser with the commanding officer of the Security Police and SD in the Hague, major-general of the Police, Dr. Harster) reported to my department in Berlin that, of the originally announced 140,000 Jews, 68,300 Jews had in the meantime left the country. Of these, 6,000 through emigration and exodus; 4,000 to Reich German concentration camps; 300 to Theresienstadt, and 58,000 in special trains to the east.

A note of SS Brigadeführer and major-general of the Police, Dr. Harster, of 6 May 1943 has survived in which it is stated that Himmler wished that in this year as many Jews as possible be transported to the east. Since in the west a Buna[6] factory had been destroyed by aerial bombing a new Buna factory had to be built in Auschwitz. So a maximum of Jews from the west would be required in May and June. A figure of 8,000 (from Holland) was to be striven for in May. Train arrangements would be made by the commanding officer of the Security Police in the Hague with the Reich Security Head Office.

All Portuguese Jews (Sephardim) were to be gathered together in a special barrack of the Westerbork concentration camp so that they could be examined on their origins by SS Gruppenführer and the chief of the Race and Settlement Head Office. The SS Reichsführer intended to construct a camp in Germany for approximately 10,000 Jews of French, Belgian and Dutch citizenship who, on account of their relations to foreign countries, were to be held back as a means of exerting pressure. Possibly they could be allowed to emigrate later in exchange for German repatriates.

It was reported to the Foreign Office on 29 June 1943 by its representative in the Hague that the commanding officer of the Security Police in the Hague informed his Reich Commissioner in a secret report that, in the meantime, the hundred thousandth Jew had left the country.

In the same year, Dr. Harster informed the representative of the Foreign Office in the Hague that the Reich Commissioner for the occupied Dutch territories had determined, in agreement with Himmler, that the Jews living in mixed marriages in the Netherlands would be free of the obligation to wear the Jewish star on proof of sterility. The sterilisation would be carried out by Jewish or Dutch doctors, whereby the test of sterility lay with the chief doctor at the office of the senior SS and Police Chief.

---

6   The synthetic rubber works established by I.G. Farben at Auschwitz

Belgium

To this I must state additionally that this news burst like a bomb at that time even in the Reich Security Head Office, a novelty that was unique up to that time and was never imitated till the end of the war.

On 28 February 1944, Reich Commissioner Seyss-Inquart turned personally to the Chief of the "Chancellery of the Führer", Reichsleiter Bormann. A powerful man of that time, a man of decisive influence on Hitler. A man who was respected by all, including Himmler, Goebbels, Göring, etc. He informed him that of course the Jews were to be extracted from the Dutch national body, but the question of Jews in mixed marriages was still open. He said that they had indeed gone further in Holland than in the Reich territory and imposed on these Jews also the obligation to wear a star and that he had also ordered the deportation of Jewish partners of childless mixed marriages to the east, that his security police handled some hundreds of such cases, but then the order came from Berlin not to carry out these deportations any further. So there remained for him some thousands of these Jews in the country and therewith the problem of mixed marriages was raised. In particular he set out four "solutions as possibilities".

But it seems not to have changed much therein, for Envoy Bene gave in July 1944 a standard half-yearly report to the Foreign Office and informed that the Jewish question for the Netherlands could be designated as having been resolved. He gave the figure of deportees as 113,000, 4,000 Jews had died, 2,500 were declared to be of mixed race or Aryans, some 8,600 lived in mixed marriages, some 9,000 disappeared in the Netherlands, there were around 3,600 evangelical Jews. Altogether 140,711 Jews.

Belgium

On 11 June 1942, Himmler had ordered the deportation of 10,000 Jews from Belgium to Auschwitz. The German military administration intended to carry out the desired deportation and the director of the office of the Foreign Office in Brussels informed its Berlin central office on 9 July that the head of the military administration was at present at the head quarters to discuss the matter with Himmler. Certain doubts were expressed, however the military administration believed that their worries could be set aside if a deportation of Jews with *Belgian* citizenship could be avoided; for the police forces available would not be sufficient for coercive measures.

False Gods

Himmler had agreed to the proposals of the chief of the military administration and, on 24 September, Bargen, the representative of the Foreign Office in Brussels, was able to announce that altogether 10,000 stateless Jews would be evacuated by 15 September, and the German security police hoped to be able to deport around 20,000 of the people in question by the end of October.

Thus the visit of the chief of the military administration to Himmler's headquarters resulted in a doubling of the originally ordered number. However, again a report from Bargen to the Foreign Office of 11 November 1942 indicates that up to that time around 15,000 Jews were deported. Around 42,000 Jews above the age of sixteen had registered on the basis of the Jewish regulation of the military commander of 28 October 1940. Of these, 38,000 were of non-Belgian citizenship. Altogether 52,000 to 55,000 Jews had to be registered in Belgium. Recently illegal emigrations to France and Switzerland had been reported and he estimates with caution that 3,000 to 4,000 Jews had emigrated to Switzerland.

Now the under-secretary of state in the Foreign Office, Luther, intervened and issued a decree to the office of the Foreign Office in Brussels on 4 December 1942, in which it said, among other things:

"If today Jewry remaining in Belgium ignores the regulations of the military commander and further attempts with all means to obliterate its Jewish character and thus creeps into nooks that are difficult to cleanse and if, finally, attempts on the part of these Jews to participate in the active resistance against the occupying force have been determined, then a vigorous attack should prevent the further spread of this dangerous group.

I would therefore like to request the consideration of the possibility - after consultation with the military commander - of now extending the measures taken to *all* Jews in Belgium and of gathering these together in collection camps until the possible implementation of the transports.

Individual questions regarding the exceptional treatment of Jews in mixed marriages, those of Christian faith, or with children, can be solved through consultation with the Security Police. In any case, a comprehensive cleansing of Belgium of Jews must occur sooner or later."

Belgium

Leon Degrelle, Belgian Rexist leader who later joined the Waffen SS.

According to instructions, Bergen in Brussels had discussed this matter with the military commander, the chief of the military administration and the regional chief of the Security Police. But he had to inform his new chief in Berlin that, according to the opinion of the military administration, a deportation of Jews could not be undertaken before spring 1943 as a result of a lack of railway wagons.

In the meantime, the preparations for the further deportation were undertaken and the foreign Jews concentrated in a camp. However, as a result of a lack of camps, all Jews could not be concentrated. Since, in the resumption of the deportation, a deportation of around 4,000 Jews of Belgian citizenship was intended, the intentions of the military administration should agree with the wishes of the Foreign Office.

False Gods

Once again Under-Secretary of State, Luther, cautioned his Brussels office in a further letter of 25 January 1943 by calling their attention to the fact that, from the start, care should be taken that, in the case of the concentration in camps of Jews settled in Belgium, not only Jews of foreign citizenship but also Belgian Jews were to be arrested.

The Reich Security Head Office too received a copy of this letter. One notes therein that it is requested "to initiate that which is necessary even from that side". What else then remained to be initiated? Others had already initiated everything up to the last detail.

On 9 April 1943, Himmler communicated to the Chief of the Security Police and SD, Kaltenbrunner, the following:

"The most important thing for me is still that the Jews be deported to the east now as far as possible. In the short monthly reports of the Security Police I wish just to be informed how many have been deported monthly and how many Jews remain at the moment."

The Reich Security Head Office had to send out this Himmler order to all offices of the Security Police and SD, and so one reads in a "mission plan" of the office of the commanding officer of the Security Police in Brussels of 1 September 1943 that, on the night of 3 to 4 September, for the first time the capture of Belgian Jews for the eastern mission that had been ordered by the Reich Security Head Office had begun with a large operation.

Italy

The documents already partly discussed in the chapter on "France" showed quite clearly, first, the attitude of Italy to the Jewish question, but they also showed equally clearly which personalities of the past National Socialist regime played an executive role here. They showed further the efforts of the former German Reich government to force a change in the Italian attitude. This occurred basically only towards the end of 1943.

Envoy Moelhausen telegraphed Ribbentrop on 6 October 1943 that SS Obersturmbannführer Kappler in Rome, (as commanding officer of the Security Police in Rome he was to a certain extent under the commanding officer of the Security Police in Italy, Major-general of the Police, Dr. Harster, who had his office in Verona), had received a

Italy

special commission from Berlin. He was to have the eight thousand Jews living in Rome arrested and taken to upper Italy where they were to be liquidated. The city commandant of Rome, General Stahel, informed Envoy Moelhausen that he would permit this operation only if it was what the Reich Foreign Minister intended.

He personally was of the opinion that it would be better if the Jews were used for fortification work and he, along with Kappler, wished to present this to Field Marshal General Kesselring.

On 9 October 1943, Ribbentrop answered that, on the basis of an instruction of Hitler's, these 8,000 Jews should be taken to the concentration camp in Mauthausen as hostages.

On this procedure Kappler said, as a witness under oath on 27 June 1961 in military prison in Gaeta (Italy), that he had no knowledge at all of the existence of such a telegram of Moelhausen's to Ribbentrop. He had seen this telegram or knew of its existence for the first time during his trial in 1948. Of course, Kappler remembered a telegram signed by Himmler in which he insisted on the necessity of solving the Jewish question in Rome too. He remembered further that he had on this occasion for the first time become acquainted with the concept of a "final solution of the Jewish question". This expression was however new to him and he did not succeed in figuring it out. At that time an SS captain Dannecker came to him and said he had the authority to implement a Jewish *razzia*.[7] This authorisation had been signed by the general of the SS (Police), Müller.

Kappler had, according to his testimony, heard of my name only after 1945 and he had also received neither any mail nor any instructions that bore my signature.

During an informative discussion between Müller and Dr. von Thadden of 16 October 1943, Müller told the legation councillor of the Foreign Office that he in no way closed himself to the arguments of the Foreign Office which spoke in favour of a sudden operation especially in view of the attitude of the Catholic Church. But the forces available were not sufficient to carry out such a thing in all of Italy. One would therefore necessarily begin with a resolution of the Jewish question immediately behind the front line and gradually force it northwards. Legation councillor von Thadden observed on that, in his lecture notes

---

7   Police raid

False Gods

for his secretary of state, that Müller too clearly had certain concerns on his part on account of the practical implementation of the Hitler order concerning the arrest of 8,000 Jews in Rome. In fact, the Roman Catholic Church in Rome had, through Bishop Hudal, approached General Stahel with a letter to the city commandant of Rome and vehemently opposed the arrests of Jews of Italian citizenship with the wish that these arrests should be immediately stopped in Rome and the surrounding areas since the Pope would otherwise publicly oppose it. The Curia was therefore particularly sad as the procedures had "taken place" as it were "under the Vatican's windows", the German ambassador was told by the Holy See.

Excerpts of a copy of this letter came from the Foreign Office also to my department. In any case, I forwarded it immediately to my boss. Regardless of all this, the Italian government had in the meantime proclaimed a law that all Jews in Italian were to be transferred to concentration camps.

At the same time, the Reich Security Head Office in Berlin ascertained that the operation ordered by Himmler in Italy had not led to any results worth mentioning. The objections coming from different quarters had delayed the required steps so long that the majority of Jews had been able to go into hiding.

Wagner, Luther's successor, who had been sent to a concentration camp on account of some apparent intrigue, wrote on 14 December 1943 to the Chief of Office IV of the Reich Security Head Office, Müller, "that the German ambassador Rahn was instructed to express to the Fascist government the satisfaction of the Reich government on the very definitely necessary law regarding the transfer of all Jews to concentration camps. On the other hand, the handing over of the Jews concentrated in the camps for evacuation to the eastern territories did not seem useful. Such a proposal should be withheld for tactical and political reasons until the operation of the rounding up of Jews by the Italian agencies has been completed, for the Foreign Office believes that it should suppose, on the basis of its experience, that the success of the rounding up operation would otherwise be impaired, if not thwarted.

With the deficient eagerness of the Italian offices shown in the last months for the implementation of the anti-Jewish measures ordered by Mussolini the Foreign Office considered it urgently desirable that the implementation of the measures be supervised from now on by German officials. Therefore the incorporation of a part of the forces belonging

Italy

Jewish children from Naples arrive in Palestine.

at the moment to the 'Italian' Einsatz Command into the Italian organisations disguised as advisers seems advisable and necessary."

Finally, the Foreign Office requested the 'Italian' Einsatz Command to accordingly inform and permit Hauptsturmführer Dannecker – on account of the possible incorporation of advisers – to get in touch directly with the plenipotentiary of the Reich, Ambassador Rahn, or his representative.

During his prosecution address at my trial in Jerusalem in 1961, the Israeli state attorney said, among other things, that many authors must, on the basis of the information obtained in the trial, subject their works published so far to a revision. I am of exactly the same opinion. I myself wish that where people have thoughtlessly and simply emphasised me as the responsible person – quite simply as a result of a fabrication, of an assumption, and allowed this to be reflected as true currency – they may from now on determine the historical truth according to documents on the basis of the trial information. Everybody will understand this wish of mine, for I am indeed not a Herostratus.[8]

---

8 Herostratus was an arsonist who set fire to the Temple of Artemis in Ephesus in 356 B.C.

False Gods

I myself have therefore sought in the composition of this work to base myself quite strictly, wherever I dealt with factual events, on the official documents of that time. I have in the main restricted myself in the content of this book to the documents that deal with the main course of events. The great abundance of incidental documents in which I also naturally play a certain role, I have ignored in these observations since they - first, due to the constant repetition of a subject and, then, because no fundamental importance can be attributed to them that can yield any new viewpoint - would operate in a tiring manner on the reader. A comprehensive treatment including the smallest details must be reserved to specialist scholarly studies.

Norway

On 17 November 1942, a law was passed by the Norwegian government on the obligatory registration of Jews. Therewith the possibility was created of a general rounding up of Jews with the aim of their deportation from Norway.

These Norwegian conditions were significantly more comprehensive than the German anti-Jewish laws. Thus, in Norway, even such persons who were of mixed race were treated legally as Jews. In November 1942, 532 Jews and, in February 1943, 158 Jews were deported from Norway to Auschwitz.

It was pointed out to the commanding officer of the Security Police at the office of the Reich Commissioner for the occupied Norwegian territories by the Reich Security Head Office that certain groups of Jewish people, including also people of mixed Jewish origin, who were not considered Jews should not be deported.

Denmark

The Foreign Office informed the Reich Plenipotentiary in Denmark, Dr. Best, on 17 September 1943 that Ribbentrop requested him to prepare proposals on the manner of conducting the deportation of Jews from Denmark. This was a matter that had basically already been decided and he may particularly consider how big a police force he would require for it. Four days later Envoy von Grundherr made a proposal to his secretary of state in the Foreign Office in Berlin in which he stated that the commanding officer of the Security Police, SS Standartenführer

Denmark

From Denmark less than 300 Jews were sent to the Theresienstadt concentration camp. All of the remaining Jews in Denmark either went into hiding, or they managed to emigrate to Sweden via numerous small boats.

and colonel of the Police, Dr. Mildner, who had newly arrived in Copenhagen, had opposed the deportation of Jews from Denmark and had approached Himmler with the consent of Dr. Best.

Mildner himself said in a statement under oath on 22 June 1945: "I flew immediately to Berlin to personally consult the Chief of the Security Police, Dr. Kaltenbrunner. The chief was absent. I went to the Chief of Office IV, SS Gruppenführer Müller, who dictated in my presence an express telegram to Himmler regarding my proposal; shortly after my return to Copenhagen, Himmler's definitive order to the Chief of the Security Police, Dr. Kaltenbrunner arrived: "The Jewish operation is to be carried out immediately."

On 1 October, at 18.30, the Plenipotentiary of the German Reich in Denmark received a letter from King Christian X. Dr Best sent this at 19.30 of the same day to the Reich Foreign Minister. That was at 20.10 in the Foreign Office. The letter from the king stated:

"Your excellence, Although, according to the communication of the commanding officer of the German troops in Denmark conveyed to me on 29 August of this year, the executive authority has been transferred to the German army, I am still concerned to emphasise to you – after hearing a report according to which it was planned by the Germans to undertake steps against the Jews in Denmark – not only out of humane consideration for the citizens of my country but also out of fear of the consequences for the future relations between Germany and Denmark, that special measures against a group of people who have enjoyed full citizenship rights in Denmark for more than 100 years could have the most severe results. Christian X."

Dr. Best then immediately made a report to Ribbentrop on the situation, especially with regard to the state of emergency imposed by the commander of the German troops in Denmark, and concluded with the words: "The operation begins today at 21.50 hrs."

Altogether no more than 284 Jews were seized. My representative in IV B4 of the Reich Security Head Office, SS Sturmbannführer Günther, had received orders from the Chief of Office IV, SS Gruppenführer Müller, to go along with some officials to Denmark to get the deportation to Theresienstadt under way.

Dr. Best, the plenipotentiary, reported on 5 October to the Foreign Office that the direction of the Jewish operation in Denmark lay solely in the hands of the commanding officer of the Security Police, SS Standartenführer Dr. Mildner, who issued all regulations for the deportation. He further informed that it was true that the commanding officer of the Security Police had ordered that shuttered houses should not be broken open.

In this context a statement given under oath of the former legation councillor of the Foreign Office, Dr. von Thadden, given on 16 April 1948 in Nuremberg, is interesting, according to which my then "regular representative" in the department, the previously mentioned SS Sturmbannführer Günther, had, following the "Denmark operation", reported that the latter had presumably been sabotaged by the embassy in Copenhagen. I had apparently already reported to Himmler and wanted the head of the saboteur. Günther refused to give more detailed information on the method of the sabotage and only mentioned incidentally the prohibition against opening shuttered homes. Such a thing is sheer nonsense as one has perceived from Best's own reports. Mr. von Thadden has doubtlessly been subjected here to a deception. Quite calmly and courteously and with no word about a discovered sabotage, I negotiated according to the orders of my boss, the lieutenant general of the Police, Müller, on 3 November 1943, in Copenhagen with the Reich Plenipotentiary, Dr. Best, in order to obtain proposals which resulted in the fact that Jews above 60 years were no longer arrested and deported, half-Jews and Jews of mixed marriages were released and brought back to Denmark, and that the Jews deported from Denmark remained in Theresienstadt and could be visited by the representatives of the Danish central administration and the Danish Red Cross.

Since I was not authorised to take any decisions, I promised Dr. Best to present this matter to my boss in the Reich Security Head Office and to forward the proposals to him.

The very cautious Dr. Best inquired on the same day at the Foreign Office if the matter had followed the course that had been discussed. Wagner could shortly thereafter report to him that it was so.

Slovakia

The first Germany envoy in Slovakia was Manfred von Killinger. His main task was to initiate the political-organisational alignment of the young Slovak government taking in view the goals of German foreign policy. It was he too who introduced the "adviser system". In a report on the political situation in Slovakia to the Foreign Office on 13 August 1940, he criticised the fact that the advisers had not yet begun since most of them had not yet arrived.

In September, his report gives information on the situation of Jewry in Slovakia. A Slovak governmental ordinance of 18 April 1939 established who was to be considered a Jew according to the law. He further mentioned to the Foreign Office materials on the state of the total Jewish assets in Slovakia that had been determined at the time of reporting by the Slovak authorities. According to the official estimation, 90,000 Jews lived at that time in the Slovak Republic.

The successor of Von Killinger, who went as envoy to Romania, was Ludin. Under his leadership the adviser corps was completed, and among them also the adviser on the Jewish question, SS Hauptsturmführer Wisliceny.

In a number of decrees and agreements between the Reich Foreign

False Gods

Hlinka Guard marching in Bratislava 1941.

Minister and Himmler, as well as between his head office chief, the appointment of both the Police attachés and the advisers was most precisely confirmed.

The advisers were without exception assigned as aides to the Police attachés and placed under them. Both came from the Reich Security Head Office and were transferred to service abroad at consulates or embassies.

The Police attachés were, as regards their activity abroad, basically under only the head of the mission and, in his absence, the current representative. These attachés had, according to the arrangement, to carry out service commissions of the chief of the mission. Possible instructions of the offices of the SS Reichsführer had to be forwarded to them through the Foreign Office by the head of the mission, who therewith took the political responsibility for the foreign political suitability of these instructions, for he could use his power of veto.

From this state of affairs it becomes understandable, for example, that if the Reich Security Head Office summoned an adviser to a meeting in Berlin, the head of the mission however had to first obtain permission from the Foreign Office for that and, on its issuance, the adviser could then follow the summons.

Slovakia

On 8 and 9 July 1941, the adviser for social policy and the one for the Jewish question from the Pressburg consulate travelled to eastern Upper Slovakia to visit Jewish work camps there. They were accompanied by several high officials of the Slovak Ministry of the Interior and the central economic office. This visit was supported by the embassy since similar constructions were to be made in Slovakia.

Ludin reported to his Berlin office on 22 October that the Slovak Ministry of the Interior did not intend any expulsion of Jews from the territory of Slovakia but strove for an internal concentration of Jews in certain places within Slovakia. Here it was a matter of a formation, inspired by the German adviser, of ghettos according to the model of the Generalgouvernement. But, in the midst of these preparations, there exploded a demand of Under-Secretary of State Luther from the Foreign Office that, as a result of the measures for the final solution of the Jewish question in Europe, the German government was ready to immediately remove 20,000 young Slovak Jews and take them to the east, where there was a lack of work force.

On 16 February 1942, Envoy Ludin received a commission to bring about the agreement of the Slovak government. A handwritten note on the copy of the telegram addressed to Ludin found in the Foreign Office after 1945 states: "Slovak government: proposal accepted with enthusiasm. Preparatory work can be initiated." Even Himmler seems to have personally intervened in this matter.

In April 1942, the Chief of the Security Police and SD, SS Obergruppenführer and general of the Police and Waffen SS, Heydrich, who at the same time had also the position of "Deputy Reich Protector for Bohemia and Moravia", paid a visit to the Slovak prime minister Tuca. It was, first, a courtesy call that one neighbouring governmental head made to another and, then, it was Heydrich's wish to stimulate the Jewish deportation matters that had been interrupted and move them forward.

Even now I was ordered by my superior to prepare myself for an official journey to Pressburg, and the Foreign Office announced this to its consulate in Pressburg on 13 March 1942. I was, on the orders of the Chief of the Security Police, to carry out preliminary discussions with the relevant offices in Pressburg for the evacuation of 20,000 Jews from Slovakia after the agreement between the Foreign Office, the consulate and the Slovak government that had in the meantime been obtained in this regard.

False Gods

Now, since the Chief of the Head Office, Heydrich, himself travelled, it had become superfluous to order me to Slovakia with the German wishes. Only at the end of May did I have to convey to the German envoy Ludin both further wishes of my boss and a handwritten letter of Heydrich's to the Slovak prime minister in connection with the mutual arrangement. Here I was asked by the German envoy not to refuse the invitation of the Slovak Minister of the Interior, Mach - whom I still remembered vaguely from the years of my stay in Vienna, long before he was Minister of the Interior – to me that had been issued to the consulate, to dine with him in the evening.

Even Wisliceny had to admit in one of his many statements after 1945 that I had been required to undertake such an acceptance. In fact I avoided all such things whenever the possibility of avoiding them existed.

Now, of course, it was a private invitation and the food was certainly not bad, and Mach and I bowled, sometimes "all nine", sometimes "travel-ticket",[9] while orderlies offered refreshing drinks and smokes. But already early in the evening Mach informed me that he had just received news from Prague that a bomb had been hurled at Heydrich. I remained a little while longer as the now constant bulletins about the assassination attempt arrived and I finally drove on the same night to Prague. A few days later Heydrich was dead. I do not know what became of the letter I gave Ludin.

A note of Luther's of 29 March 1942 announces that, according to information from Ludin, the Slovak state council had decided the evacuation of Jews from Slovakia. A member of the state council had indeed offered opposition, but a bishop had then held a very positive speech. Thereupon the proposal to agree with the evacuation had been unanimously accepted. One restriction was made, namely that baptised Jews were to be excepted until a certain cut-off date.

Further, Envoy Ludin informed Luther that three evacuation transports had already left and the others would follow without any delay, and as soon as the first 20,000 Jews were evacuated the evacuation of the remaining around 70,000 Jews could be begun. Luther added that the Chief of the Security Police and SD should be informed of this immediately.

---

9   Bowling games

Slovakia

Luther wrote to Ludin at the beginning of May1942 that the Reich government was ready to accept another 20,000 Jews fit for work – out of the announced 70,000 in all - in the course of May from Slovakia and take them to the east. The details would be regulated as before.

An accurate overview of the matter is provided by a letter of 15 May 1942 of my then "regular representative" as divisional head of IV B4 in the Reich Security Head Office, SS Sturmbannführer Günther, to the legation councillor Rademacher in the Foreign Office. According to it, from 25 March to 29 April 1942, the first 20,000 Jews had left Slovakia for Auschwitz and on 4 May 1942 the deportation of 20,000 more Jews had been effected.

The provision of rolling stock by the Slovak government made the technical implementation of the evacuation considerably easier, since it would not be easily possible, on account of the strained traffic situation, for the German railways to make the required special trains available.

On 26 June 1942, Ludin informed that the continuation of the deportation had, through the Church's influence, reached a "stalemate". Prime Minister Tuca however wished to continue them and requested the Reich government for support through sharp diplomatic pressure. Ludin requested instructions on whether he could proceed in this direction.

In a discussion with Tuca on 30 June Ludin advised a 100% solution. Of course, very recently the papal pro-nuncio, Msgr. Burzio, had called on the Slovak prime minister to protest on behalf of the Holy See against the continuation of the deportation. However, at first he did not at all accept the protest since in this case there was for him a higher authority than the pope namely, his, Tuca's, father confessor. The latter had asked him if could justify to his conscience the Jewish deportation as being in the interest of the nation. When Tuca answered this question in the affirmative, the father confessor apparently had no objection against these measures. Tuca related this to Envoy Ludin.

On 21 July 1943, Reich Foreign Minister von Ribbentrop rejected Weizsäcker's proposal and had Ludin announce that SS Oberführer Dr. Veesenmayer would soon call on Prime Minister Dr. Tiso and would have to present the matter of the Jewish deportation on this occasion.

False Gods

On 22 December 1943, Dr. Veesenmayer was able to announce that Tiso would personally offer the guarantee that the operation would be implemented and completed as quickly as possible.

In the meantime, however, there was in 1944 a general uprising in Czechoslovakia and, in the course of the suppression of this, drastic steps had been taken by the Germans. Agreements were made between Envoy Ludin and the commanding officer of the Security Police, Dr. Witiska, who had been installed in Slovakia in the meantime, on the one hand, and with the Slovak government, on the other.

According to these, the German offices were in agreement with a concentration and supervision of the Jews on Slovak territory.

On 4 October 1944, the Slovak prime minister intervened through Ludin saying that he had heard that they had, without notifying the Slovak government, gone about deporting the Jews from Slovakia, but diplomatic difficulties would doubtless result through that. Ludin told him that the Jewish question must in any event be resolved in a radical way now and he advised that in the case of difficulties he should simply point out that the Reich government demanded a radical solution from the Slovak state. The Foreign Office then sharpened Ludin's advice a little further by formulating that the strong involvement of Jews in the uprisings and partisan movements inevitably made a radical solution of the Jewish question necessary in the interest of the security of the Slovak state.

Insofar as it was absolutely necessary for the position of the Slovak government, it may be added that the Reich, as part of the partisan crackdown that took place on the wishes of the Slovak government, had also vouchsafed its help in the solution of the Jewish question.

On 6 October 1947, the former envoy Ludin made, among other things, the following statement on oath before the examining authorities in Bratislava:

"I can state that the Jewish deportations in 1942 took place on orders from the Foreign Office. I myself received the order for this in 1942. In 1942 then some 60,000 Jews were deported from Slovakia. The last Jewish deportation was undertaken by the commanding officer of the Security Police."

Greece

The German commanding officer of Thessaloniki-Agäis had, in agreement with the Greek Generalgouverneur of Macedonia, issued an ordinance on 7 July 1942 on the work deployment of Jews for the construction of the Thessaloniki-Katerim-Larissa highway.

On 3 January 1943, my representative, SS Sturmbannführer Günther, flew on the orders of the Chief of Office IV, lieutenant general of the Police, Müller, to Thessaloniki to conduct negotiations there on Jewish matters. Under-Secretary of State Luther wrote to his envoy Altenburg in Athens "that Günther naturally may work with him".

The same Günther informed the Foreign Office on 25 January 1943 that, after the required discussions with the Plenipotentiary of the German Reich in Greece, the consul general in Thessaloniki and the army group, as well as with the military commander of Thessaloniki-Agäis, on the implementation of evacuation measures from the territory of Thessaloniki had been conducted, a deputation of the adviser for the Jewish question working in the Germany embassy in Pressburg was necessary. Agreement was requested. A corresponding instruction of the Foreign Office was issued to Pressburg on 5 February 1943.

On 6 February 1943, the military commander of Thessaloniki-Agäis issued through his military administration an identification and ghettoisation ordinance. He directed this ordinance to the Jewish religious community in Thessaloniki "by virtue of the legal powers lent to the commander of Thessaloniki-Agäis".

A further ordinance of the same office of 13 February 43 stated that the president of the Jewish religious community in Thessaloniki had to be in charge of all Jews in the entire territory of the military commander of Thessaloniki. On the same day the military commander ordered further, through his military administration, that Jews are not authorised to leave their place of residence without permission. "Trespassers will be shot on the spot." Trams and other means of transport were forbidden to Jews and equally forbidden were the use of telephones, access to streets and public places as well as attendance at public events after nightfall.

On 15 June 1943, the military commander of Thessaloniki-Agäis informed the Generalgouverneur of Macedonia that, according to higher instructions, the entire Jewish property that had been, or still

False Gods

Jews in Ioannina, Greece, waiting to be deported.

was, in his commanding region had been transferred to the Greek state represented by the Generalgouverneur of Macedonia. Wisliceny in the meantime arrived in Thessaloniki and was there placed, according to the official seals used, under another commanding officer, namely the commanding officer of the Security Police and SD, who was in turn functionally placed under the German military commander of Thessaloniki-Agäis. On the basis of the decrees of the military commander Wisliceny now announced the implementation conditions for these. How big the Jewish identification mark had to be, who was to be considered a Jew according to the law, etc.

The escape of a single Jew caused the military commander to order on 21 March 1943 that 25 Jews be arrested as hostages. In the case of the least contravention of the prescribed obligations these would be shot. Further, Jews were allowed to leave their houses only between 10 hrs and 16 hrs., even within the ghettos. Trespassers would be shot immediately; German and Greek police commandos would supervise this regulation especially strictly.

There were around 55,000 Jews in Thessaloniki. The greatest part of them were deported. From a circular decree of the Foreign Office to the German missions in Budapest, Lisbon, Rome and Ankara of 30 April 1943 it is to be learnt that urgent military and security police reasons necessitated the extension of general measures against Jews even to the northern Greek territory occupied by German troops.

Yugoslavia

Who solely decided on the start or stop of Jewish transports and who thereby observed the tactical issues is shown by a telegram of the German envoy Neubacher, from Athens, to the Foreign Office of 27 November 1943: "Please suggest to the Chief of the Reich Security Head Office that the deportation of the Jews here is still awaited. At the demand of the Security Service, out of approximately 8,000 Jews, around 1,200 have registered, the remainder have fled or are in hiding. After the deportation of the Jews who have registered and who apparently represent the most uninteresting contingent, there is no more prospect of getting hold of those who are for us politically more interesting than those who have registered.

The senior SS and Police Chief and Chief of the Security Service are of the same view. Request decision to me in Belgrade and to the senior SS and Police Chief in Athens."

Neubacher was at that time the plenipotentiary of the Foreign Office for the entire south-east. The adviser in department D III of the Foreign Office, legation councillor Dr. von Thadden, forwarded this telegram to me with a request for the corresponding comments of the Chief of the Reich Security Head Office, the general of the Police and Waffen SS, Dr. Kaltenbrunner,

Mr. von Thadden provided the copy of his express letter to me on 4 December 1943, which was found after 1945, with a handwritten note that stated that he had discussed the matter with me and I had informed him that Kaltenbrunner had in the meantime settled the matter by telephone directly with those involved and the deportation would therefore be carried out.

Even this example shows, on the other hand, that my role in matters in the Reich Security Head Office was that of a conveyor of news and orders. Contrary to the press and the literature, as well as many untrue so-called witness testimonies, I have never maintained anything else.

Yugoslavia

On 10 April, the German troops marched into Zagreb and on 12 April Belgrade was occupied. With the troops was incorporated an Einsatz Group of the Security Police and SD. Their commander was the SS Standartenführer and colonel of the Police, Dr. Fuchs. Under this Einsatz Group were two Einsatz Commandos, one in Zagreb

False Gods

under SS Sturmbannführer Beisner, the second in Belgrade under SS Sturmbannführer Kraus. After the establishment of a German consulate in Zagreb under Envoy Kasche, SS Sturmbannführer Helm was assigned to it as Police Attaché. The Yugoslav territory had been divided into three regions. The Slovenian part, of which some districts were incorporated into the Reich territory, Croatia, which was proclaimed an independent state, and Serbia, which was occupied by German troops.

Slovenia

Heydrich received orders from Himmler to immediately begin with the "settlement of the nationality question" in the territories newly obtained by the Reich in the south-east. Basically, it was a question of the evacuation of 260,000 Slovenians to Serbia; this was an originally ordered number which, as far as I can remember, was not reached even approximately.

At that time I received orders to send out invitation letters to all German central authority offices to a meeting fixed for 6 May 1941 in Marburg under the chairmanship of Heydrich. Thus, to the Foreign Office, the Reich Ministry of Economics, the Reich Ministry of the Interior, the Commissioner for the Four-Year Plan, the Reich Finance Ministry, the Chancellery of the Führer, the Race and Settlement Head Office, the Reich Transport Ministry, etc.

The evacuation activity ran under the auspices of the SS Reichsführer and Chief of the German Police as Reich Commissioner for the Consolidation of the German Nationality. The goal of the conference was that all the participating central authorities had to assign their representatives to the implementation of the Hitler order according to the resettlement regions and to take care of their departmental work on location.

My task was to take care of the constant reporting from "the top to the bottom" and vice-versa.

The resettlement regulations were themselves a matter of Office III of the Reich Security Head Office as well as of the Race and Settlement Head Office.

Yugoslavia

Serbia

On 11 May 1941, the military commander in Serbia issued an invitation, to a discussion of Jewish matters, to the Commissioner General for Economics in Serbia, Consul General Neuhausen, the Commissioner of the Foreign Office in Serbia, Envoy Benzler, the Chief of the Einsatz Group of the Security Police and SD, Dr. Fuchs, the Field Commander, Colonel Keisenberg, and the director of the administrative group, senior war administrative councillor Dr. Rantze. Five days later, the Jews of Belgrade were ordered to report on 19 April 1941 at 8 a.m. to the city Security Police. Thereafter several demands were issued by Envoy Benzler and Veesenmayer to the Foreign Office in Berlin for the removal of these Jews from Serbian territory.

On 8 September 1941, Benzler and Veesenmayer wrote to the Foreign Office: "... It is therefore urgently requested that the speedy securing and removal of at least all male Jews be seen to now. The figure in question here should amount to 8,000 Jews ..."

On 10 September 1941, Benzler and Veesenmayer announced from Belgrade: "Quick and draconic settlement of the Serbian Jewish question is the most urgent and most expedient demand. Request from Mr. Reich Foreign Minister appropriate instructions to be able to exert appropriate pressure on the military commander of Serbia. No resistance is to be expected from the Serbian government and population, especially since partial measures up to now have been maintained very well. A similar order of the SS Reichsführer to the Chief of the Einzatz Group of the Security Police, SS Standartenführer Fuchs, would advance the matter significantly.

At first it was a matter of taking these 8,000 Jews to some Danube island belonging to Romania. This was however rejected by Ribbentrop since it could not be implemented without the agreement of the Romanians. Under-Secretary of State Luther communicated this on 11 September to Benzler and remarked that it was left to their discretion to secure the Jews in work camps. But immediately, on 12 September, Benzler answered that the accommodation in work camps was not possible since, as a result of internal conditions – uprisings –, security could not be guaranteed. There remained only immediate deportation to the Generalgouvernement or Russia, which however might cause considerable transport difficulties. Alternatively, the Jewish operation must be postponed, which is contrary to the instructions issued by Ribbentrop.

On 13 September, legation councillor Rademacher presented his under-secretary of state a remarkable note:

> "I cannot understand the necessity of the deportation of 1,200 male Jews wished for by the office of the Commissioner of the Foreign Office in Belgrade, if not to Romania, to the Generalgouvernement or to Russia. Russia is a field of operation fully unsuited for the acceptance of Jews. If they are already a danger in Serbia they would be a greater one in Russia. The Generalgouvernement is already oversaturated with Jews. In my opinion, it must, with the necessary hardness and determination, be possible to retain the Jews in camps in Serbia itself. If the Jews still foment unrest there they must be dealt with by a tightening of martial law. I cannot imagine that the Jews will continue to conspire if a large number of hostages are shot."

Benzler sent on 28 September a new urgent telegram, personally, to the Reich Foreign Minister. He reminded him of his promise to help him to convey the Jews, Freemasons and Serbians belonging to England, either down the Danube or to concentration camps in Germany or in the Generalgouvernement:,

> "The immediate solution of the Jewish question in Serbia is at the moment the most politically important task and the precondition for the initiation of the removal of Freemasons and anti-German intelligentsia. The military operation now taking place for the combating of the uprising has now produced the right moment for the start of the operation. In addition, General Böhme as well as the military commander have again expressly requested, for their part, that the immediate deportation of Jews out of the country be effected. At first it is a matter of some 8,000 male Jews whose commitment to camps is impossible since these camps must be utilised for the accommodation of 20,000 Serbs from the uprising areas."

The remaining 20,000 Jews and family members they would have to manage themselves; the deportation to an island in the Danube delta seemed the simplest solution in terms of transport, and Benzler, along with Veesenmayer, finally requested urgent support in this matter.

To this Luther commented on 2 October – in a submission through the secretary of state to the Reich Foreign Minister – in the following manner:

Yugoslavia

"If the military commander is agreed with Benzler that these 8,000 Jews most of all prevent the pacification operation in the Serbian Old Reich, the military commander must, in my opinion, see to the immediate removal of these 8,000 Jews. In other places other military commanders have taken care of a substantially greater number of Jews without speaking of it. In my opinion we cannot expect the Romanian state leader, who already has enough worries with the deportation of his own Jews, to take over another 8,000 Jews from foreign territory.

I therefore request authorisation to discuss this question with Obergruppenführer Heydrich, who will, in the next few days, come to Berlin from Prague for a short while. I am convinced that we will in consultation with him be able to come to a clear solution of this question."

On the same day, at 22 hours, Ribbentrop announced that he would immediately clarify the question with Himmler whether he could send the 8,000 Jews to eastern Poland. It was agreed with Heydrich that a special commissioner of the Reich Security Head Office would come to Belgrade for the settlement of the question. Three days later, Luther wrote to Belgrade that I would start the journey in the company of legation councillor Rademacher. On 15 October, this plan was given up, for Luther had to inform Belgrade that not I but some others would come as representatives of the Reich Security Head Office along with Rademacher.

But even here something seems once again to have occurred in the meantime, for Rademacher travelled - as the application for permission to travel officially which he directed to his authorities declares – for the purpose of the liquidation of 8,000 Jews, apparently alone to Belgrade, for his detailed travel report contains nothing about other participants in his official trip; even the files say nothing in this regard. In the meantime, the following happened in Serbia:

The commissioned commanding general in Serbia, general of the Infantry, Böhme, issued on 10 October 1941 an order according to which it had become necessary to carry out the orders of the High Command of the German Army in the sharpest manner. As a result, everywhere all male Communists, Jews and a certain number of nationalistic and democratically minded inhabitants were to be taken as hostages.

False Gods

The Grand Mufti of Jerusalem, Haj Amin el Husseini, reviewing the Bosnian Muslim SS Division in Neuhammer, Germany. November, 1943.

For every German soldier or ethnic German killed or murdered, 100 prisoners or hostages were to be shot; for every wounded 50 of them.

The Chief of the general staff of the commissioned commanding general in Serbia ordered, on 19 October 1941, the execution of 2,200 of those arrested for 10 fallen and 24 wounded German soldiers.

Rademacher wrote in his official travel report of 25 October 1941 that his first talk with Envoy Benzler and state councillor Turner at the office of the military commander had as a result that already more than 2,000 Jews had been shot as retaliation for attacks on German soldiers.

In detailed negotiations with the experts on the Jewish question, SS Sturmbannführer Dr. Weimann from the office of the state councillor Turner and the director of the State Police office (he means here the chief of the Einsatz Group of the Security Police), SS Standartenführer Dr. Fuchs, and his Jewish expert, it came about that

1. "The male Jews will have been shot by the end of this week; therewith the problem broached in the embassy report will have been settled.

Yugoslavia

2. The remaining around 20,000 Jews (women, children, old people) as well as around 15,000 gypsies, the males of whom will likewise be shot, should be concentrated in so-called gypsy quarters of the city of Belgrade as in a ghetto."

But now it became too much for the state secretary in the Foreign Office, Mr. von Weizsäcker, in Berlin, and he wrote on 22 November, on the basis of a memo of department D III of his office of 7 November that, according to the Führer decree of 28 April 1941, the commissioner of the Foreign Office was responsible for the handling of all questions of a foreign political nature emergent in Serbia and that, accordingly, Envoy Benzler and, with him, the Foreign Office, have to deal with the deportation of Jews from Serbia to other countries, but that, on the other hand, it was beyond the scope of Benzler's office and the Foreign Office to participate actively in this. He had orally told Envoy Benzler the same today and it would be advisable to instruct him accordingly in writing.

On the other hand, Under-Secretary of State Luther put forward in his defence, in a note for his state secretary on 12 December 1941, everything that he had undertaken according to Ribbentrop's instructions and he therefore had to assume that it was the intention of Mr. Foreign Minister that the Foreign Office should involve itself "in this delicate matter".

This "in-house" conflict seems to have been the reason why the following remarks are found in a telegram of Benzler's to the Foreign Office on 12 September 1941: "Please speak immediately with the Reich Security Head Office, then a report. Luther, 12.9."

"According to information from Sturmbannführer Eichmann, Reich Security Head Office, IV D VI, acceptance into the Reich territory and Generalgouvernement impossible. Not even the Jews from Germany can be accommodated there. Eichmann proposes shooting.

Rademacher, 13 September."

To that Rademacher stated the following, on 30 July 1948 in Nuremberg:

"On the basis of Luther's note of 12 September, I was summoned for a talk on 13 September. I still remember precisely that I sat opposite him when I telephoned the Reich Security Head Office and that I wrote out in handwriting keywords of Eichmann's answer and pushed them across to Luther during the phone call. Eichmann had spoken to the effect that the military officers were responsible for order in Serbia and just had to shoot rebellious Jews. To my clarificatory question he repeated simply: "shoot" and disconnected."

Now, I have never made such a statement; it has been freely invented by Rademacher. I would also have not had any authority for that.

For much smaller matters hundreds of letters were exchanged between the Reich Security Head Office and the Foreign Office. Taking care, with a marked bureaucratic pedantry, to have mutual comments always properly recorded in the files according to the bureaucratic prescriptions.

Further, imagine that two men sit in the Foreign Office facing each other. Both know each other well. One of them knows the telephone partner very well officially, the other knows him well officially. The phone call was made quickly. Both know to whom and where. Rademacher presents the matter. Luther sits opposite him at the time. Rademacher writes out the information in the file.

I therefore ask, from the standpoint of the criminal investigator: in my opinion, in such a case a person can hardly begin to start writing: "According to Sturmbannführer Eichmann's information, Reich Security Head Office, IV D VI ..."

Luther knows all this, for he sat opposite me and he knew me for a long time. It cannot also be correct that, during this supposed telephone call, Rademacher pushed my supposed information across the desk to Luther for, if one checks his notes and statements, the matter does not tally.

Furthermore, I am not mentioned even once in the course of the further file handling in relation to this, which however would have been very obvious. No, it is as I said – here, as a result of Weizsäcker's reprimand, an additional "exonerating material" was subsequently produced as quickly as possible, the way things were wont to be practised within the central authority offices. And finally in this context even the statement of Weizsäcker during the Nuremberg Trial is not uninteresting circumstantially. Apart from the fact that my service designation was not IV DVI but IV BIV.

Yugoslavia

Croatia

The German envoy of the Croatian Republic in Zagreb, Kasche made a telephone call to the Foreign Office in Berlin, in which he informed that the Croatian government was basically in agreement with the deportation of Jews. He therefore considered it right to begin with the deportation and indeed for the entire state territory. One could therefore play it by ear if difficulties would arise in the course of the operation insofar as it was a matter of the Italian-occupied zone.

On 24 July 1942, Luther made this information the object of a submission to Ribbentrop.

On 16 October 1942, Kasche reported that the Croatian Finance Minister Kosak had already declared he was ready to make available to the German Reich thirty Reichsmarks for every deported Jew. The written confirmation as well as the manner of payment would be arranged with the Foreign Minister Lorkovic. The preparatory work for the deportation of Jews from the Italian occupied zones would be carried out by the Police Attaché. He requested that the Reich Security Head Office be notified.

But the Italians had reserved to themselves the implementation of this task and rejected a transfer of Jews to Germany.

In the meantime, an SS Hauptsturmführer Abromeit had been placed under the Police Attaché as an assistant, who had to undertake the deportation of Jews from Croatia, insofar as the latter came into question for an evacuation, and order the transport trains from the German railways.

The rounding up of Jews would be carried out by the police chiefs who were responsible in the districts at the time in accordance with an instruction of the chief administration for public order and security.

On 22 April 1944, Envoy Kasche made a report on the Jewish question in Croatia to the Foreign Office in which he stated that this had been "to a large extent settled" in Croatia; it was now a matter only of measures in the coastal territories. As a document he attached a report of his Police Attaché. As is well known, the Jewish deportation from Croatia was – so it says in this report - carried out in late autumn 1942 by the responsible Croatian authorities with the involvement of the advisory activity of the Police Attaché. There is a letter of the Reich

Security Head Office according to which, on Himmler's orders, the Jewish question in Croatia should be settled in the shortest time. On the basis of the Himmler order, the Jewish question would be once again thoroughly examined by the commanding officer of the Security Police in close cooperation with him.

Romania

On 7 August 1941, the German envoy in Romania, Manfred, Baron von Killinger, requested from the Foreign Office that the adviser for the Aryanisation and Romanianisation question, SS Hauptsturmführer Richter, who belonged to the Reich Security Head Office, might be sent back to Bucharest.

A request to that effect from the deputy prime minister Mihai Antonescu to Himmler was likewise sent to Berlin.

And Luther was able in a detailed situation report to Ribbentrop to remark, among other things, on this that, in spite of the resistance of the Reich Security Head Office, it was possible for Richter, who had been withdrawn from Romania, to be sent back to Bucharest on the application of the Foreign Office.

Richter straightway had two significant conversations with Mihai Antonescu, one on 12 December 1941, the second on 23 January 1942.

In both discussions it was a question primarily of the agreement that the Romanian government might, based on the Himmler order of October 1941 regarding the prohibition of emigration of Jews from Germany and the occupied territories, for its own part issue such a prohibition for the Romanian sovereign territory. Richter wrote regarding this in his report that the chief of the Security Police and SD (Heydrich) had personally informed the adviser (that is, him) of it. The chief of the Security Police now wished that the emigration of Jews from Romania too be under all circumstances stopped.

On 30 August 1941, an agreement was made in Tighina between the high command of the German army, represented by Major General Hauffe and the representative of the Royal Romanian General Staff, Brigadier General Tatarascu, on the securing, administration and economic utilisation of the territories between the rivers Dujestc and Bug and Bug and Dujepc. This agreement was based on, among

Romania

Romanian nationalist leader Horia Sima is saluted by members of the Iron Guard.

other documents, a letter "from Hitler to the Romanian state leader Antonescu" of 14 August 1941 and the reply letter of "Antonescu to the Führer and Reich Chancellor of the German Reich, Hitler". In point seven of this agreement it says "Deportation of Jews over the Bug is not possible at the moment. They must therefore be concentrated in concentration camps and deployed to work until, after the conclusion of operations, a deportation to the east is possible."

In April 1942, the Reich commissioner for the occupied eastern territories informed the relevant central authority offices in Berlin that regional Romanian offices had recently deported some 10,000 Jews over the Bug into the Reich commissariat of Ukraine and the deportation of a further 60,000 Romanian Jews was to be feared given the present circumstances. Even the Reich Security Head Office received such a complaint.

Following the orders of my superiors, I subsequently wrote on 14 April 1942 to the Foreign Office that an immediate stop of these illegal Jewish transports was to be effected through the regional Romanian offices by the Romanian government. Since it was supposed that the Romanian government would unconditionally comply, initially Security Police measures would be desisted from for the purpose of avoiding a sharpening of the tensions already arisen among the regional offices on account of the illegal transport of Jews.

False Gods

In case, however – I had to add this according to instructions – the Romanian government does not comply or regional Romanian offices act against an instruction of the Romanian government, Security Police measures remain reserved.

In May 1942 these Jews deported over the Bug were liquidated in the Ukraine. They were killed by the regional offices following a *higher* instruction. The literature has noted here especially my statement relating to the "Security Police measures".

Everybody who can even partly read can without the least effort understand that these measures of a Security Police nature were *not* to be brought against the *Jews* but against the Romanian regional offices that carried out the deportation measures. And anybody working in border services knows that by such measures is meant a closing of the border, words that are rephrased in this sharp form as Security Police measures in mutual correspondence, and even generally.

In order to forestall criticism - not that the then Reich leadership had been against a deportation to the east. On the contrary, in the middle of 1942, there were especially sharp orders of Himmler's for the intensification of Jewish deportations to the east, but apparently Rosenberg, the Reich Minister for the Occupied Territories, had raised a protest at the highest office in "his" territory against such a "disorderly and uncontrolled" deportation.

For, at around the same time that this commotion blew through the forest of Berlin authorities, Müller wrote to Luther that it was envisaged that from now on even Jews from Romania were to be transported to the east in special trains from around 10 September 1942. The group of people to be rounded up extended at first to Jews fit for work so long as they did not fall under the privileged exceptions. The same information went to Himmler, however with the remark that those capable of work would be assigned to work-deployment, and the remainder would be subjected to special treatment.

Thereupon Luther replied to Müller that basically there were no objections from the Foreign Office that from now on even the deportation of Jews from Romania to the east should begin. Regarding the range of the group of people to be rounded up and the attitude of the Romanian government there were still negotiations, after the conclusion of which they would return to this matter.

Romania

On 15 September 1942, Killinger sent a telegram to the Foreign Office informing that, since the Romanian government had not yet replied to the verbal notice of the German ambassador of 27 August, a date for the start of the deportation operation could not be determined.

A notable and energetic correspondence arose in this matter between Killinger and Luther in the course of which the often uncontrolled Killinger proceeded blindly with complaints against others without making an effort to undertake an objective examination. The cause of this was his own SS Untersturmführer Richter, who was under him, who became a little later his Police Attaché. The latter had shown a handwritten letter from the deputy prime minister of Romania, Mihai Antonescu, according to which Romania was in agreement with the deportation of Jews to the east.

Now, Richter was a man who not only came from the information service but who at that time stood firmly in it. A painful observation of bureaucratic niceties, methodical handling of files, absolute adherence to the official channels and whatever else prescriptions there may have been were not particularly dear to him. He was likewise not interested in negotiations with inferior authorities like divisional heads. He negotiated and communicated with the office that *he* considered right and these were always the *chief's*. So he was the only adviser who attained the promotion of becoming accredited as Police Attaché.

Naturally, the manner of obtaining such a handwritten letter from such a high official post did not correspond to the normal diplomatic conventions. And it is not very surprising if Luther may have expressed his surprise regarding this, on behalf of the Foreign Office, to Envoy Killinger.

Killinger reacted to this very badly and was not sparing with criticisms. How could the Foreign Office suppose that he would allow such sorts of important questions to be settled exclusively by an SS officer; or, it was self-evident that the adviser had done the preparatory work on his orders.

But, on the other hand, he did not understand that when such a high official of the Romanian government as the commissioner for Jewish matters, Lecca, went to Berlin for negotiations, the latter was to a certain extent dealt with callously by the Foreign Office, which must quite doubtlessly lead to resentment.

False Gods

In his blind wrath he wrote about the official postal channel between the Embassy-Foreign Office-Reich Security Head Office, and also in reverse order, and accused me of not adhering to these prescribed official channels. That is a nonsense; it cannot be proven in any way that I allowed myself here to be guilty of a formal mistake in bureaucratic terms; indeed, I did not have anything at all to do with this matter, because Richter carried out the matter in agreement with his own envoy, which Killinger significantly confirmed at the same time in his own writing. Faced with the tenacity of his envoy, Luther himself finally wrote resignedly in a file that Killinger just did not want to understand.

And all this when Lecca, at the same time, wrote in a report to his minister that the Reich Security Head Office was exceedingly cautious.

On 9 October 1942, ambassadorial councillor Dr. Seltzer inquired about the verbal notice of 27 August. Mihai Antonescu hurried to assure him that he had not yet forgotten it. Even his discussions with the Reich Foreign Minister in his field headquarters had moved in this direction, it was therefore left to Germany now to make concrete plans.

So Richter called on Mihai Antonescu on 22 October. The latter stated – very frankly to Richter's surprise – that he had agreed to the deportation of the Jews from Romania, and negotiations had also been undertaken in Berlin in this regard, but, on the other hand, the deportations over the Bug had been prohibited. (see, in this regard, the letter which I had to prepare according to orders and in which I had to threaten with Security Police measures if the deportations over the Bug were not stopped). In his opinion there was a contradiction here. Richter came to the conclusion that the state leader Marshal Antonescu had deferred the deportation of the Jews, and Richter got hold of a photocopied order of the Marshal in which it said:

"The evacuation from Siebenbürgen[10] is *only* being studied. The implementation has been deferred. It will be begun only when the favourable moment arrives. Until then preparations will be made in fullest detail by the Ministry of the Interior on the basis of the instructions issued by Mr. M. Antonescu. Marshal Antonescu."

---

10 The German name for Transylvania (in central Romania), which, in the twelfth and thirteenth centuries, consisted of seven cities established by Saxons.

On 14 December 1942, Luther wrote to the consulate in Bucharest regarding its report of 26 November that the fact of the stoppage with regard to the a Jewish deportation from Romania was for the moment of no great importance since a deportation during the mid-winter months is anyway undesirable. At the same time he adopted a positive position to an invitation which – apparently through the mediation of the consulate – was issued by the Romanians to me. In the following January I refused on account of excessive work an official form that was at that time customary. More truthfully and correctly, I received an order to refuse the invitation. Since nothing is more burdensome than to accept and to survive official invitations – at least for me –, it was one of my most pleasant duties when I could refuse these. Finally, on 2 November 1943, the legation councillor von Thadden wrote to me, or to my representative:

"The German embassy in Bucharest has, among other things, stated: The proceedings against the Jews have basically become dormant. One only takes money from the rich Jews and seizes poorer Jews for work-deployment. The embassy draws the conclusion that the Romanians give free rein to Jewish activities in order not to offend the English and Americans. A change of Romanian conduct can only be obtained when a stabilisation of the eastern front has been reached and the concern to make an attempt to get on the right side of the Anglo-Americans before the Russians reach Romanian territory no longer seems justified."

Bulgaria

This country had Jewish legislation similar to Germany. From 1942, the concept of who is a Jew was determined by an enabling law, identification with the Jewish star, restrictions on names and housing were introduced, the possibilities of business and economic freedom restricted and the liquidation of Jewish assets pushed further.

On 27 November 1941, the Bulgarian prime minister Popov and the German Foreign Minister von Ribbentrop spoke about the Jewish question on the occasion of a reception in Berlin, whereby Popov proposed to solve it according to European standards. In his report of 21 August 1942, Luther informed his foreign minister what introductory steps he had initiated with regard to the order issued to him which was conveyed to him after the Popov-Ribbentrop conversation.

False Gods

Already on 15 October the discussions between Germany and Bulgaria had flourished to such an extent that Luther could wire Envoy Beckerle in Sofia with reference to these negotiations that he should approach the Bulgarian government in order to settle the question of a deportation to the east of the Jews who were ...[11] according to the new Bulgarian ordinances. He further proposed denaturalising these Jews in the interest of a property legal declaration analogous to the Reich Citizenship Law of 25 November 1941. Depending on the acceptance of this proposal, he suggested further that it should be communicated that they were ready to place an adviser at their disposal.

Beckerle's reply arrived in the Foreign Office already on 16 November. The Bulgarian prime minister basically welcomed the measures to send the Jews to the east and welcomed further, with gratitude, that, before the deportation, a German adviser would be assigned to Sofia so that the latter could help with the implementation.

A correspondence followed now between the under-secretary of state of the Foreign Office, Luther, and the Chief of Office IV in the Reich Security Head Office, SS Gruppenführer and lieutenant general of the Police, Müller, in the course of which it was agreed that SS Hauptsturmführer Dannecker, working in Paris as adviser to the commanding officer of the Security Police, should be transferred to Sofia. There he was placed under the Police Attaché, as his assistant.

The Bulgarian government had already established a Jewish commissariat and named commissioner Belev as its director. He was under the Ministry of the Interior and Health. Beckerle reported on 8 February 1943 that he had spoken, before the introduction of Dannecker, with the Bulgarian Minister of the Interior Grabowski who had confirmed to him his firm intention of deporting all Jews.

Grabowski declared that he was ready to deport with German support Jews from the new Bulgarian territories, Thrace and Macedonia, to the east, but that there was no question of a deportation from the old Bulgarian part for the moment.

The planning and all individual questions should be discussed with the Jewish commissioner Belev. In the meantime, Belev had submitted a proposal to the Minister of the Interior for approval by the ministerial council. This was accepted in all its details on 12 February 1943,

---

11   lacuna in text

and without waiting for the decision, Belev had sent commissioners to Thrace and Macedonia to investigate there the possibilities of the concentration of Jews in camps.

He promised further an announcement, in the first days of May, of the departure stations and the number of Jews to be deported from here. He reckoned that the deportations could be conducted around the end of March 1943 and the entire number would amount to around 20,000 Jews.

On 26 March, Beckerle reported that the vice-president of the Sobranje,[12] Pesheff, had conveyed to the prime minister a petition signed by him and 42 other deputies in which the deportation of Jews was opposed.

Thereupon the prime minister made a request to Pesheff to express his suspicion. The majority of the deputies voted against Pesheff. As a result Pesheff had to resign from his position as vice-president of the Sobranje.

On 24 June 1943, Police Attaché Hoffmann reported through Envoy Beckerle the conclusion of the deportation from Thrace and Macedonia with roughly 20,000 Jews.

Hungary

It must have been around the 10 March 1944 when my Chief, the SS Gruppenführer and lieutenant general of the Police, Müller, met me at a work-place some 80 km east of Berlin, in the Wustrow district. I had orders to build there a barracks village as a temporary place for a possible consolidated Secret State Police Office. He found everything good and proper. In conclusion he said, "Eichmann, report immediately to the commanding officer of the Security Police and SD in Hungary, Standartenführer and colonel of the Police, ministerial councillor, Dr. Gentke, in Mauthausen. You have been assigned to him for service as an adviser. The SS Reichsführer and Chief of the German Police has ordered, for strategic reasons, the evacuation of all Jews from Hungary, combing it from east to west."

---

12   The legislature of Bulgaria

False Gods

I tried to point out the work was far from completed and requested permission to be able to bring this to an end, but the uselessness of this request had become clear to me already at the beginning of his speech.

I now handed over the department totally to my "regular representative" up to that time and set off to Mauthausen. There the commanding officer of the regular police and of the security police were busy with the formation and grouping of their commandos. A field-march adjustment was issued and the commandos were armed and ammunitioned. The motor-vehicle park for that was set up and the commandos then drove off in three groups in the direction of Hungary. The fast advance unit of regular police and security police under SS Obersturmbannführer Krumey and, some 24 hours later, the large one – likewise of regular police and security police – under my command; finally the commanding staff travelled with the commanding officers. When we arrived on the marching route I was moved behind the 1st Panzer Lehr division[13] and marched behind this advance guard according to the marching orders.

Once arrived in Budapest I disbanded the marching order according to orders and the several units of my marching unit – (for the unit was under me only during the march and during possible battle deployment, in case the march in should for some reason not proceed without friction) – reported for service to their several offices and chiefs.

One who trusts the many publications about me up to now must necessarily be of the opinion that I began here to crank things up in order to deport the Jews at lightning speed personally with my commando. But if he has certainly been surprised to read that I disbanded the marching commando when I arrived in Budapest – there remained to me only about 15-20 men including vehicle drivers and guards – he will certainly be even more surprised to read the following pages, in which I adhere strictly to the official documents.

The former legation councillor Dr. Eberhard von Thadden, who was interrogated in Germany in 1961 as a witness, declared: "The deportation of the Hungarian Jews was, as far as I know, arranged between Hitler and Horthy during their meeting in the Klessheim

---

13 The Panzer Lehr Division (tank training division) was an elite armoured division of the German army formed in 1943 and composed of elite training troops.

Hungary

castle. At the meeting between Hitler and Horthy, Ribbentrop and Himmler were present. Today I know that an ultimatum was presented to Horthy." This meeting took place on 17 March 1944. On 19 March at 13 hours, Veesenmayer wired the Foreign Office: "Arrived in Budapest after a smooth journey at 11 hours and have taken over the business. Envoy von Jagow informed the Reich administrator this morning that he had been recalled with immediate effect and had taken leave of him after informing him of my appointment as Reich Plenipotentiary and envoy."

The witness Dr. Wilhelm Höttl declared on 24 April 1947 in Dachau: "The decisive discussions with the Hungarian prime minister Sztojay as well as, presumably, with Horthy were conducted by Dr. Veesenmayer himself. Only through the arrangements resulting from these discussions was the evacuation initiated. That Sztojay himself told me. Even the creation of a special Hungarian office for it, namely that of State Secretary Endre, resulted from Dr. Veesenmayer's wishes, as the then Hungarian Minister of the Interior Andor Jaross recounted to me."

During this initial stage, as the documents reveal, SS Hauptsturmführer Wisliceny, as expert, and SS Obersturmbannführer Krumey, who indeed stood incomparably higher in rank than Wisliceny but had no idea of the specialist work, operated at the office of the commander of the Security Police in Budapest, an SS Obersturmbannführer and senior governmental councillor Trenker. 'In case of possible complaints turn to Krumey and Wisliceny', so it said in an order to the Jewish functionaries in Budapest of 20 March. Only the commander of the Security Police had sole command over the Pest Israeli religious community.

Of course this document has neither a letter-head nor signature, it neither bears a book number nor is it fully complete; but I remember that Wisliceny got together with the Jewish functionaries even at the start of his arrival in Budapest and I also know that the executive activities were performed by the offices of the commanders of the Security Police in agreement with, and after previous consultation with, the Hungarian Secret Police and the relevant regional Hungarian gendarmerie commando central offices.

The organisational structure of the Security Police and SD in Hungary had at its top the senior SS and Police Chief as the regional representative of the SS Reichsführer and Chief of the German Police.

False Gods

He was the highest authority of all German SS and Police units in Hungary and its judge. So the commanding officer of the Security Police and SD in Hungary, Dr. Geschke, too was under him.

The former general of the Police, von dem Bach Zelewski, said, as a witness in Germany in 1961: "In those areas in which a commanding officer of the Security Police belonged to a senior SS and Police chief, he was under the senior SS and Police chief. The senior SS and Police chief never obtained orders from the Reich Security Head Office. When an order of this head office was issued to the commanding officer of the Security Police and the latter presented it to the senior SS and Police chief, there was a possibility that he had obtained Himmler's decision."

The commanders of the Security Police and SD, of whom there were conceivably 4 or 6 in all of Hungary, were under the commanding officer of the Security Police and the "Eichmann" Special Einsatz Commando was under my direction.

The origin of the name of this commando is as simple as it is remarkable. A special commissioner of Himmler's in Budapest, of whom I shall speak more later, stuck to buildings that seemed suitable to him a piece of paper with the inscription "Eichmann Special Einsatz Commando". This name could no longer be obliterated. The action of this special commissioner was unauthorised, but he was covered by his Himmler commission.

For a special Einsatz Commando it will sound remarkable that this consisted of only around 20 men. It was later officially named "Eichmann Special Einsatz Commando-Hungary" since the name clearly became ineradicable, as a letter of the Chief of the Security Police, Dr. Kaltenbrunner, to the mayor of Vienna, Blaschke, of 30 June1944, about which I shall speak later, proves.

SS Obersturmbannführer Krumey was appointed my "regular representative". Our chiefs were Dr. Geschke, who had in the meantime been promoted to SS Oberführer, and the most senior German SS and Police Chief in Hungary, the general of the Police, Winkelmann. The latter was, in political matters, under the Reich Plenipotentiary, Dr. Veesenmayer. It was in principle the same hierachical organisational form as in all the other occupied territories except that Veesenmayer and Winkelmann had a bad relationship with each other professionally since Winkelmann found it difficult to be a subordinate. To express it

Hungary

Jews in Koszeg, Hungary, await deportation to Auschwitz

briefly and commonly, each aspired to commanding the other. For us subordinates it was best that one did not worry about the conflicts of the great, since one might thereby only be "squelched", but did one's service stolidly as one was ordered.

On 31 March 1944, Ribbentrop had great worries and his personal representative Ritter transmitted by "special cryptograph" to the Reich Plenipotentiary, Dr. Veesenmayer, in Budapest the following telegram: "Mr. Reich Minister has learnt that Obergruppenführer Kaltenbrunner intends to be present in Budapest during the next fortnight. Mr. Reich Minister requests from you on this occasion a confidential report personally to Mr. Reich Minister on what duties Mr. Kaltenbrunner has and conducts there with General Winkelmann, who is under you. Is he personally involved in the regulation of the Jewish question or with what other special questions? Mr. Reich Minister is still worried that the SD could attempt to intervene in the duties and rights assigned to you and requests you to be especially careful that this does not happen."

So it is now presented in black and white. General Winkelmann is, whether he wishes it or not, under the Reich Plenipotentiary. Finally, no German general can dance around as he would like to even in Hungary. But now there begins in the succeeding period a race between Veesenmayer and Winkelmann for hegemony with regard to the Jewish deportation, a race in which Veesenmayer, by virtue of his authority and accreditation with the Hungarian government, fully wins.

False Gods

And already on 15 April, Veesenmayer reported that his demand, which had been made to the Hungarian government, to make 50,000 Jews available for work in Germany by the end of the month was accepted and *he would arrange the details of the deportation with Obergruppenführer Winkelmann*. However, he requested the Foreign Office to issue immediate instructions on where the transport should be directed to in the Reich. The Foreign Office informed him in response that the assignment of wagons and the travel-plan would be regulated by my office *as soon as the final instructions* from Obergruppenführer were obtained. I received these instructions from the Reich Security Head Office on 22 April. And through the bureaucratic channels came a letter of the Reich Security Head Office in which it pointed out to the Foreign Office that the commanding officer of the Security Police in Hungary was informed by express telegram of Veesenmayer's negotiations with the Hungarian government and was asked if, considering the transport difficulties, an involvement of the Reich Security Head Office in the Reich Transport Ministry would be considered necessary.

In spite of everything and on account of the cumbersome bureaucracy, it did not go fast enough for the Foreign Office and, as if they feared rebuke from above, Ambassador Ritter recommended to Veesenmayer on 27 April that, in the event of a further delay of the deportation, he should state clearly in his telegraphic report that *from his side* everything possible and necessary had been done for the quick implementation of the operation but that the deportation of the Jews was delayed by the fact that the offices responsible for the deportation and acceptance of the Jews had not given the necessary orders.

On 29 April, Veesenmayer reported to the Foreign Office that the first transport from Budapest had departed, and on 11 May he was able to report further that a travel-plan conference would be arranged on 6 May. The deportation of around 325,000 Jews from the Carpathian region and Siebenbürgen began on 15 May. Four trains with 3,000 Jews each were planned daily, for deportation to Auschwitz. The 100,000 work-force required by the OT for work-deployment in the Reich had to be requested from the SS Economic and Administrative Head Office *which had the Jews sent for deportation under its charge*.

On 22 May, legation councillor von Thadden arrived in Budapest. He had to get a picture of the state of affairs on location. On the question of the handling of assets he presented his opinion to Envoy Veesenmayer, but the latter explained to von Thadden that the question was not yet official; as soon as he considered the situation favourable he would tackle it. The envoy pointed out that the subject of the discussion was not at all proportionate, in terms of magnitude, to the haul initiated by Himmler's offices. On this extraordinarily delicate matter he had sent his best colleague, consul Rokowski, to Himmler. Mr. von Thadden maintained in his report on this matter to the Foreign Office that, as far as he could gather from Veesenmayer's suggestions, it was a matter of secret contracts that Winkelmann had prepared behind Veesenmayer's back and with which the envoy was not in agreement.

Now, what were these matters about? Since I experienced them myself and partly worked out and partly also offered suggestions on them, I shall best describe the matters in the manner in which they, as far as I know, came about.

Shortly after I was in Budapest in March of 1944, an SS Obersturmbannführer of the Waffen SS, Kurt Becher, appeared one afternoon in my hotel room – (I worked and lived at that time in my room in the hotel, since no official accommodation had yet been assigned to me). Since we were both of the same rank, there was from the start a relationship which must customarily be the same in most countries of the world among men of equal rank of the same uniform. At that time I could not have any idea that this same Mr. Becher would, after 1945, in order to save his own skin, in such a shameless way, distort the facts, defame me and narrate to the Allies and their assistants who were at that time ostracising their defeated enemies in Nuremberg, whatever they most wanted to hear, regardless of its truthfulness. Even in 1961, as a witness of the Israeli prosecution interrogated in Germany, Becher clung to falsehoods almost "to a breaking point".

That he was thereby guilty of perjury obviously did not interest him at all and he seems not to have noticed it in the haste of his fabricated untruths, even though the "witness questions" were made known to him one or two days before the trial. Really, a "fair play", as a result of which his atrociousness promises to enter the history of jurisprudence.

This former SS Obersturmbannführer Becher informed me at that time that he was Himmler's special commissioner in Budapest and that it was his task to secure assets for the Waffen SS; more clearly, in order to provide items of equipment for it.

False Gods

What was interesting about his visit to me was the date of the start of the deportation. I could also not give him any *other* information at that time but that which he may have known anyway since he came rather "fresh baked" from Himmler.

In the subsequent period we saw each other quite often and gradually I was also able to give him more precise details; for he was, after all, Himmler's special commissioner. Thus I was able to tell him that Veesenmayer and Winkelmann were busy with negotiations with the Hungarian government to discuss the deportation plans and phases and I was able to convey to him very precise details on the operational preparations through the Hungarian gendarmerie since I was constantly informed of these in order to give my boss the latest situation through reports - as I had been ordered to. To that extent we got along well. Only when, one day, Mr. Becher began to push, because he could carry out his Himmler orders quicker, better and more elegantly in a deportation atmosphere, in an overheated atmosphere, and when this pushing increased, did I become – as one says – embarrassed. For no official works "in a jiffy", even the Hungarian gendarmerie, no matter how solid and powerful this body may have been, was no exception to this.

Red tape everywhere requires its time, no matter if in Germany or in Hungary. Besides, and this was the best, I could neither start nor stop it, neither accelerate it nor delay it. Thus I found his accusations unjustified and with the caution of a bureaucrat I hastened to draft a service report to my superiors since I could not suppose anything else but that he would do the same through his official channels. His official channel was indeed short since he was at that time directly under Himmler.

My anger increased when, one day, he began to allow Jews to emigrate upon the surrender of their assets. The emigration of Jews was at that time strictly forbidden by an order of Himmler's, and only he himself or a chief of the Security Police could make exceptions. How much more astonished was I when Obersturmbannführer Becher was now likewise able to authorise this on the basis of his own decision.

I, who had been centrally involved in the Jewish emigration for years and was officially preoccupied with it, until the above mentioned prohibition, had to grope around with deportation travel-plans with the Reich Transport Ministry; and here a person from outside the Police was placed beside me - who had to go through a "schooling"

Hungary

lasting many years in deportation experience, even though I was not able to issue such authorisations. On the contrary, I had to allow myself to be pushed by this person from outside the Police to begin with the deportation so that he could "pick the cherries from the cake", knowing full well that only the Reich Plenipotentiary, the senior SS and Police Chief, Himmler, and Ribbentrop could decide on deportations; and perhaps also Kaltenbrunner. I was furious; a fury that was so much worse in that Becher, on account of his connection with Himmler, was actually untouchable. He did have orders to authorise everything in exchange for assets.

In addition, at that time the German aversion to payment of foreign exchange likewise allowed Jews to be smuggled abroad. But I had to sit there like a pickaninny and in a few weeks, days, I would have to issue telegrams to the ordered offices with information about the transport trains that had departed. Reports to the commanding officer of the Security Police for the Reich Security Head Office, notifications to the senior SS and Police chief; and in between, once again, acquisition of detailed information from the Hungarian Ministry of the Interior or to the directors of the Reich Railways in Vienna, for the arrangement of a travel-plan conference to which I was ordered. In between, I had to calculate for the commanding officer of the Security Police, on the basis of the travel-plans, the number of the ordered transport guard teams, which he had to confirm in consultation with the commanding officer of the Regular Police, and the complicated correspondence relating to the variations in the treatment of Jews of different foreign citizenships and whatever other bureaucratic work of the sort there may have been.

And so I began to ponder. I thought to myself, what they can, I also can. I sent Obersturmbannführer Krumey and with him SS Captain Wisliceny. I had the Jewish functionaries sounded out about what sort of emigration approval would be offered for say 100,000 Jews. Foreign exchange was offered. But this did not help at all; it was nothing new. The Defence and the Special Commissioner were anyway working on this.

How I came into touch with the Jewish functionary Joel Brand, who arranged this, I can no longer recall. I only know that one day he sat before my desk and we discussed together a plan; or better, I described to him my plan. In that short period I travelled back and forth a few times between Berlin and Budapest.

False Gods

At that time somebody had put forward a figure of 10,000 cargo lorries. Was it me, was it my boss in Berlin, lieutenant general Müller, was it Himmler or Becher - I cannot say precisely any more. I know precisely that I held a talk with my boss of many years, Müller, about transporting 1,000,000 Jews to some points chosen by the Jewish organisations. For this was demanded 10,000 lorries, winterised, with trailers, with the guarantee that these would not be deployed on the western front. 10%, thus 100,000 Jews, were to be deported as an advance - if Joel Brand returned from abroad with a favourable response - as soon as this response was obtained.

It makes you laugh and cry; laugh, when I think that this plan was approved by my superiors, Himmler himself approved it; cry, ... but more of that later. Now everything moved fast. Joel Brand was able to pick up from me a delivery of foreign exchange that had come from abroad to the sum of some 120,000 dollars, including foreign mail charges. The mail was not even checked, though every item of foreign mail for everybody was checked at that time. I was thinking of other things. So I wasted no more time. During my trial Joel Brand said, as a witness for the prosecution, that he did not know how it happened to him; 120,000 dollars, mail, 100,000 Jews in advance, flight to Istanbul. A courier plane of the German air force took Joel Brand to Istanbul.

Krumey, as the highest ranking officer in my office, received orders from me to take Brand safely to Vienna. The commanding officer of the Security Police and SD in Budapest determined which person Brand had to accompany, a Bandi Grosz. Krumey brought him too punctually to the plane. So I thought to myself: this matter is anyway going well; nothing more can go wrong. And I did not bat an eyelid when the first deportation transports rolled. For, news from Brand could come any day; Brand himself might come, and the travel-plan was redirected to Spain, Portugal, Romania. The Jewish organisations would indeed look to the rest.

What surprised me greatly during my trial was the fact that Joel Brand, as witness for the prosecution, spoke about the process precisely and truthfully except for a few things. It is not true that I said that the deportation transports would be stopped during the time of the decision or that the Jews would be "put on hold" in Austria. I said to everybody that wanted to hear it that, according to orders, I had to say that the transports would continue to run according to the scheduled travel-plan until the decision came.

Hungary

How would I, as an Obersturmbannführer, have been able to suspend, speed up or cancel what half a dozen higher and the highest superiors of mine, in the different agencies and central offices, had ordered. Name me one man in any European country who, in my office, during the war, would have been able to do something like that.

Brand said that Krumey had told him as the plane took off that there were also other SS officers like Eichmann. There were also other Krumey's and Wisliceny's. He might think of that when he was with his friends abroad. Even though the former SS Obersturmbannführer has himself been placed for a long time as an accused person in a German detention centre, he stated – even when questioned as a witness about that – that he had never said such a thing. It is credible, for it certainly would not have been an incrimination for Krumey if he had confirmed Brand's version.

Now, during my trial in connection with this mission a series of documents from the Israeli secret archives were introduced and placed before the court as evidence by the prosecution. It is not my task here to explain this matter in greater detail. There may also certainly be similar or even supplementary documents in the secret archives in England and North America which are preserved for a possible publication in the future.

There remains for me only the sad task of stating that Brand – not due to his own fault – never returned and that a sort of confirmation was never received. But others let the deportations continue to run, as the next documents will show. Only Joel Brand and nobody else – I think – will be able to feel my anger and my pain that the matters went in this way and not otherwise; and in turn I can feel, likewise at first hand, the anger and the pain of a Joel Brand that paper-work, which is otherwise so patient, was obviously not useful in this case. For, the initiation of at first only 100,000 Jews willing to emigrate without any foreign reciprocal action would have resulted in a completely different picture. With these or similar words I concluded my remarks relating to this before the court during my trial.

Now, the other point, of the secret arrangement made by Winkelmann behind Veesenmayer's back, that was broached by Mr. von Thadden, was an arrangement made by the commissioner Becher. He pocketed to a certain extent the armaments works of the "Hungarian Krupp" - the so-called Manfred Weiss works in Budapest - in exchange for the emigration of the entire family of this Jewish industrialist to Portugal.

False Gods

The Chief of the Economic and Administrative Head Office of the SS Reichsführer, SS Obergruppenführer and general of the Waffen SS, Oswald Pohl, under whom stood all the concentration camps, issued a telegram on 24 May 1944 to Himmler in which he requested permission for the OT organisation, the German state large-scale construction company, to employ Jewish women from Hungary for its projects. Himmler signed this telegram with his characteristic big "HH" and it is to be supposed that he granted this to Pohl.

Sometime in May/June, the persons in charge of planning began to deal with a deportation of Jews from Budapest. Mr. von Thadden wrote to Veesenmayer that the press department of the Foreign Office intended to suggest to the Reich Foreign Minister that one should create external reasons and bases for the operation such as, for example, the discovery of dynamite hoardings in Jewish clubs and synagogues, sabotage organisations, revolutionary plans, attacks on police officers, and huge foreign exchange profiteering with the aim of undermining the Hungarian currency system. The keystone in such an operation should be an especially blatant case to which the large-scale pogrom could then be attributed. Veesenmayer was requested for a telegraphic response, but the latter had to request urgently the avoidance of all propagandistic actions, since it was well known everywhere that Jewish clubs and synagogues had been for weeks under the strict control of the Hungarian Police or had been partially confiscated. Jewish assets were likewise confiscated or blocked, and the Jews were very restricted in their freedom of movement.

Blaschke, the mayor of Vienna, wrote on 7 June to his friend Kaltenbrunner that he would like to have the Jewish work-force. Thereupon Kaltenbrunner, as Chief of the Security Police, granted to him 4 transports with 12,000 Jews altogether and wrote to him that roughly 30% thereof might yield Jews fit for work. Both the Jews fit for work and those unfit were to be committed to guarded camps. He could discuss finer details with SS Obersturmbannführer Krumey of the Hungary Special Commando.

Guidelines were then discussed in detail for the deployment of these Jewish work groups, who were divided into some 20 political districts of Lower Austria.

"Whereas up to 19 March numerous Jews emigrated from Slovakia to Hungary, now a reverse migration took place. It would considerably lighten the local work if now steps were taken against the Jews in a

Hungary

fundamental way even in Slovakia. If corresponding instructions are issued, I would meet Ludin in Pressburg for a discussion in connection with this to work out practical proposals together. Veesenmayer wrote this on 14 June to the Foreign Office, and some days later General Winkelmann issued a personal letter to Himmler. "Most respected Reichsführer, In the last week many things occurred here that might indeed have raised concerns in other places." He begins to speak of the Jewish question and the attempts to solve it and on Hungarian internal political matters, he characterises individual personalities of the political life and then maintains: "The best naturally would be if the Führer summoned the Reich Administrator to express his opinion clearly. But it should also proceed in such a way that Veesenmayer finally receives strict instructions to put his foot down. With his way of handling things he is really not getting far." On 4 July – he writes further – he, Winkelmann, took part in a discussion which Becher (Himmler's special commissioner) had had with the Hungarian Minister Imredy on the "Manfred Weiss works". Among other things it dealt with the nationality of its managing director. The Hungarians wanted a Hungarian. Becher declared that such a demand was totally unacceptable for only a man who got his orders directly from Himmler and who had his full trust could become the managing director. The letter ended "the Reichsführer's most obedient Winkelmann".

In the meantime, von Ribbentrop wired a message personally. He requested Veesenmayer to inform the Hungarian government that it was not opportune to enter into all the different foreign offers in favour of the Jews and he requested a proper settling of the matter.

And what was I doing at that time? What were the people of my commando doing? People will hardly believe me if I said that I never had more free time and less to do in all the preceding years than during the Budapest months. And yet it was so. The reader who has followed the certainly very dry sequence of documents in their chronological order will have seen and will continue to see that everything, literally everything that was of any importance, was handled personally either by Veesenmayer or by Winkelmann. If, during my Berlin years, I had avoided making use of the meagre executive authority at my disposal that every divisional head was apportioned, and if I had made it my custom to obtain instructions from my superiors in all matters, very seldom did I need to do *even this* in Hungary. For, constant worry ruled the Reich Administrator as well as the senior SS and Police chief, that the other might supersede him in authority. So this worry alone impelled both of them, and caused them to order and handle things which they would in normal circumstances have transferred to their subordinates. Even the commanding officer of the Security Police had in Hungary, in contrast to other occupied territories, personally very little to do with these matters for the mentioned reason. Which is very striking in comparison with other countries. Of course, I must correctly admit that the machinery of the Hungarian internal authorities functioned in a way that could seldom have been claimed by any other authorities in other regions. It functioned not only in Jewish matters but simply in all its official duties, and more than once I said to myself, "God, up to now you thought that exact precision would prevail only in Germany; here you see at least the same painfully clean accuracy. At that time I admired the Hungarian internal administration not with regard to the settlement of the Jewish matters, but I speak quite generally from a bureaucratic point of view.

Krumey often went out in the early forenoon for tennis playing; and around June/July he was transferred to Austria, for there was really precious little for us to do.

Even in 1961 he said, when interrogated as a witness, about this: "I observed that his (Eichmann's) typist did not have much to do. Eichmann himself spent little time in the office. He came and went as he wished. He had a remarkable and relaxed private life.

Indeed I did not even have personal authority over the hardly twenty members of my command; even this work was taken care of by others, as Krumey confirms further. Already in Mauthausen he saw and heard that Dr. Geschke directed the Security Police. He received his commissions from him and he stated further that he was transferred from Hungary, where he was my "regular representative", by the commanding officer of the Security Police in Hungary, Dr. Geschke, and not by me.

Now, I can well understand that all this is not yet an answer to the question about what exactly I was then doing, both privately as well as officially.

Officially: so long as the transports ran according to travel-plans I had to send telegraphic notes according to the received notifications of departures to Auschwitz, through the commanding officer of the Security Police in Hungary, to the Reich Security Head Office; keep statistical records, report orally to my superiors daily in Hungary, and also give at least once a week a situation report in writing. For that I

Hungary

had to acquire the documents from the Hungarian Ministry of the Interior, as a rule directly from the secretary of state, Endre.

I received communications daily from the gendarmerie; in short, everything connected with the ordered report was my duty, and in addition all that bureaucratic work that I spoke about in the beginning. The entire organisation was constituted of five or six men. Another eight men belonged to the guard, and were drivers and typists. The remainder were in the provinces and had to see to it that Jews of certain foreign citizenships were not deported, as the order stipulated.

After the misfortune of Stalingrad, I began to occupy myself with the manufacture of an engine. Unfortunately I understood too little of the construction side of it to be able to push this matter forward alone since I was not an internal combustion engine builder. The only thing I could do was, first, obtain the relevant latest literature and devote myself to its study.

Unfortunately, I had at that time also too much bureaucratic business around me, and the increasing intensity of the bomb attacks did not in any way advance the matter. Nevertheless, after some hours of study, I got in touch with an expert in the field of rotor construction, Professor Flettmer, the inventor of the Flettmer rotor, the constructor of small rotors for our submarines. He told me one day that the idea of the so-called aerial delivery bomb was to be attributed to his daughter for, inspired by the propeller-like fruit of the sycamore tree and its fluttering fall to the ground, she arrived through pondering the problem at the aerial delivery bomb.

In short, the man seemed to me to be the right person. And he was indeed enthusiastic about my idea, especially when I explained to him the special military equipment possibilities but, as a result of our shortage of non-ferrous metal, the horse power of the German engine was, for example, lower in comparison to a US engine. I think I can remember that there was a difference between 30 or 35% or even higher compared to the German engine. But he promised to consider the matter, study it and keep me informed. That was agreeable to me. Since I did not want anything for myself but for the matter at hand, it was a matter of indifference to me who reaped the possible recognition or fruits from this matter if only the idea could be brought closer to realisation and an operational relief were provided to the troops. Therefore it was also completely superfluous to make out a contract. He had only to swear to silence in relation to unauthorised persons.

False Gods

My special interest at that time was more in the reduction gear engine, the transmission of rotary motion and other relevant things than in anything else.

Flettmer then visited me a few times in my office; I visited him in his small factory and examined with interest his small rotors that were being built. I really wanted the same thing, only a very small rotor, or a device like a small rotor, or, as I expressed it at that time, a "motor-rotor" with all the necessary trappings.

Then the Hungary post gradually came about and I had lots of time. But Flettmer was far away in Berlin, and I thought that I must force things. I sketched, studied, and slogged away at how one could "motorise" one or two divisions in this way. But Flettmer remained silent and matters did not advance. Then came the V1 rocket and immediately I thought consolingly that nobody now needed the nonsense with the "motor-rotor". And I thought to myself that, at this hour, the stupidest sow would laugh me out if I had opened my mouth. One day, in the middle of 1943, I presented the idea to my boss, lieutenant general Müller, but I might as well have narrated it to his waste-paper basket. He listened patiently, looked at me and laughed a little and then led me back into reality with an official matter. This was one of my unfortunately fruitless occupations in Budapest.

This was at the beginning of 1944. Veesenmayer had to report to Berlin that Prime Minister Sztojay informed him that Horthy had stopped the continuation of the Jewish operations, and Sztojay requested him to approach Ribbentrop so that the several foreign offers in favour of an emigration of certain groups of Jewish people could be considered more seriously. At Ribbentrop's suggestion Hitler approved some of these offers under the condition that the emigration of Jews to the Reich that had been stopped for the moment by Horthy be conducted as quickly as possible.

But things always got complicated; a few days later, on 16 July, Ribbentrop again wired Budapest: Hitler is aware that Horthy is thinking of recalling the present Sztojay government and setting up a military government in its place. He has learnt this to his displeasure. With greater displeasure has Hitler heard that Horthy had issued arrest warrants against some ministers and secretaries of state of the Sztojay government who had recently carried out measures against Jews. He threatens the immediate recall of Veesenmayer and the imposition of measures that would exclude a repetition of such incidents once and

Hungary

for all. In this case Hitler would in future have no mercy at all. Hitler however hopes that Horthy would see that every deviation from the path decided upon in Klessheim would entail complications.

The deportation transports were accompanied by regular police or, when there was an extreme shortage of personnel, mixed with members of the office of the commanding officer of the Security Police. The latter, however, as far as I can remember, turned up very seldom. The negotiations for the removal of these forces from the regular police were carried out directly by the commanding officers of these police units at any time.

During a transport, on Slovak territory, I understand there occurred excesses on the part of the transport escort against the Jews. The German consulate in Budapest reported on 2 August to the Foreign Office, "The matter has been investigated by the commanding officer of the Security Police and SD in Hungary – the Special Commando of SS Obersturmbannführer Eichmann is responsible exclusively for the technical implementation of the Jewish transports – who has reported on the results to the Reich Security Head Office."

I thought that I had to make use of this document since it revealed strikingly that my men had nothing to do with the executive matters but limited their activity exclusively to matters that I have already described substantially.

And how little my commando could decide even in technical matters is shown by the fact that, even when I received authorisations for emigration, I was bound to Himmler's orders which had been communicated to the Security Police. Veesenmayer will have learnt confidentially that I had once again approached the Reich Security Head Office with a request to get Himmler's final decision on whether the departure of a so-called "Swiss operation" through Romania to Palestine might be approved. I had hitherto proposed in Budapest that this be authorised only to Lisbon through western Europe, for I could not after all alter any order of my superiors through my own authority. But this route to Lisbon was approved by the arrangement between Ribbentrop, Himmler and the Mufti.

There was also finally - as I very often said to the Jewish functionaries in Budapest - the "green border". For that nobody needed an approval and, since the executive part did not concern me, the "green border" did not interest me.

False Gods

In August began the tug-of-war between Veesenmayer and the Hungarian government related to the commencement of the deportation of Jews from Budapest. I was thereupon informed by the Hungarian Ministry of the Interior that it had begun, then again a contradictory order was announced, in short, it went back and forth. The result was finally that Horthy forbade the deportation. This prohibition was transmitted to Berlin by Veesenmayer on 24 August at 10.20 hours.

On the next day, at 11.15 hours, he was able to report to the Foreign Office that Winkelmann had just informed him by telephone that Himmler had given orders by telegram at 3 a.m. to strictly forbid every deportation of Jews.

On 30 August it started once again from the beginning. Veesenmayer wrote to Ribbentrop that, following the swearing-in of the new Hungarian government, a ministerial council meeting had taken place in which the evacuation of Jews from Budapest was the main subject of debate. It was decided to initiate the operation immediately.

I myself with my commando had for a long time not been in Budapest, for the commanding officer of the Security Police, Dr. Geschke, had issued orders to me to go with my commando to the region of Greater Nikolsburg to save, through evacuation, 10,000 ethnic Germans there from Russian capture. A small commando of mine evacuated a German army hospital from New Arad, which was temporarily freed of Russian occupation. And on 22 September 1944, according to orders, I dismantled the commando with a final appeal. I was ordered back to the Reich Security Head Office, but was however instructed to remain a week longer in Budapest and then to report back to Berlin.

In the meantime, Veesenmayer reported to his Berlin central office that the Hungarians had up to then not yet complied with the obligations entered into for the solution of the Jewish question in Budapest. Legation councillor Wagner as Gruppenleiter of the home division II of the Foreign Office proposed to Ribbentrop on 12 October, in view of the recession of the front, that the German position should be fundamentally altered and the evacuation of the remaining Jews be implemented on their own or through the application of appropriate pressure on the Hungarian government.

Under-Secretary of State Luther had in the meantime worked on the Hungarian envoy accredited in Berlin, who was travelling on

Hungary

18 October to report to Budapest and intended to present the entire matter to his prime minister and the Reich Administrator.

Besides, he held out to the Hungarian government the prospect of an official action from the German side and now gave Veesenmayer instructions to see to it that the measures against the Jews in Hungary were to be carried out further in an appropriate manner. On 14 October he wrote that the goal in Hungary must be:

1. To exclude, through progressive legislation, Jews, without distinction, from the cultural and economic life

2. To facilitate the appropriate governmental measures through immediate identification of all Jews, and to give the people the possibility of a clearer distancing

3. To prepare the resettlement and deportation to the east.

The reader of these lines will gradually begin to wonder why I, as the writer and to a certain extent as a contemporary chronicler who found himself in the midst of the events, always recount the actions of the Reich Administrator of the Foreign Office and, at best, also those of the senior SS and Police Chief. Did other offices too – he will ask himself – not have more of a direct hand in the matter than is represented by this writer? Does the writer wish to deliberately distance Himmler, Kaltenbrunner, his own direct superior, Müller, in short, names that come up everywhere, from the issues in Hungary? Perhaps for the reason that he himself was working there?

I should reply to that that this was not so in any way. Hungary was essentially the "Foreign Office's contest", not that of the Security Police or of Himmler. I have made use of all the documents that were presented here in Israel in my trial and to which I granted some significance with regard to the course of events or its better understanding. There is nothing *more* about it there. One cannot also say, well, the Reich Security Head Office burnt its files in 1945. This is of course true, but the other central authority offices did not do this. And after 1945 all the letters were discovered of which the copies were burnt by the Reich Security Head Office. It may certainly be that, in the course of time, one or another document will still be found; but the total picture cannot be changed any more by that.

Hardly had I, after a few holidays (insofar as one can still speak of

False Gods

holidays in this advanced stage of the war), been back in Berlin with my family than there came to me my boss' orders to return to Budapest. What had happened? The senior SS and Police Chief pressured the German envoy! The Reich Plenipotentiary pressured the Hungarian government! The Reich Foreign Office and Veesenmayer pressured each other! Why? The deportations had been stopped there. Himmler had prohibited them, even Horthy had prohibited them.

In Hungary, in the meantime, the Arrow Cross people under Szalasi had come to power, and Veesenmayer reported to the Foreign Office on 18 October in the following way:

"With the changed political situation, the Jewish question has entered a new stage. Obersturmbannführer Eichmann, who has been brought back *on the orders of the senior SS and Police Chief here and the command of the Chief of the Security Police* has undertaken negotiations with the Hungarian government that 50,000 male Jews fit for work should be transported from Budapest to Germany for work-deployment.

From the publications of the new government it may, moreover, be perceived that even Jews who had been excepted up to now have been obliged to wear the star."

On the same day Veesenmayer reported further: "In spite of Szalasi's basic statement which has already been issued about not having any Hungarian Jews deported any more to the Reich, the Minister of the Interior will attempt to obtain an exceptional agreement to the requested temporary handing over of 50,000 male Jews fit for work who should be deployed in the Reich territory for the Jäger[14] programme and for the relief of Russian prisoners of war who are needed urgently elsewhere. The transport should take place as a footmarch accompanied by German commandos. The Eichmann Einsatz Commando will, apart from a partial assumption of the supervision of the footmarch, work alongside only in an advisory capacity, while the operation should otherwise be carried out by the Hungarian gendarmerie under the direction of the commissioner for the Jewish question up to now, senior lieutenant Ferenczi, and the senior direction of the state secretary in the Ministry of the Interior, Laday."

On 24 October, a Reich Secret dispatch was sent by Veesenmayer to

---

14   See p.213

Hungary

Hungarian Jewish women are rounded up by police for deportation.

the Reich Foreign Minister in which he reported to his minister: "... I inform you that yesterday, on SA Obergruppenführer Winkelmann's repeated urgent request, I requested Szalasi to make available to us at least 25,000 working Jews on loan for half a year for use in the German Jäger programme. SA Obergruppenführer Winkelmann by himself made a request for 50,000 working Jews but this has up to now failed due to the resistance of the Hungarian government offices. I considered it right to realise at first a partial demand with the intention of presenting our wishes again possibly later."

Szalasi agreed immediately to this request, but at first only pointed to the fact that Hungary itself needed the most part of the Hungarian Jews for navvy work and requested me to initiate a further arrangement of the matter between Obergruppenführer Winkelmann and Minister Kowacs.

The senior SS and Police Chief Winkelmann repeatedly approached Veesenmayer saying that 50,000 working Jews had to march into the Reich territory. He also got into touch directly with the Chief of the Security Police and SD, Dr. Kaltenbrunner, with a demand for my immediate recall to Hungary. I received the order for that. I had to obey. I could not by any means say: "No, I do not want to, find somebody else." I could not pretend to be sick since I had sworn an oath of allegiance. Besides, I looked too healthy to pretend to be sick.

False Gods

What was the Jäger programme? The last effort to drive away the enemy bombers from the German skies. Thousands and thousands of one-man turbine Jägers with fantastic speed and manoeuvrability were used. When they were ready, they stood like hornets on the highways, fields, airfields, at the edges of woods. But they hardly took off. Shortage of fuel. The Allies had – through systematic painstaking work, often in low level attacks - destroyed the German refineries – dozens of small refineries skilfully and securely camouflaged like small swallows' nests in ground trenches and on mountain sides against enemy planes. But it had not yet reached that point. The order still was: the Jäger programme. For that Winkelmann had raged against God and the world. For that I received orders to conduct detailed discussions with the Hungarian Ministry of the Interior.

Were these the actions of responsible leaders directing according to a plan? Nonsense; these people only thought of the moment. They gave orders! According to the motto: better a stupid order than none. And what did the same general Winkelmann say in 1961 when interrogated as a witness in Germany? "Himmler had declared to him that he was not interested in the Jewish question in Hungary."

To that I must ask: why then had Himmler ordered the deportation of Jews by scouring the country from east to west, was it for strategic reasons? Why then was Himmler present at the Hitler-Horthy meeting in the Klessheim Castle where these matters were determined? Why then did Obergruppenführer Winkelmann, as senior SS and Police Chief, not intervene *against* the deportation? He was indeed the highest SS and Police authority as Himmler's representative in Hungary. Why was he repeatedly present at Veesenmayer's on account of the deportation of the Jews? Why then did he bring me back to Hungary by applying pressure on Kaltenbrunner? And then I read his statement: "Eichmann had, in his subordinate's manner, overstepped his authority when he thought that he could thereby act in accordance with those who gave him orders."

A word or two on that, Mr. General: I would ascribe such a thing to your advanced age that you have in the meantime reached. But when I consider what a silly and foolish man I must have been to follow your orders in 1944 I am even today filled with rage at myself, and sympathy for you, Mr. General! I sit here in this Israeli prison but I have the courage to tell you this. You will therefore understand that, given such an attitude of my superiors of that time towards their subordinates, I rely all the more precisely, and solely, on the wording of the documents. Certainly my views too have changed in the last sixteen years, but I would never adopt such an attitude to one of the men, junior officers or officers who had been at that time under *me* as you today, my superior general at that time, adopt towards me - unless he clung to falsehoods the way you do. These, Mr. General, were the words that I wanted to convey to you. And how did things proceed?

"I request you, in the implementation of all measures that compromise them in the eyes of the enemy not to deal with the Hungarians in an obstructive way but to rather support them in every way; it is especially in our interest if the Hungarians proceed against the Jews in the sharpest way possible." Ribbentrop wired this personally to the envoy as a secret note, under Reich Secret Matters, on 20 October.

Should Winkelmann and Veesenmayer for this reason not have effected a planned proposal for the establishment of food depots, overnight camps, etc. in that they themselves were now involved in detailed negotiations with Minister Kovacs? Personnel!

On 31 October, the director of the Inland division of the Foreign Office, legation councillor Wagner, presented to the Reich Foreign Minister a situation report on the Jewish question in Hungary. In Hungary there had been around 900,000 Jews. Of these, 437,402 had, up to 10 July, been deported to the eastern territories. After the start of the Szalasi government, now at first 25,000 Jews were to go the Reich for work-deployment and Envoy Veesenmayer intended to negotiate about a further 25,000. The relevant secretary of state in the Foreign Office, thus Ribbentrop's closest colleague, was now a Mr. von Steengracht. He was interrogated by the International Military Court in Nuremberg and there he stated, among other things, the following:

"There were offices in Germany that conducted and carried out the Jewish operations. These organisations encroached also into foreign countries and removed people from there without the *knowledge* of the Foreign Office and without its *cooperation*."

One might think that the writer has made a mistake. No, no I did not make a mistake. It was as I wrote and it can be looked up at any time in the sources. I had many, many years ago a Latin professor who also struggled with me. I have not retained much. But he certainly was right when he thrust the following "common saying" more than once at me: "*Sitacuisses philosophus manisisses*"

False Gods

But even this, in spite of frequent professorial use, I would not have memorised up to now if his very handy free translation had not promptly followed the Latin quote every time: "If you had held your tongue you would have remained a wise man." One cannot say more about this Steengracht fairy tale.

The Foreign Office reported to Veesenmayer that, according to a report from me to it, up to the date of the report, around 27,000 Jews fit to march and to work had been ordered to march to the Reich territory. In Budapest, in the mean time, the following had occurred: after Veesenmayer had obtained the approval for the foot-march from the Hungarian state leader and Winkelmann had discussed the details with Minister Karacs, it was determined that this foot-march was to be carried out exclusively by the Arrow Cross, supported by units of the executive. German support, German supervision and German transport escorts on Hungarian territory were refused by the Hungarian authorities.

In the first days too they seem to have mainly held to the Veesenmayer-Winkelmann demands with the exception that not only male marchers but also women were included; but later whatever Jew could be found was ordered to march.

Since I, the writer, was most heavily attacked on this point – very unjustly, as one will see –, I do not wish to use my own words to describe the situation but bring forward a document and let it speak for itself. A document which must be beyond every doubt if one knows of what sort it is. It is a protocol of a meeting in the Swedish consulate in Budapest on 22 November 1944 at 6 in the evening.

The participants were legation secretary, Raoul Wallenberg, commissioner of the Swedish consulate, N. Krausz, commissioner of the Swiss consulate, Dr. Körner, commissioner of the Portuguese consulate and Police captain Batiztalvy.

The Police captain, who requested confidentiality, stated that the Jews arriving at the Hungarian-Austrian border were handed over to the commissioner of the Germans. He stated further that 10,000 Jews had disappeared on the country roads. Fled, died or shot. Nothing, or little was prepared in advance.

Then there followed a report of the envoys of the Swiss consulate, Dr. Leopold Breszlauer and Ladislaus Kluger, on the experiences that they

Hungary

had gathered during their official trip from Budapest to the Austrian border between 23 and 27 November 1944.

According to the report, of the 25,000 Jews deported up to 22 November, 10,000 were handed over to the Germans, 6-7,000 should be handed over in the coming days, and a further 6-7,000 were shot on the way by the Arrow Cross. Some Jews succumbed to their exertions and some through sickness.

The Hungarian gendarmerie senior lieutenant Ferenczi had, as a result of the protocol of this meeting, command over the entire foot-march.

The Jews were removed from the streets and houses in Budapest by the police, but chiefly by the members of the Arrow Cross Party.

The supervision was principally under the Police, but in fact public authority was exercised by the members of the Arrow Cross Party.

The deportees were then, regardless of age and sex, conducted on foot in the most diverse directions, but mostly to the Hungarian-Austrian border. During the march Hungarian gendarmerie accompanied the marching groups under the control of members of the Arrow Cross Party.

The commission could determine that the Germans at the border refused to accept persons who were unfit for work, old or sick, as well as pregnant women.

In general we were able to determine – the report continues – that those Jews who worked within the country directly under German commandos were properly fed and treated decently; on the other hand, those Jews who had to work under the supervision of the members of the Arrow Cross Party were treated in the cruellest way and very badly fed. Of a group of 4,000 Jewish workers, some 2,000 were shot, the remaining 2,000 arrived on foot at the Hungarian-Austrian border in bad physical condition, half-naked, without food and had been subject to many blows. This group was first disinfected by the Germans in Germany, then clothed and set to work. The handing over and acceptance of the Jews in Hegyashalem (Hungarian-Austrian border) was performed by the gendarmerie, with which the Hungarian Honved[15] collaborated.

---

15   The Hungarian army

False Gods

The report ends with the declaration of the commission that the goal of the present Hungarian government was doubtless to annihilate Hungarian Jewry completely and, according to a declaration of Szalasi's to the papal nuntio, they would not ask for mercy, but they would also not grant any mercy.

An envoy of the International Red Cross completed the make-up of the commission. Dr. Leopold Breszlauer and his commission colleagues gave in their report a large number of names of those persons who were responsible for the matter. Dr. Leopold Breszlauer also appeared as witness for the prosecution in my trial in Israel. The witness did not mention my name at all in connection with this foot-march. Dr. Breszlauer would certainly have done so, he would have had to do it, if I had had any involvement in the matter.

According to a declaration on oath, it remained reserved to the SS General Jüttner on 3 May 1948 in Nuremberg to cook up a fairy-tale:

"When we arrived we drove directly to the senior SS and Police Chief. Winkelmann told me at that time that he was completely powerless in this matter. And he told me that he would be very grateful to me if I would object to what I had seen. I now demanded that the man responsible for the implementation of the transport be brought to me. I was told that it was Obersturmbannführer Eichmann. I ordered that he be brought to me, and indeed I wished to speak to him in the presence of the senior SS and Police chief and Becher. Eichmann was not there. A representative arrived, as far as I know a captain, I do not remember his name any more."

He reprimanded with sharp words and demanded an immediate response.

"This Hauptsturmführer replied to me in a callous way that he only obeyed orders and that I did not have to order him anything." Jüttner wanted to get in touch immediately with Himmler, which he apparently did.

The then SS and Police Chief General, Winkelmann, was interrogated on this in 1961 in Germany. He confirmed Juttner's statement insofar as it related to the description of the foot-march. But he could not remember if the name Eichmann was mentioned.

To the general of the Waffen SS, Jüttner, I have only one thing to say:

Hungary

Mr. General, you seem, as far as I know, to be the only general in Prussian-German military history who allows himself to be replied to by a captain callously, "You do not have to order me anything."

If one of my captains had really told you this at that time, you would and should have immediately locked him up. Besides General Winkelmann, who according to your report, was also present, and who was responsible for this captain, would have handed over the latter immediately to the SS and Police court because he should have done so. To the other nonsense that you presented in your sworn declaration I cannot state anything else – since I sit in an Israeli prison – but recommend that you study the report, or better, the protocol of the Swedish, Swiss, Portuguese and Spanish consulates of 22 November 1944, on the foot-march, and also the report of the German envoy and Reich Plenipotentiary, SS Gruppenführer Veesenmayer, to the Foreign Office and ask Mr. General Winkelmann how things went at that time with his negotiations with the Hungarian minister Karacs relating to the details of the march. I do not wish to have anything more to do with you than to say to you: You should be ashamed, Mr. General.

If the last Hungarian Minister of the Interior, Vajna Gabor, had known the consular protocol of the representatives of the neutral powers in Budapest, and also the Veesenmayer report to Berlin, he would certainly not have written in his statement of 28 August 1945 to an office of the Allies: "In Budapest Eichmann wanted to deport even the women, children and old men, against which I repeatedly took a stand. Finally he declared: 'Then the Germans will take over the deportation of the Jews'."

In the meantime *history* has branded this gentleman as one of those whom one is wont to call, in common speech, a liar.

There was a fundamental change in the method of evacuating Jews from Budapest. This was telegraphed by the German envoy from Budapest to Berlin. Szalasi ordered that the evacuation should take place no longer as foot-marches but by means of transport. Considering the lack of the latter, this order was practically tantamount to a stoppage of evacuation.

On 23 November 1944 Veesenmayer reported to the Reich Foreign Minister that he had on that day, according to instructions, informed Szalasi, and the latter had wanted to energetically continue the evacuation of the Budapest Jews in spite of the technical difficulties.

False Gods

He would see to it that, through continuous scouring of the land, the wishes of the Reich Foreign Minister would be substantially complied with.

The former legation councillor, Dr. Grell, temporarily assigned to the German consulate in Budapest, was the only one who had the courage during a witness interrogation in 1961 in Germany to speak out; of course, in Nuremberg things were foisted onto those who were dead or not arrested. This was possible in those times, first, since there was a lack of documents, and, secondly, it is quite possible that a subordinate officer should do such a thing if it corresponded to his plan. However, in the case of a commanding general or a state secretary, the Reich Plenipotentiary or such high personages who gave orders, initiated and planned at that time when the events occurred, such an attitude is, in my opinion, to be considered only as shameless.

Today, thanks to the research of the last one and a half decades, there is already such an abundance of genuine documents available that a "foisting off" is no longer possible in any case. They form the basis for future historical researchers and these will one day present an objective picture of the events free of all attachment to emotions and subjectivity, of all considerations of political and propagandistic interests.

I may say about myself that I think that, as the accused, I attempted during my trial in Israel to present a somewhat objective attitude to things even though it is very hard for someone accused even to speak. Wherever I had to blame myself because I once received the relevant orders, I did this without faltering or hesitating. But wherever falsehood, the cowardice of former superiors or some interests of many publicists during the last 1½ decades dumped their intellectual rubbish onto me, I, on the other hand, took a stand and spoke against it. My best defenders here were the documents insofar as I found them genuine and unobjectionable; and these were, apart from a few exceptions which may have got mixed up in the post-war years in an obscure way among the genuine papers, by far the majority; in short, almost all of them.

In the representation of the course of events in the activity of the Jewish persecution, I have mainly based myself on core documents. The focus on those responsible was thereby automatically crystallised and, through my reference to the documents, I have offered the possibility of having my lines subjected to an examination regarding factual matters.

Hungary

Unknown Jewish couple wearing the yellow star, Budapest, Hungary.

In this section I have dealt with twelve countries; what we called at that time the countries occupied or controlled by us, and the reader has seen that the former Reich Foreign Minister Joachim von Ribbentrop and his aides were energetically concerned to defend their authorities. They did not allow any uncontrollable intervention of the SS Reichsführer and Chief of the German Police into the planned handling of the problem or into their documents.

I have demonstrated the dance of death of the false gods. Those false gods whom I also served. Apart from a very few exceptions, they danced in all the countries of Europe. It is not my intention at all to defend this hectic catastrophic politics even with one stroke of the pen; for here there is no defence, there is only a confession. Even though here too it was the effect of a cause. Nationalistic super-egoism of the victorious powers after the first world-war. That egoism that led to Versailles, that egoism that was born of economic envy and fear of competition. Without these facts National Socialism would not have been born. Yes, National Socialism, that greatest catastrophe, in truth, for all nations.

And I? From youth on I had an innate drive for intellectual freedom, freedom of personality, which I carried around with me in accordance with my education. The saying "where there are stronger people, they

False Gods

are never on the side of the weaker" was often repeated to me by my father. Through this same education I had to get used very early also to being part of an external order.

It was these acquired values which later drove me forcibly and pressingly to the side of those who, still as a minority scorned and mocked, developed their drive for freedom in the battle against the ignominious Versailles dictate and campaigned against it in speech and writing. In this way I was subjected to a ...[16] that dominated one's will, to which I was finally bound through the binding means of an oath, and I became the servant of the false gods decorated with the tinsel and epaulettes and the order and badge of honour on account of which I was considered worthy. It sounds like a joke that just those people who decorated me at that time in this form with these things and thereby obstructed and prevented my way *out of* the central service to these false gods themselves, could, in their witness statements in 1961, on account of their fear and worry, follow no other path than that of a mockery of me, their former subordinate, and that of falsehood, in the very stupid idea that they would be believed; in their vain hope that they could in this way save their body and also their soul. And again I must foolishly rebuke myself on account of my excessive folly and inadequacy that I once allowed myself to be clasped by the *idée fixe* of serving these false gods along with all their demi-gods dutifully and faithfully. Perhaps there is nobody alive whose eyes witnessed the intensified horror, the infernal apocalyptic storm to such an extent as it was my destiny to witness.

For the words of the false gods are smooth and their words tempting. And while I warn my sons of such and similar "gilded" preachers of obedience with their exhortative phrases of nationalism, holy war, and whatever other seductive words there may be, I warn – on the basis of my own experiences – all young people, those of today and those of tomorrow, of these dancing false gods.

Perhaps there is nobody alive whose eyes witnessed the intensified horror, the infernal apocalyptic storm to such an extent as it was my destiny to witness.

So the youth may believe me that my warning words are of considerable weight and arise from a concern ... again serve such a dance of death of false gods.

---

16   lacuna in text

Hungary

On 24 December 1944 at 3.30 in the afternoon I left Budapest according to the orders that I received. Through bone-hard frozen streets and fields past German and Hungarian units that were shot, flattened and hacked to pieces, to the Hungarian-Austrian border. After New Year's Day, I reported back to my superior in Berlin, the lieutenant general of the Police, Müller.

Berlin was at that time a witches' brew. Every day and night Anglo-American bombers dropped their blessings on the sea of houses. It smelt of decay and rot, burnt flesh, and putrescent corpses. One could no longer think of any orderly official work. I too with my men prepared for defence, for the enemy tanks pressed into Berlin. The field of ruins around my office offered a good building for tank traps and defence nests. I was incorporated in the "Wehrkanal" defence sector.

The weapons stockpiles were replenished, ammunition stocked up, and rations set up. One order followed another. Himmler had sought refuge in those times in the world of cares and fancies of "Old Fritz".[17] And if the death of the Tsarina rescued the latter from destruction, Himmler perhaps hoped for such a twist of fate corresponding to the contemporary circumstances. Through his middle-men he had extended his feelers with regard to possibilities of ending the war.

His lack of ideas resulted in the fact that he ordered me to transfer 100 or 200 prominent Jews from Theresienstadt to Tirol, which was part of the planned "Alpine fortress". He wanted to keep them there as hostages and needed these as security guarantees with regard to his planned negotiations with Eisenhower.

When I consider this, I must ask myself today if he really gave me this order or if I just imagined it. So childish and devoid of all reality, empty, without any plan, it even seems stupid to me that the Chief of the German Police, the senior commander of the SS, could have given me such an order; "as a safety guarantee for his negotiations with Eishenhower".

Of course, only Schellenberg, the then Information chief of the Reich Security Head Office, may have had *all* his "trump cards" in this connection. But I must have followed the order without any doubts since I travelled thereupon through Prague and Linz to Innsbruck.

---

17   Friedrich II (1712-86), King of Prussia, was nicknamed "Der alte Fritz".

False Gods

In Linz I told my father about the "Hubertusburg peace treaty"; he believed that Himmler had told me that but he did not think that Himmler meant the words literally.

In Bixlegg I experienced a rather nasty bomb attack. It was 17 April 1945 for, at the very moment that I was in the place, the bombs of the first wave of attacks swooshed down. The attack hit the heavy water works, as I was told later. The place was quite devastated. I had lain down at a garden gate and hidden my nose in the soil because the bomb splinters whizzing around forced one to such an action. After some waves had unleashed their load, it seemed too stupid to me and, since my car was, as if by a miracle, still in running condition, I drove away. When I came again to Linz on my return journey, this city also had, in the meantime, received an attack. In Prague State Secretary K.H. Frank told me – I did not meet any other commanding officer, they had left their offices and apparently got other positions – that I could no longer get to Berlin, as the "Russians" had broken through.

I learnt that Kaltenbrunner was in Altaussee and had received orders to have me report to him. The Himmler order could no longer be carried out. Once I arrived in the Altaussee region, I was to conduct a partisan battle in the mountains. Weapons and ammunition were available in sufficient quantities, but a few days later Kaltenbrunner gave me orders not to shoot at the English and Americans. I had already let go a large part of the men who hung around my neck as they were not suited for the mountains, but as there were only Americans all round I could not, according to my orders, do anything but dismantle the partisan commando unit.

I departed with my adjutant; we wanted to get to Hannover, but I was out of luck. I fell into American custody, from which I freed myself only at the beginning of January 1946; that is, I made an escape with the approval of my imprisoned officer comrades. It was an SS prisoners' camp in which some 300 members belonging to many divisions were held in custody. I was interrogated and recorded in the files there as SS lieutenant "Eckermann".

After my escape, I worked as a wood-cutter in the Miele forest in the Celle district near Hannover, and later as an independent wood-seller and, finally, as a poultry-breeder. Here I called myself Otto Henninger, born in Breslau.

Hungary

In May of 1950, however, I started to travel and thought of travelling through South America to East Asia. After many difficulties – I have described my postwar experiences in greater detail elsewhere – I reached Argentina, and there I remained. After a two-year long stay there, I had my family, who lived in Altaussee, come over.

I was in this beautiful country for ten years. Working most of the time as a technical employee, finally with "Mercedes-Benz Argentina". In between I managed a farm belonging to a distant relative of my wife, an agricultural business, as its administrator. I worked in North Argentina, in the isolation of the primeval Aconquija massif, a huge mountain range many of whose peaks towered up to five thousand five hundred metres. I had to conduct hydrological studies there and I had to work repeatedly at a height of five thousand two hundred metres. My family lived at one thousand six hundred metres in Rio Potreso, at the border of Tueuman and Catamarca.

Part III

My Capture and Trial

On 11 May 1960, I travelled, as I did daily, from my house to my daily work. Of course, I did not return home any more, for an Israeli commando unit apprehended me on my return from my office, made me incapable of resistance and took me to a country villa which lay on the northern route. From there, without me being able to offer any resistance, I was flown out of Argentina in a four-engine plane and brought to Israel. Naturally, it was not pleasant for me; something like this is no picnic for the person concerned, that is clear, but I was treated correctly and decently. In any case, I had expected the opposite.

On 11 April 1961, my trial began.

It is the middle of August and the oral pleadings of the prosecution and the defence are coming to an end. The indictment against me includes 15 charges.

I am accused on *four* counts of crime against the Jewish people, a crime according to section 1(a)1 of the Nazi and Nazi accomplices penal law 5710-1950 and paragraph 23 of the Criminal Code Ordinance 1936;

- *Seven* counts of crime against humanity, a crime according to section 1(a)(2) of the Nazi and Nazi accomplices penal law 5710-1950 and paragraph 23 of the Criminal Code Ordinance 1936;

- *One* count of war crimes, a crime according to section 1(a)(3) of the Nazi and Nazi accomplices penal law 5710-1950 and paragraph 23 of the Criminal Code Ordinance 1936; as well as

My Capture and Trial

Eichmann's trial judges Benjamin Halevy, Moshe Landau, and Yitzhak Raveh

- *Three* counts of belonging to an enemy organisation, a crime according to section 3(a) of the Nazi and Nazi accomplices penal law 5710-1950.

To the judge's question whether I confessed that I was guilty as charged, I declared about all 15 counts, "No, not as charged."

And the question of my defence counsel if it was true that I had signed a declaration that I would answer before an Israeli court I answered with a "Yes." The next question of my defence counsel, whether I had given this declaration voluntarily I answered with a "No."

The reading out of the indictment lasted up to 6 July, and the hearing of the witnesses for the prosecution, and also the defence.

From 7 to 24 July I was cross-examined by the state attorney general, Dr. Hausner. My defence counsel, Dr. Servatius, told me that it had been the longest cross-examination in the history of jurisprudence.

During the cross-examination I expressed my satisfaction that this had been my only opportunity up to then to publicly counter the untruths that had been unloaded on me in those long 1½ decades through the statements of witnesses in the post-war years before the military courts and through a certain type of journalism.

False Gods

I admitted everything that I had at that time believed I was obliged to do according to the orders issued to me, all other accusations I dismissed. To my defence counsel's question about my feeling of guilt, I stated the following in the court:

"That is today one of the most difficult questions, the question about the feeling of guilt, and I think that, in answering it, I must here make a distinction between a *legal* view and a view considering a *human* guilt.

First: In the case of the acts of which I was accused, it is a question of cooperation in the deportation. Since this was even a *political* ordinance I believe that a person can only feel guilt here in a *legal* sense who bears responsibility for the political decision, for:

Where there is *no responsibility*, there is also *no guilt,* and the result of my reflections is therefore that the responsibility is to be examined in a *legal sense*.

So long as human cohabitation in a political sense has not led to any global solution, orders and obedience are the basis of any state order. No state system can be built in an emergency on spies and traitors. For higher security, the state leadership makes use of a binding means, the *oath*. But the *responsibility*, conscience, must be felt by the *state leaders*. It was constantly preached to us, in speech and writing, *"Trust in the leadership"*. In the case of a good state leadership, the subordinate, the recipient of orders, is lucky. In the case of a bad one, bad luck. *I did not have* good luck. The then state leader gave the order for the annihilation of the Jews.

My cooperation in the deportation arose from the fact that the "senior judge" of the SS and Police jurisdiction under whom I stood, Himmler, gave the deportation orders to my judge, the Chief of Security and the SD. The latter commissioned my direct superior, the SS Gruppenführer and lieutenant general of the police, Müller, with its implementation. From him then I received the orders insofar as I was responsible for them according to the work assignment plan of my department. The penal code of the SS and Police jurisdiction indicates that disobedience would result in death;

Concerning the instructions about classified information, the orders to secrecy, the matters important to the state had their clauses relating to imprisonment and the death penalty. I had personally exhausted all legal possibilities of obtaining an order to another service; my transfer

My Capture and Trial

from the SD to the Secret State Police office in autumn 1939 indeed came about against my will, according to received orders. I had to obey. I bore a uniform. It was wartime.

Indeed, even when 1950 approached, and I toyed with the idea of travelling out of Germany overseas, I did this not because of a feeling of guilt in the legal sense but because of the political situation and for family reasons. My attitude is the same as that of millions of others who had to obey. The only difference is that I had a *much more difficult* commission that I had to carry out according to orders.

All those involved who maintain that one could have effortlessly, or without great danger, *withdrawn* from the fulfilment of an order give no details about their own case.

They say that there is always the possibility of shirking and of feigning some illness. A general has here many possibilities. A subordinate does not have such possibilities. For, if it is ascertained that the illness is an excuse, that will have its consequences. Besides, such an action is against the oath of allegiance. Himmler, for example, says in the Posen speech,[1] and *only* in relation to the *SS generals*, that they could be transferred if they feel they are not capable. But if the order is maintained it is to be followed. A man in a *smaller office cannot* escape. Especially not when he is the bearer of the highest secrets. He can shoot himself, this is true. Those who say that one could have *opposed* the implementation of the orders themselves declare for the most part that they did not know anything about any annihilation of men. They were thus not bearers of secrets. *The SS and Police jurisdiction* placed on the lower offices a very sharp standard and would have had to issue a corresponding judgement in the case of a blatant refusal of orders.

Guilt in the *ethical* sense, a confession of guilt before one's *inner "self"*, this is quite another thing. It lies in regions that are removed from the clauses of a legal ordinance. *Here each person has to contend with and judge himself. I so myself, and still do it.*

Finally, there remains for me the declaration and confession: "I regret and condemn the annihilation activity against the Jews ordered by the German state leadership of that time."

---

1   Himmler made two speeches, on 4 and 6 October 1943, before SS officers and party officials in the town-hall of Posen (Poznań) in Poland. The speech Eichmann refers to is the first.

False Gods

I was only an instrument in the hands of more powerful forces, and of an unfathomable fate." This declaration I offered at the end of the defence, before the cross-examination began. As I sit in judgement on myself many inner voices tell me many things: Could I have laid down my business? Could I have simply refused to carry on working? Would this have been mutiny? But what does mutiny against murder mean? Mutiny stands *against* the oath of allegiance and the oath of office! What is murder ordered by the state and what is an oath?

Does the maintenance of an oath belong to the realm of ethical values? To the subject of ethics? Does it belong at least to the *margins* of morality? What is morality? That morality is a part of ethical values I can no longer believe! Unless the oath were a necessity, an obligation to become, if necessary, the accomplice of the state.

So there seems to be something wrong here. For, most states, no matter what form of state, distort in their tyranny, manifested in war-time, the logical thought of minds. They demand from their recipients of orders, in the name of the sacredness of the oath, the recognition of heroic courage, readiness for self-sacrifice, obedience and discipline as ethical values. And on the basis of this demand they order murder, death and annihilation.

Moreover, the state in wartime encourages its recipients of orders through a series of decorations which they hold in readiness to the perpetration of the crimes ordered by it. It clouds the brains of its recipients of orders with crusade slogans, slogans of liberation, commitment and readiness to defend. On both sides, the instruments are blessed by appeal to stronger forces and powers, for each side commits its crimes for a so-called "just" matter. So there really seems to be something wrong here. So what is truth and what is justice?

Eugen Kogan writes in his book, *Der SS-Staat*, "But what would the twelve to fourteen million people driven out be able to narrate, who were "resettled" in the eastern European countries, often in the most barbaric manner, and driven to Germany in closed wagons, in trains of misery, as individuals, groups and herds! One may try to explain to a mother who has lost her children, to a man whose wife was violated, adolescents whose parents were beaten, to all those who experienced death and cruelty in their own bodies, that these – in a proclaimed better world – are indeed nothing but the sad consequences of mass injustice that had previously been committed, which affects the guilty and innocent without difference. And one may explain to a people that it is neither hypocrisy nor cowardice that emphasis was not placed in the declarations of Yalta and Potsdam that the "resettlements" should be conducted "in an orderly manner". Even the National Socialists did not drag millions through eastern Europe.

If I add also the names of Hiroshima, Nagasaki and Dresden, and mention the countries of Korea, Indo-China, Egypt and Algeria, then I have little more to say about that; at most just this: the decision to punish war criminals was announced at the Moscow foreign ministers' conference on 20 October 1943.

On the side of the Allies, however, not a single individual was brought to trial and punished for the orders they carried out. Double standards! Double justice! Nationalistic egoism everywhere, on both sides.

On Knowledge and Will

If a man wishes for inner peace and a certain internal balance, he will – and I speak from wide experience – begin to put the internal disorder into order, or at least try to do so.

For example, a sheet of paper, with iron filings strewn on it. These small pieces of iron lie in a scattered confusion in every direction. This is how it looks to me when I lack inner peace, when I strive in vain to bring order into the matters of my inner life. But if I move a magnet under this sheet of paper, then this confusion of iron filings orders itself immediately within the range of the magnetic field into an – I might say almost militarily ordered – pattern.

But what is the use of all desire for order if my knowledge cannot be translated into action, if I cannot make use of this magnet, when I myself am only such an iron filing that is ordered within this magnetic field. If stronger forces prevent me from acting according to my will and, moreover, according to orders issued by a state, my activity has to stand in opposition to my inner will, to a will that, according to the perception of my feelings, must arise from the realm of ethical values, I will, as an individual, be able to record inner peace and inner balance for me only from the egoism that is instinctively given to me.

I am neither a philosopher nor a physicist. I occupied myself, for love of the subject, in the manner of interested lay people, from time to time with the former as well as with the latter subject. It gave me pleasure and it was, at the same time, instructive. Just as the stamp-collector goes through his collection from time to time I gladly bought now and then a specially recommended work that dealt with these subjects. I could revel in it like an esoteric bibliomaniac. It was the same for me as Sunday morning service for pious church-goers, a compulsive thirst for inquiry into the *final* truth, for real things, the higher meaning of life. Knowing well that I could only penetrate to a very modest extent, but every little item of new knowledge satisfied me most deeply. This curious wish to know adhered to me many decades. Of course my interest in these two subjects occurred only in later years and was also interrupted by long pauses, whether through the bustling fast pace of daily life which robbed me of all leisure or through the temporary lack of enthusiasm caused by bodily exhaustion and fatigue, the last especially during my Argentinian summer.

Already my religion teacher in Linz an der Donau laid the foundations for my temporary preference for Kant. The evangelical priest – born an East Prussian – was a specialist in matters relating to the Königsberger and it is surprising that he succeeded in awakening in our youthful brains such a sympathetic interest in a subject that often bores even adults. However, to a young boy he brought it to life with many examples from daily life.

A friend of my youth, loved at that time this "philosophy of technology". My friend must have perceived the aesthetics and ethics of the creative will from his numerous sketches of bridge constructions, for he brought forth ever new designs and ideas and we were both delighted by the beauty of the lines. We both attended at that time a technical high school. He then transferred to a philosophical class. I was very glad to receive greetings sent from him through my defence lawyer in prison in Israel, and I am grateful for his kind thoughtfulness and know that I have received from him an answer to my work. Whether it is positive or negative I thank him for it equally. Yes, my dear Brother Bernadus, you can see how things happen to a man. We could not have dreamt of such a thing when we were together the last time at the Hinsdorf abbey and a long time before in the Traun castle or in the high school in Goethestraße in Linz.

The war had broken out. I bought the *Critique of Pure Reason* in the pocket edition, for I could thus hide this "Critique" in my uniform jacket. But I cannot say that I fully understood Kant at that time even if I had been older, for my understanding was not adequate for it yet. I strove to absorb that into myself which I thought I could recognise

On Knowledge and Will

in him and to live my life according to it. With philosophy it was, and is, for me as with a ring on which many keys hang; and I always tried, and try, to find the correct key for locked doors. Sometimes a key worked immediately, at other times I had to search for long. At times I must refine a little more out of it with, or even without, dexterity.

It is said that, in spite of efforts lasting thousands of years, philosophy has not succeeded in discovering a universally recognised line of thought which might unite all philosophising minds. For, up to now, there have been "ifs" and "buts" to every insight. Some expressed their doubts gently and full of woe, other scholars, like Schopenhauer for example, criticised vehemently. But such talk cannot draw the philosopher out of his equanimity. For, he argues, what was generally recognised already does not have anything in common with real philosophy since the latter is a universal scientific insight and firmly valid. Of course, I often thought, My God, how fine it must be to be able to give *true knowledge* to the one searching for ultimately valid things. But it is nothing but at most a belief in a supposed knowledge according to the imagination of the individual. The one who can develop for himself a world-view, who works it out and derives his inner peace from this representation and considers this in itself as valid for the moment is to be called a fortunate person.

The war, with its atrocities and the post-war events; especially, in those days, the efforts in the battle for existence abroad, less the physical stresses from the climate and all the unfamiliarities - this is true of thousands of people – than, rather, the psychological stress conditioned by personal anonymity, and finally the abduction from Argentina, and my gargantuan trial following it.

I have often asked myself how I could have survived all this without killing myself in order to cover everything with the gracefully covering shroud of a voluntary and desired ending of one's life. But thereby I would have confessed to guilt, which I did not, and do not have.

The more I escaped into philosophy so much more did my curiosity, my thirst for knowledge exceed the distress of the moment that held me in its grasp; I steadily obtained a distance from the sufferings of daily life and my personal worries seemed to be of no importance. I recognised that there was no end for me and, as little, a Nothing. Time will lose itself in space in the most distant finitudes; I know that for me new "times" are ready for me again. And then I perceive how the restricted narrowness of the moment leaves me. The sorrow of the day

False Gods

flees; only I remain surrounded by the rays of the vivifying effulgence of suns that protect me forever.

I was brought up, from childhood, with a Protestant education, and when I had been in the SS, indeed almost three years in the Security Head Office, I still adhered with conservative tenacity to the faith of my fathers. Only in 1937 did I announce freely and of my own accord, at some legal office in Berlin-Neuköln, my departure from the Evangelical religious community. There were no political considerations; quite simply I could personally no longer consider the contents of the Bible through faith as *that* which it claimed to be able to communicate, namely the final truth of ultimate matters.

A raging and vengeful god had become unimaginable to me; such a thing seemed to me to be too human, not at all divine. The more that I inquired into things at that time the looser was the structure that I had up to then considered as a solid basis. I thought I perceived that that which I had up to then believed in was the result of polemical dogmatic and bigoted Church Fathers of the first centuries A.D., who merely philosophised about the dogma of the Trinity, or the conflict between the doctrines of the divine or human nature of Christ, and many other such things.

Even the Luther-Melanchthon[2] reform of this philosophical system was, to a large extent, based on the intellectual heritage of the classical philosophy of ancient Greece, and also mixed with other religious philosophies. And after even the Evangelical Church could not convey any *knowledge* but announced beatification through *faith,* I thought it was safer and simpler if in future I got together alone with the Lord God without making use of the mediation of Evangelical priests, especially since *they* too were subject to human weaknesses, exactly as Protestantism itself is a human creation.

Therein nothing has changed in me up to today and nothing *will*. Besides, the Luther-Melanchthon doctrine has brought enough calamity on humanity, when I consider, for example, the history of the Thirty Years' War?

When during my trial in Jerusalem I was sworn in – as a witness on

---

2 Philipp Melanchthon (né Schwartzerdt) (1497-1560) was a great-nephew of Johann Reuchlin (see above p. n) who collaborated with Martin Luther in the establishment of Lutheran Protestantism.

On Knowledge and Will

my own behalf –, I had to swear the oath, according to the normal custom, with my hand on the Bible. According to my convictions I declared that I would not swear on the Bible but on God, for I believe in God. This is right, for I do. But I cannot personify Him.

I believe in a supreme and all-powerful creative force, the ruler of all that was, is and will be. In *the* God! and I, man, and compared to his Will and his Tolerance, simply an element that flows along in the flow of Becoming, in life.

I said that I approached the SS voluntarily. This is correct, and I have already mentioned the reasons that impelled me. What an abundance of unimaginable battles did I have to face. I was like a swimmer who has fallen into a body of water full of seaweed and vines, trying to free themselves from all this confusion in order to swim. The body of water was – for the sake of comparison – the SS; the confusion into which I entered was that complex which the "world-view" of that time formed. Because the intellectual borders of this world-view coincided, I might say, with the borders and interests of the Reich, one should better call this more appropriately and accurately "the Reich world-view".

If I had, at that time, followed the advice of my religion teacher and had further pondered Kantian insights for the purpose of achieving a free course of thoughts, who knows what effects the condition of my inner conflicts would have had. I know that it is idle to think about "ifs" and "buts", for the fact is that I did not do it. For a while I still tried to accommodate the Kantian demands to my National Socialist convictions of that time and I must say that it went quite well for a while. Of course, only within the modest scope of the intellectual capacity of my brain. But then the moment arrived when I had to make a decision and every effort at accommodation was in vain, that moment when even the little sophistry which I often made use did not help me.

It was the time when my boss ordered me to go as a reporter to the different places of the killings. But I allowed myself to lack, I must say this, in the subsequent period of time, that ethics of convictions which one might reasonably expect of a man who undertook such thought processes. But it is always easy to speak and to argue, since there were, on the other hand, again external bonds to which I had to subject myself. For, apart from the oath which I strove to fulfil faithfully, my superiors had obligated me, after my transfer in late autumn 1939 from the army records office, to war service at the Secret

False Gods

State Police. I had to bow to such an obligation for such was at that time – as now in similar cases – a prevailing law from which one could not withdraw legally. But how did the body of water with seaweeds and vines look, that complex of my views at that time with which I had to inwardly battle? A shot of nationalistic egoism mixed with self-interest. In addition, there was some Romantic idealism and even a bit of reasonable, sober objectivity was not occasionally lacking for the purpose of seeing things objectively. Moreover, it soon developed into a collective thought, and individualistic tendencies that were present earlier were gradually sacrificed to this following the sworn obedience. On occasion I saw the irrationality of the state leadership because it propagated its special interests and, because I no longer progressed with my idealism, I took refuge in a materialistic Naturalism. My basic disposition however became, in spite of everything, increasingly more pessimistic. Of course, my personal views on life diverged from a part of the official "world-view" that was preached, but gradually I absorbed into myself, temporarily, everything that was presented. To be sure, I could almost never muster an unconditional inner receptivity as a fanatic will for *all* National Socialist goals, for that there were too many doubts in my heart.

I could no longer follow in all their consequences my clear inner principles after my withdrawal from the Church. I worked in myself and on myself like the "Schopenhauerian mountain climber" who figures out an unsafe mountain path without a guide but receives in return a feeling of freedom. And it is certain that in normal times I would have succeeded in obtaining the balanced inner peace and security that I always strove for. I had been placed in extraordinary times in extraordinary circumstances for which what was valid and practised up to then was no longer valid.

My personal work on myself was transposed and pressed by totalitarian state measures of a sort that I rejected and to which I myself was subjected against my will. So there was a split between my inner self - with only a small part of which I served my leadership - and my external self, which I devoted almost entirely to my leadership, for it was war-time. I practised a sort of willed and conscious schizophrenia.

This divided condition was caused by inability to understand the manner of treatment of blameless civilians by the then German state leadership, their arrogance with regard to civilians of foreign citizenship especially, and then the inability to go along any more with the mass murder of Jews ordered by the state. Since I was not

On Knowledge and Will

directly involved in it and my activity in conducting the deportation neither corresponded to my will nor could be stopped by me and I could not even so much as influence such a thing, my limitations did not in the main lie within my *inner* self.

My outer self, which was bound anyway, obeyed the state leadership faithful to my oath, for Germany's enemies had – so it was preached to us and we saw it too – set as its goal the destruction of my fatherland. And following the conception I had at that time of the oath of allegiance and oath of office, there was for me only the *legal* way as far as a change of my war service assignment was concerned. For the will to destroy of our enemies of that time invoked, in spite of the follies of one's own state leadership, my patriotic conscience of that time.

The mistake, apart from principles, was that the leadership of that time placed me in a position that I was quite unsuited for, and which I could not change of my own accord except through the path of desertion. But I rejected that way. All this created in me an inner turmoil, that I had developed for myself precisely the opposite of that which I thought was equivalent to, or even *better* than, the lost faith of my youth. This I had from 1937 to the end of 1939. But from this time on the curve of my inner peace sank sharply downwards. And if I had at that time still been within a church community, even this would not have been able to change my internal condition or my external obligation. It was the time after I was transferred to the Secret State Police Office.

I did not even have to combat those inhibiting personality blocks like envy, greed, cruelty, hatred or revenge. To that I was immune, thanks to the education of my youth and the fact that I never *fully* gave up working on myself. For that reason I now saw death in its frightful forms in all corners and ends. The only insight that I found confirmed at every turn at that time was that the world in which I had to live as a manifest being had to be not at all the best but the worst that one could imagine.

I considered the human condition to be meaningless for, however hard I researched, I could not recognise any higher meaning in the workings of Nature both on the friendly and on the enemy side; indeed, could not even apprehend any common incidental design. And I silently envied the wearer of the yellow Buddhist clothes for he sought to derive at least for himself the best from his pessimistic attitude to "the things of the world" and did that apparently successfully – unlike me.

False Gods

And when I considered everything rightly, what a sunny gay nature, carefree, optimistic, without any conflicts, I had had just some years before …

My harmonious balance gave way increasingly to the disharmony of an inner cramp and there remained to me as the only consolation the fact that other worlds standing before me could not in any way be worse than those that I had now to endure as a man, a world of forced complexes. But according to any providence – so I thought – since higher workings of nature could not get lost in negativity – coming worlds of life had, as far as I knew, necessarily to be better; for of all organic life none is known to me that deliberately posits the bad – apart from man.

Of course, nobody could prove this – about good and bad worlds – but it was still consoling. (And to my pessimism was added during the war an appropriate shot of fatalism, which I have not cast off from me up to today.) This produced for me anyway a glimmer of hope. And I was so bound by such thoughts that, for example, during the bomb attacks, I went to the shelter that we were ordered to only when I thought I could, for reasons of discipline, not get away from them.

My egoism and my self-interest belonged contextually and consciously for most part to my people and my fatherland. It were better called national egoism.

The initial spark was called "Versailles", that cannot be changed. This engine once set in motion was further propelled in my environment. My natural attitude to National Socialism, my people and the state was developed from the situation which surrounded me. The further development of the relationship of my "self" to the "Reich" occurred from now within that realm in which the idea of national self preservation gradually played the dominant role and culminated in the propagated thesis: "Justice is that which benefits the nation".

Self-interest drives man as one of the chief instincts to which he is subjected from the beginning. Ever since those distant times when as a lone-wolf or in hordes he had to conduct a personal battle and war against everything just to maintain his life. Later, much later, men then united, partly under pressure, partly without it, into a state. They obeyed the tribal or state leader; their existence was clearly better guaranteed in this collective than they could ever have guaranteed it earlier. What the leader of their community considered right was

On Knowledge and Will

justifiably good; everything else was bad. Through the different forms of human communal life this attitude has not essentially changed up to today.

The prophecies of the downfall of one's own people if one did not fulfil one's duty which were spread by the state leadership through propaganda were believed in, even I believed them. And they were moreover not so incorrect.

Obviously, I also wished for the removal of the injustice of Versailles; I wanted the removal of the many catastrophic consequences of this dictate. I was also one of those who hoped and longed for a great and free and strong Reich. For this reason I had abandoned at that time all my life's comforts, which I could have clung to. And I thought that a strong Reich with a unified people was in itself the guarantee that to this people and Reich something other than "Versailles" would be shown.

Through the disregard of everything non-National Socialist, through the trampling upon every other will by the impatience factor of the National Socialist Reich government, a fact that is as regrettable as it is painful, there necessarily arose in the subsequent period the complications and catastrophes whose sadness is, in its scope, perhaps unique in history up to now. I think that there were only few who had thought that the words and threats of the speakers of the party's struggle time would become reality after the seizure of power. Everybody rather thought that the development promised after the revolution by the leadership was to be taken at face value. And that then a peaceful federal governance within the circle of the European family of peoples would begin after the insight of the other side led to concessions to the benefit of Germany wherewith then all hovering problems would in the course of negotiations find a settlement through administrative channels.

A "dancing congress" would arise again. But, unfortunately, irrational intolerance manifested itself here, combined with power hungry ambition on the part of the leadership of the Reich. This is a fact that cannot be denied. Their procedure was comparable to the powerful rulers of nations of ancient and rather extraordinary times. But they did not consider adequately the bonds and relationships that had in the meantime become extraordinarily intricately ramified and on which they were dependent and that here every disturbance of this sensitive machinery *had to* lead to conflicts. Rather, they were demoniacally

False Gods

possessed by their power and did not consider the especially emotional thought of our age. They remained without advancing, indeed they pressed themselves back into the absolutist thought of a "master morality".

Considered in retrospect they were gamblers who, without any forced necessity, thoughtlessly threw with their dice the happiness and freedom of nations. I say considered in retrospect, for my personal judgement at that time was, as a result of the subordinate position which I occupied in the hierarchy, a very limited one.

Naturally, I had at my disposal more information material than the average colleagues of that time, but I too had no connection to higher places. My personal opinion was not of interest and remained so until May 1945.

I was not allowed to become an unconditional yea-sayer to *all* the measures of the former Reich government on account of the cherished remnants of the Romantic Idealism that had been saved in spite of everything. Before I became acquainted with National Socialism, this was my preoccupying penchant; indeed, even more, it gave me a feeling that was in a position to conjure up in me joyful ideas of happiness. It had nothing to do with the Romanticism of youthful fraternities. I would rather characterise it as a *primitive* Romantic idealism; a condition in which I could freely devote myself to natural reverie without limits and restraints and obtained in it a wonderful feeling of inner peace. And I am not ashamed if I distort words by saying that I had the Romantic idealism of a primitive. For I was at that time, in any case, more unspoiled and happier in that than later, when I found myself in the quagmire of inner bonds and had to grapple with half a dozen or more different views.

I was then able to seek refuge in this world of beautiful experience when I thought I was no longer able to figure things out from end to end and could no longer manage things. It was a sort of medicine cupboard that I maintained. And an Adalbert Stifter and a Peter Rosseger[3] offered me pleasure. Rosegger's exciting description of Good Friday on the mountains lay on the desk of my private room during all my years in Berlin: "When I was still a boy of the woods". I read it over and over again. A completely unassuming little story

---

3   Peter Rosegger (1843-1918) was an Austrian poet and novelist whose works depict the Alpine life and landscape of Styria.

On Knowledge and Will

but if somebody should dally with negative thoughts or thoughts of ambition or power then he should read this narrative with care and the peace of a woodsman. The virgin beauty of the Bohemian woods, the soothing silence of solitude in the world of mountains and the thoughts and fancies that I interpolated and contemplated here, on the changes of life in the course of time and my own relation to these changes, allowed me to forget all doctrines and present events that annoyed me through an immersion in this world.

Even today, in prison in Israel, I resort once again to this tested method, for being imprisoned and life in imprisonment bring with them such an abundance of inconveniences that I was often pessimistic at the break of a new day which forced me to go through life anew. There is no doubt that death is better than imprisonment, but a man does well not to avoid his fate. And anyway the forces of these glorious imaginary worlds were always strong enough to constantly "lead me to other thoughts". I do not wish to talk now about my present feelings but try to transpose myself back into time past.

That I needed such "flights" for an inner pacification, for an inner balance, was certainly a sign that something was not right here. This is certain. But I could not change anything about it, for I was neither the cause nor the effect; I had become the plaything of circumstances. I often had to obey against my desires, against my will.

Most of the recipients of orders of that time said to themselves – when it once again went against the grain - "Oh well, the Devil has a devilish child; I have to plod along with my service, and after me the flood." I shall be open and admit that I too more than once fortified myself with this remedy which was supposed to bring pacification. Only it was without any inner effect at all.

So I rather lost myself in my observations, which however were becoming increasingly more confused. Of course, the standpoint of the realist had something to it, for he accepted things as they offered themselves to him. But I did not have the robustness of feeling that would have been necessary for that. Naturally, I could also step out of my quixotic pastimes into reality, I could also abandon my thousands of doubts and then doubtless achieve much progress. For instance, there were no more unemployed at that time. Assets were developed in the field of construction and in the field of production, which was once again boosted. Whether the manner of the work and the vehemence with which it was impelled forward – considering the

False Gods

increase of mistrust, the envy and greed of foreign countries – was dictated by reason, this I could not at that time judge for I did not even think of it. Today I must justifiably doubt it. Even if it was, and would have remained, really an internal German matter, had not our then leadership in its foolishness represented its "defiance" in such a sabre-rattling manner, an enterprise that had to make our neighbours suspicious. The handling of the Jewish question by the then German government did even more to strengthen the isolation and boycott of Germany.

The initial successes seduced the elite of the Reich to callous and thoughtless activity presented in the form of ever new demands. And war had to finally break out in Danzig, and this city was to become the fate of Germany and its people. But not only the political leadership of that time was to blame for the entire disastrous development process – even though it bore the decisive responsibility, but also the German high finance of that time. The leadership stoked and drove exactly like international high finance, this is beyond doubt.

Now, considering how things were at that time, there were many things to which one could maintain a positive attitude; but at least as many things happened in which for a man like me only the immersion into other worlds made an escape from daily life possible. This eternal searching and not finding lacerated me more than I could hope for alleviation from it. And the conclusion was: since I could *not* decide, then better to fully "immerse" oneself in collective thought, in thinking with the crowd. The crowd was for me at that time the SS. It was, in addition, the NSDAP and, if one wishes to continue, the majority of the German people, which was also essentially not asked and did not give orders and could not stop anything.

Here in the collective was the opportunity to disappear as an individual and to feel ideologically one with mass thought. I was not uncomfortable with this thought since I anyway did not at any point in my life want to take up more responsibility than I thought I had to for the existence of my family. Beyond that not an iota more.

I was not endowed with any ambition or hunger for power. It is possible that I got along well for the most part with all colleagues, comrades and superiors since I was not at any time an obstacle to their personal ambitions. It is possible that, for this reason, I remained stuck as a lieutenant-colonel for four years while colleagues with whom I was of equal rank for a long time were in the meantime promoted to generals.

On Knowledge and Will

It is possible that, for this reason too, I got along well with the Jewish functionaries and they with me. I say "it is possible", because I never claim to know anything.

To be sure, the collective was nothing but a militarily organised instrument; the strictest order and system seems to appertain to every collective more or less. Uncritical blind obedience, discipline and readiness to sacrifice. In material terms the SS promised in exchange a safe existence in peace, and in war very possible death. If one has resigned oneself to collective thought, it is then a relatively comfortable life; I mean now less from the standpoint of physical life; rather, I have in mind the inner life.

Of course, such a thought demands finally a certain willingness to be superficial. Some people have from the start a propensity for it, in others it will be instilled without their being fully conscious of it, and the third group – I would like to express it figuratively – seeks refuge in this readiness because it – thinking in an egoistic manner – thinks that in this way it can be free of all inner personal problems with all the wearying doubts that never allow it to find peace. The worldly collective of the SS sort demanded the performance of the work that had been ordered and the affirmation of the "world-view of National Socialism". But since the latter was still something half-baked, something cobbled together from all possible ideas and imaginations there was really also no intellectual or "world-view" overview that could have determined or promoted any deeper developments of this confession, that could have conveyed intellectual information according to definite plans in a guiding and directing manner. Of course, there were the Ordensburgen,[4] and also the SS-Junkerschulen.[5] But, for one thing, these institutions were temporary and committed to purely warlike matters and, for another, they were things for the younger generation. Nobody worried about the problems of the "old". Finally nobody also needed to worry about them, since neither I nor other people asked for nursing aid. But, to the extent that the state leadership deviated from the traditional legal norms – just for the duration of the war, as they said – and had subsequently had even an authorisation from the

---

[4] Ordensburgen were originally mediaeval fortresses built by the Livonian Brothers of the Sword and the Teutonic Knights to protect their conquests from the Livonian and Prussian natives. During the Third Reich the term was used for the elite training schools for National Socialist leaders.

[5] SS Junker schools were military training schools for the Waffen-SS during the second World War.

parliament given to them for this, the person who otherwise did not require any nursing aid could have a desire for a regulating statement especially when he was assigned against his will to authorities who had to direct such deviations from legal norms into executive channels.

The cardinal demand was a unique one and it was: to obey. Every single person had, in war times, to obey in some way, no matter in what position he was; this is true everywhere.

A freeing from this collective, rather like - in the past - from the Church membership, did not exist anymore now. In any case, I would not have done such a thing so long as enemies threatened the fatherland through war. The only thing that I did was my efforts to be transferred to another office of the collective. Perhaps to the front or at least to the general police administration. It was of course a collective built on the "Führer principle". But the compelling stubborn necessity to obey in *all* things, and the waiting for the orders and regulations of any time, removed all personality values or caused it - as a result of pressure or as a matter of habit, under the influence of the law of inertia - to be repressed.

So it really was in my case, for, since I was now *anyway* no longer master of my own will, this meant for me the only possibility of escape, of avoiding the anyway fruitless attempt at a solution of problems and complexes. I learnt from experience that when one must, bound by fate, live in a horrible present situation and cannot be a regulator but is someone regulated, the incorporation in a collective is increasingly less easy to bear, since the individual can no longer manage "himself and his difficulties". Of course, individual thought suffers a setback in favour of group consciousness, but the latter is, in times of war, rather an advantage for the sensitive person, for disregard of thought and division of responsibility offers him a certain protection from the pressure of the conscience.

The collectively organised consciousness occupied with commands and orders of course loses in personality values, but the individual anyway renounces this often very gladly, for the individual can survive at all only with a cessation of all the spiritually burdening points. Unless it is a question of men to whom a deviation from the legal norms would signify a higher meaning, or any meaning at all, or some obligation. But I think that such people are only in a disappearing minority.

On Knowledge and Will

I still found the imprisonment in a collective in view of the circumstances and conditions to be the only mollification and therefore accepted all the collectively conditioned disadvantages. It was for me as for a contemporary person living in a technical collective whose electric lights suddenly go out. Such a person imprisoned in a group then merely determines if they went out only in his place or if he can determine the same also in the neighbouring house. If he is not the only victim of the blackout, then he will declare, grumbling and complaining, that these eternal disruptions are an absolute scandal but he will finally resign himself to his fate with the thought that he is powerless and as an individual cannot do anything about it with any success. He will ask himself why this is necessary or how it could happen; indeed he will under circumstances make plans, how such an unpleasantness can be stopped in future, he will point to the damage that arises through such measures, and whatever else of the kind. One has observed the result of such efforts more than once at one's own electricity station. Now, to this one may reply: fine, then I shall leave this technical collective, buy a petroleum lamp and be free. To be sure, I shall be a somewhat poor man, but nevertheless independent.

Yes, in normal times this is all right. But in war times there is neither petrol nor candles in the cities, and the possible intention of moving to the country to be able to live more freely is aborted through a more or less tight restriction of freedom of movement for everybody for the duration of the war. Now there were also a few who shut up shop and did not cooperate at all; they set themselves against the system. The consequences are of course well known; the result as well. During my SD Head Office time in 1938, I got hold of a lot of Masonic literature on Giordano Bruno, the former Dominican monk who had to burn at the stake for heresy. His pantheistic doctrine contradicted the principles of the Church of that time.

Apart from the fact that I was no "Giordano Bruno", a possible *public* opposition on my part – perhaps against the manner of solving the Jewish question – would have produced the same result insofar as I would have been made to disappear and made no longer vulnerable; another person would have been moved into my place.

It is naturally easy to say today, "Man is always master of his will", "the preservation of one's personality values", "the ethics of one's convictions" and other things like that. The idea of the freedom of the individual also hovered before me; I also once stood against all intellectual slavery. I could for a time intoxicate myself with dreams of desire and daydreams. But then I had to understand and was able to say: let anybody try it in reality. In the middle of a murderous war, under a totalitarian state leadership, as a recipient of orders.

What a difference there is here between theory and practice. The desire of the will of the individual, that is, the realisation of the moral law innate in him, comes up against an impregnable wall in his attempt at a practical application that follows from his understanding. For, through a transformation of values by the state leadership, the reverse result has been raised to a new "moral commandment". But what is a moral commandment when it can be made something changeable by the state leadership and is subjected to the political wishes of the state leadership instead of it being the opposite, with the leadership of the state subjecting itself to the moral commandment? So what is justice?

The state leadership forces its executive, the individual person to oppress. And what essential protection does the recipient of orders have if he could act according to his conscience at all? And more importantly, what practical success do the wishes of the individual recipient or orders have if he cannot act according to his conscience, because the state leadership requires readiness. What is the use of mere understanding and will alone when action has no effect? No one can say that such things happen only in totalitarian states. Even the western hemisphere provided, and provides, enough examples.

The person who is not bound to any faith hardly derives from any other fields more satisfying material *against* arbitrariness, irrationality, and efforts at deviation from the legal norms than from the field of material Naturalism, if he observes things from a higher point of view.

Of Blood and Soil

The idea of blood and soil, the continuation of life in the blood of one's progeny, the feeling of being secure in traditions are not bad ideas so long as they are not accompanied by ideas of arrogance. But nevertheless they too cannot satisfy the mind that wishes to know more, that drives forward in its inquiries; I already said once, they are values that were valid within the limits of the borders of the Reich. Questions about reason and life in the sense of an all-ordering Nature and therewith those regarding the higher sense of all organic life do not find any answer in them. Except with sophistry; with that I can indeed answer a lot of things; but then it often comes very close even to a fallacy, if it

Of Blood and Soil

is not that itself. One who considers material Naturalism even briefly and fleetingly must, for example, characterise all racial prejudices and racial discrimination as petty human folly. I was asked once during my trial if I had been an anti-Semite. I could answer this question freely and forthwith with a "no" and bring forward proofs of that. If I had been that, then I would also certainly have had my "reasons", and then I would also have explained them. Naturally I wanted – and I said this too – a solution of the question between a host people and a guest people now that the complications had been brought, through a specific propaganda on the part of the host people, to a point where they, allegedly, could no longer be solved in a bloodless and silent way, and because this matter was finally raised to an irrevocable dogma. For one thing, I had imagined a political solution and, secondly, I had no feelings of racial prejudice. A power created the universe and the power manifested itself in the universe; and in history man neither possesses a preferred status nor is he the "image of God", he cannot be that, for he lacks all-powerfulness for that.

Nature is Being and man is a small particle in it. Hardly was he created than he presumed to work in a corrective manner. No, this went against my convictions. If people at that time expressed such ways of thought as those concerning the "laws for the protection of blood", in combination with materialistic-naturalistic considerations, then I could perceive that it was a deviation into transcendental realms and an abandonment of the direction that focussed on the state and the present. Naturally I too stood on the basis of that which affirmed the present and I could also speak, in many matters, of an affirmation of the state, just for reasons of the self-preservation of my people. But the killing of civilians I could not, in spite of all my National Socialist loyalties, accommodate in any form as a regulation.

Immature minds were at work in imposing the appearance of eternal values on a heap of concepts and ideas. But even after a war that may have been won, these postulates mixed together would have needed a renaissance of a comprehensive sort and only through the development of fully newer and inwardly also more satisfying goals would one have been able at all to speak of some further continuation of this movement. Though, on the other hand, I am convinced that the state leadership of that time would even have succeeded in compensating for civilian murder and the moral pressure on a person of that time by means of appropriate psychological influence as long as the individual had not yet attained that age of clear vision which protects him from propagandistic obfuscation.

False Gods

The masses would in any case succumb to it. This has indeed been practised and experienced in other places. Such communal-systems are to be rejected as contrary to nature. And one cannot say that National Socialism represents a unique case. There are many examples. Indeed I would like to maintain that the few cases in history where this cannot be demonstrated in the different communal systems are those where the appropriate opportunities for this were lacking The battle of all against all is one of the primitive human instincts and it will last so long as we are not all "thrown into the same pot".

The only thing that I wonder about is that even Nobel prize winners and the other elite of the sciences, apart from a few exceptions, believed and believe in this really outdated system, and followed and still follow it. To be sure, it is hard when one considers for a moment that even Plato did not succeed in obtaining the tyrant Dionysius for the realisation of his ideas of the reform of state leadership. And even Plato had to recognise that state leadership is more powerful than even the wise man and that it can also paralyse his desire to act in an ethical manner.

No, it is true; the individual can only in the rarest of cases change a situation which even the will of the masses has in good faith brought about. When one was oneself only a small part of the masses and life itself contributed to the fact that such a situation could arise which one was able later to recognise as fateful, then such a person rightly criticises himself. And it is also useless, for what has happened cannot be undone, and we were not able to imagine the goal. And if someone – on whom functions were imposed under the dictatorship, within the scope of the collective, that he had to carry out or exercise – is suddenly, *after* the collapse of the collective security, alone and forced to turn to himself, then there enters an equally sudden void.

A situation in which he is even less capable of logical thought or action and in which, after overcoming the first shock, overcoming that situation in which he finds himself beneath the limits of a will to live, he attributes all evil and all the causes that led to this evil - through comparative considerations, mixed also with false conclusions and other sophistries in his total one-sidedness - at first to *the enemies* and makes them *alone* responsible for the deprivation of existence-guaranteeing security among his own people and quite simply for *everything* negative that they forced his government to undertake.

Of Blood and Soil

Only much later, through sober consideration, does he recognise that the enemy side cannot simply be made responsible for everything negative, and slowly he begins to follow a rather more objective view of things and, under the pressure of his inner questioning about alleged justice and injustice, admits outwardly, in relation to these considerations, *that* which he had already felt in an emotional or intuitive way during the period of power of his own leaders.

But only at the very end does he concern himself with the attitude of his *own* personality. But here for him the differentiation of the values regarding what was supposedly just and what unjust is still more difficult as the points of departure of his observations are influenced by a great number of factors which occupied him, his conscience, to a certain degree but only now do so fully. They range from the real or supposed obligation to which he was subjected up to the field of psychology itself. Especially when it is a question of a collective matter of a political nature. The question of freedom of will and action is here *not just* a mountain behind which he can hide. It is also a very real and decisive fact.

One thing is true: it can be supposed that, compared to the masses of all those involved, only in rare cases did a violation of the moral commandment that may have occurred in wartime arise directly through the initiative of an individual receiving orders. It was the state leadership itself that ordered such things; the leader of the state, one's chief of the Police, one's immediate superior judge. These gave the orders. I am today, still of the view that guilt in a legal sense does not pertain to me in any way, and I say this without *any* sophistry!

I was not one of those who, after the lost war, threw away everything overnight and opportunistically converted loudly to the democratic re-education and denazification and represented themselves as people who had been seduced because they had lacked liberty. I consider even today the form in which such a thing was carried out as a mischief which could not have been created by sly people. Quite apart from the fact that the conduct of certain powers after 1945 was able to allow the opinion to arise that the Devil had been driven out with Beelzebub.

An escape into philosophy alone would not have satisfied me completely, I also required a good shot at facts that were suited to support the edifice of my ideas which I had to now construct for myself anew. At first it was a weak structure which, on account of nationalistic impulses, repeatedly collapsed or threatened to collapse.

False Gods

Mostly it was procedures of a political sort, especially in the years of the "re-education" of our people, that robbed me of every desire to continue to work and allowed me to backslide. But then there came years of certain peace and I found no great stumbling blocks; it was the years of the first successful attempts to walk in space, it was the years in which even rockets had other targets than densely populated cities of the earth's population.

To the extent that I occupied myself with my ideas increasingly more intensively my planned structure obtained, without it becoming fully conscious to me, at least a foundation which satisfied my demands, which I did not in any way set very high. I only needed to consolidate it now and to build my new structure upon it.

If a man wishes to build a house for himself, he must first of all scrape up whatever money and assets he has to buy the building ground and construction material for it; for only very few people would consider such expenses as incidental expenses which they could defray without effort.

For a small man a modest house is sufficient, for his means are limited. He can indeed later, in the course of time, build up better. He can enlarge it with an annex or an addition of floors, according as his imagination and possibilities allow him to do. He has, in the meanwhile, undertaken some test excavations. He knows how the soil is constituted and how he must therefore lay the foundation. He also fences in his construction plot, he cuts it off. It is not necessary that all the neighbours watch him, they would only unnecessarily disturb him. He now begins to prepare a small plan or even only a sketch and then he thinks of laying brick upon brick after the foundation has become solid. A roof over his head, windows and doors are fitted, and already the man can, if worst comes to worst, move in, for most of the other work will take place now anyway in the interior of the house. It can be done in any weather. The outer plaster is still necessary against the inclemencies of the weather, even if this is not of equal importance for all climatic zones.

My wife and son wanted to build a house in Argentina. I then had some free time and went to the experts. I was so astonished at the things that had to be taken care of and with which one had to reckon. How the costs would be distributed and what legal conditions were stipulated. The specialist terms that were partially incomprehensible to me complicated and confused matters further.

Of Blood and Soil

I said to myself that, with such difficulties, neither my wife nor my son will have a house in their lifetime. Then one day I sat down and drafted a design. In terms of engineering it would certainly have been rather acceptable but it would have driven any foreman to desperation.

Then my sons laid the foundations and built walls, and I with them, and I think that within a year the structural work was completed. We could not work daily, we did not have time for that. On Saturdays and Sundays, and otherwise when each had some time. And it became, according to experts, a really solid and strongly built house.

Precisely in this way did I go about with the construction of my new world-view. The work and the difficulties were quite similar to the house construction just described.

Here, in the search for the truth, the validity of things, thorough clarity, one came up against such an enormous number of academic philosophical considerations, hypotheses, insights and opinions that at first one simply shrank back from it. But gradually the ancient and modern wise men provided that which is necessary for one's collection: the distancing from daily matters. When I finally had this, I could begin to build. Except for one thing: I had to build here alone.

For myself, my world-view house certainly had many technical defects and mistakes. I did not have it tested even once. Even the house that my sons and I built had some technical mistakes but they do not disturb my family for the structural engineering calculations were in no way affected by them and one can live quite well in this house. It is of course interesting to see if here or there this or that mistake has crept in; but the main thing is that one feels well in such a house.

Protogoras said around 2,400 years ago that he knew nothing about the gods; he could neither say that these existed nor could he say that they did not. Up to today we have not progressed one step further in this knowledge. Some people believe in God, others do not. Nobody *knows* God. I *believe* in a God.

Some years ago in Argentina I read a theory about the creation of our universe that captivated me. A Belgian or French priest presented it. Some five billion years ago a pulp-like mass exploded, conceivably to a magnitude of a cube of several hundred kilometres' length. Such a catastrophe is not anything new to modern astronomy and physics.

False Gods

The pulp "vaporised". The steam clouds of this explosion were flung with tremendous speed into space. They scattered in all directions and their speed increased, and is still increasing, the farther they went from the epicentre of the explosion. Rotation gave these gaseous entities form and shape and cooling resulted in condensation.

And our earth, as one of the planets of our solar system, is an extremely small particle, merely a speck of dust in the enormous number of other solar systems within "our Milky Way galaxy", of which there are similarly unnumbered others. Now such a thing is not unthinkable and seems completely comprehensible, especially after mankind has already succeeded in replicating such natural catastrophes on the smallest and most meagre scale in the form of the few atomic explosions during the last world war and during the attempts at making hydrogen bombs that followed after it.

Regarding the time calculation, there seem to be no factual objections from the professional experts that would destroy the theory. It is, besides, as one may read, in verifiable mean-times, half-life periods and radiation losses, and transformations, for example, radium into lead; they have a role in such calculations. But not only earthly witnesses give evidence of long past events, even other stars send us their messages constantly.

And so it is that the explosion of which our little story narrates is obviously not the only one of its kind. And other more powerful natural catastrophes that mock the heat of merely twenty million degrees centigrade that accompanied the birth of our worlds. And we men in the midst of our galactic worlds have a presentiment of super-galactic magnitudes going through the paths of space. All this moves in space; in the universe, as we call it.

Some people characterise space as the totality of places in which material bodies can move. Others add time to the three dimensions of space itself "It flows", "unbroken and constantly expanding". Still others see it in a rectangular way and are in opposition to those who wish to consider it as curved.

The former are of the opinion that space is an empty and total void and that it has no other possibility than to be filled, and the latter say that there is no doubt that it has a reality, even though beyond our intellect. I think that a void can also be curved, a void does not expand, it does not "flow", a "totality of places" however is a something, and that in which something can move is consequently not a void. Whether the worlds known to me at the moment and, beyond that - following my conjecturing reason - further worlds in the form of explosions that already occurred, such as the one noted in my introductory story, were flung into this something - a matter that is quite illuminating to me and seems acceptable to my common sense - or whether the cause of the creation occurred in other ways will certainly remain unknown until, one day, man is able to enter these worlds and will carry out his investigations *in situ*. This "life" of our system of the worlds in any case assumed a concrete form in a "period" which lies one to ten billion years in the past. "Life" arose through a creative act and follows its path according to the laws of the cosmos.

It is all indeed incredibly riveting and interesting, but if I want to build a house I must finally decide on a certain type and a certain implementation. Oh yes, there are a great number of finer and more splendid forms, but as a "small man" I can in the end not build a twenty-room palace for myself. And what sort of palace would I have if only the four walls were built up and no more because the finances were exhausted. Of what use to me, a man who wishes to exist, is a glowing gas ball, a half liquid fire ball or even a more solid body which, however, according to its constitution, offers no possibility of existence to organic life. What is the use to me of a half dozen other theories, very fine and interesting but unfortunately incredibly complicated and hard to assimilate.

"Being" is a single vast unbroken "becoming" as long as the condition of "being" continues, and "becoming" is an eternally lasting intertwined and fluid transformation of being, through becoming, into another condition of life, and then it reached the point that one day the 'being' state of our earth was suited to yield and maintain organic life. Plants, animals, man. Whether Haeckel,[6] Darwin or others were on the right path to an explanation of evolution has finally not been proven up to today. It is sufficient for me to know that I can attribute my entry into life to a single one of some 150 million sperms which, in the reproductive act, inseminated the ripe egg in the maternal womb.

I, man, have a wealthy origin, for the Nature to which I belong can afford an incredible amount of waste; so I do not need to worry about anything, it takes care of me with its endless plenitude. And

---

6   Ernst Haeckel (1834-1919) was a biologist and racial scientist who championed Darwin's work in Germany.

False Gods

my "becoming", and all being, is taken care of, and falling into a "nothingness" that cannot exist is not possible. And the fact is that I remain in the "life" of "being"; and "life" is a "becoming" condition of being. But so long as "being" can bear "life" I am subjected to this eternal coming and going, this eternal dying and becoming. *To this extent* indeed I *am anyway* immortal.

But this is what interests me in the subject in a pacifying way: I cannot believe that life is a burden – even though I sit in prison at the moment – and I cannot believe to what extent one must "fear death" or must be tortured by anxiety on account of a putative final destination of all organic life. Something that is the Nature-willed fate of all men cannot be anything frightful. It is unthinkable for me, when I consider the natural course of things, that the power that sets us men in its plan can have determined only futility and sorrow as the destiny of life.

Of course it is a wise Providence that allows us men to become immortal but not exactly as men. This is already very consoling. But the thought of the plenitude of living forms that I will still have to live through according to an iron law of Nature makes me cheerful, happy and gay. That we as men bear so much sorrow and care and cause this to one another mutually lies in our own deficiency. Even man is subjected to an eternal process of perfection as long as "becoming" allows it. And we men stand yet at the beginning of our formation, and much that still causes anxiety and fear to those who live today will be smoothed out by the grindstone of "becoming".

The sorrow and tribulation of men in earlier times was, in comparison, incomparably greater than today. And in future epochs our descendants will maintain the same of us by applying this comparative measure. There can and will always be temporary setbacks, even supposed regressions; but this does not affect the matter when one observes the whole. It is a sad fate for those born in such times; this is undeniable. And man should try, by virtue of his knowledge, to steer the reversal. He is by now capable of that; whether he finally will the future will show. Anyway, a good power does not at all wish dissolution. This is clearly proven to me by the fact that it gave me, a feeling for joy and cordiality. And a desire of the power that its creation be destroyed by fear, anxiety, quaking and sorrow is an impossibility.

Seen in this way, the interpretation of things that I present to myself is benign and pleasant. I cannot share Sartre's viewpoint that life and death are absurdities. Of course, I admit that they are insignificant, both life and death, considered from the point of view of *"becoming in being"* insofar as it concerns *me* as a person. I have again gained access to tranquillity and peace; values which I already had in my younger years. Of course I derive these from other realms now; but how does that affect the matter. The result alone is decisive. But the time in between I could have done without.

Epicurus says about death that it does not exist so long as he lives. If it comes, then Epicurus is no more present. And Schopenhauer thinks that death is not worse than birth. I complete myself, maintain myself between death and a birth which I do not know, and say that it is delightful to celebrate my wedding with my bride; then a "new life" begins for us both. And death does nothing else; it leads me to new lives. But the "death" of the organic entity is a necessity of the natural law, consequent upon the continuing "becoming of life" and serves the process of perfection. It is a metamorphosis into something new, nothing else. Why then anxiety and care?

Thousands upon thousands of deaths lead me to thousands of lives; in the most manifold forms of life, of the uninterrupted game. Until, for climatic reasons, the earth which bears and nourishes my life at any time can no longer maintain me. On reaching the limits of the possibilities of organic existence on our earth, this falls back once again into other forms of "being". And herewith the first cycle is closed and others follow. Until a new original causality once again gives rise to new beginnings.

Attention! To new beginnings. For nothing in the universe can be at rest and inert, and everything is always in a flux. *And there is no death as such because there is no Nothing. For the outpouring restrains itself and then flows once again.*

When I consider this system I must say that it is a design that pleases me. Everything gloomy and dark disappears and I am glad of it. *Simple*, complete in itself, it always stands before my eyes; otherwise, in the rush of daily life it would also have little practical value. For, the longer time I need to spend to have my image of the world before me using astute thought – if I could bring forward such at all - , the less it would be of use to me for household use. Thus do I understand the role destined for me which I have to play in the course of things.

This now gives me also a *distance* from *petty* daily events, and everything that was still difficult yesterday has disappeared today.

This is true freedom, born of knowledge, that no human trumpery is any longer capable of robbing me of my inner peace, and therewith my attitude as a man to men also changes at the same time; it becomes something different. Today, having an open mind, no anxious skulking, a lack of prejudice, no envy and no hatred are the most important advantages. Of course, I am still an egoist, but this time not at the cost of others. Now even my fellow human beings take part in this egoism with advantages to themselves. For contentiousness, strife, causing difficulties, contempt, calumny, and the whole litany of vexations undergo a diminution to hitherto unknown dimensions due to a lack of sufficient grounding.

The End of Nationalism

I experienced to a sufficient degree the effects of a pessimistic world-view; it can definitely be characterised as the midwife of much evil. In a logical evaluation of this knowledge, the struggle for sovereignty of small sectors, each accommodating that crowd that is called my "people" has now become of absolute insignificance.

National, narrow-minded thought has become a burden to me. Mutual mistrust, the striving for domination of one over the other, grouping of men according to values and classifications, all this is from now on part of the old system. In truth, this system, can only be regarded as a tragic situation of mankind, and through the continuation of the same, man will live his earthly life without any hope and confidence without being able to direct it into a more constructive path.

For what is the use to an individual of a world-view which satisfies him and what is the use of knowledge of the higher meaning of "being", if every day martial laws can be enforced and the freedom of action of the individual can be rigidly controlled.

Numerous are the forms of society that have been tried through the millennia with the goal of bringing a more or less satisfying system into the coexistence of mankind. But nothing from tradition seems to be really adequate for the present-day situation. To be sure, here too the matters are in a constant flux. And it may be supposed that what was the strict order of the day among a total population of around three billion possibly did not yet interest men at a time when they were able to live with a single billion. And it seems to me that ideas that deal with a global solution are favourable and good considering

The End of Nationalism

the circumstances. For, in the "becoming in being" everything presses towards the whole.

Why modern man has not yet decided on such a sort of solution in spite of two devastating world wars seems to be a puzzle. Perhaps there is a concatenation of many causes and effects and human wrong-headedness seems to me to be not the least of these.

Well, the future generations will change it; anyway, they will only have a smile of regret for our conduct. Do we of today have no smile of sympathy with regard to the conduct of our predecessors when we think of the dozens of small German states? Even Goethe travelled only a few hours by stagecoach and already he was in a foreign country and subject to other laws. But then, one day, this system of miniature states was removed. And why should not this be valid for the entire community of nations. After such a solution a peaceful mutual cooperation of men will then be brought about by itself. For, in political terms, in this manner it will necessarily come to a neutralisation of contradictions. And that significance will be bestowed on daily events which must be rightly conceded to it for the improvement of life.

The task of regional governments, which will then have only a provincial character, will be to make the nations of the earth happier in union with the central authority. And the sooner such a thing is achieved the more the personal security and independence of the individual is provided for, and every oppression of him will be prevented.

But in the case of a tendency to remain without changing, the masses will, in spite of the finest world-view ideas which the individual may have, fall back into the existential anxiety of the primitive until an external powerful impetus forces such a solution - if it is then still worth it at all.

For, in an honest observation of the situation it has been for a long, long time true that every person is his own neighbour. Conditioned by instincts, which is a basic condition. All efforts at correction in this regard have up to now not achieved any wide and lasting result. And only an *inter*nationalisation of peoples overcomes the existing basic instincts, at least one part of the *additional* hotbeds artificially created by men *through nationalisation*. And as long as this remains in the sovereignty, the desire for independence, of a state, the standpoint of "Each is his own neighbour", even in the national sense, will retain its ineradicable significance and, in times of war, the majority of the population of a state will in any case carry out what the state orders, willingly or unwillingly. If this does not happen in an easy way, then the state takes care to force it.

And all moral demands that the individual is full of, all the ethical will of the individual, remain a theory that is not in a position to practically produce any concrete results. For, the power apparatus of the state crushes all phenomena of a practical nature that stand against its goal and its will. No matter whether it is a democracy or a totalitarianism, no matter whether a monarchy or a republic. In war times this is anyway the naked reality which cannot at all be removed by philosophising or sophistry.

It is relatively easy for a man to speak about the realisation of moral laws and thereby also stand up to a state apparatus as an individual: and to say aloud: "Here I stand, I cannot do anything but say to you that what you are doing is an enormous scandal, you are murderers, corrupt, and betrayers of the nation, and I shout it out to the whole world and I myself will not work for you one more day", when the person concerned has reached the age of between fifty and sixty at least or has no family or his family is economically so secure that his duty of care in this regard may be considered as negligible.

In all other cases the individual will, in the best of cases, control himself and compromise and finally do the "duty" ordered by the state. The few exceptions confirm the rule. In more distant times, such considerations were also clearly the reason why, for example, the Roman Catholic Church imposed celibacy on its clergy. The courage and resistance in times of danger to faith becomes - regardless of the consequences for the person concerned and the earthly uselessness of his sacrifice - stronger and more stubborn through a freedom from duties of care.

That is why I said that evil must be extirpated basically, *radically*. The organisational form that can bring men to such conflicts must be removed. In mutual coexistence man does not have to accommodate himself to the organisational form but the organisational form must be tailored to man. This alone seems to be a practical application based on the bleak experiences up to now; the other is, I think, heretical nonsense. Good perhaps for inner edification, but what is the use of this when murder and annihilation can continue to be ordered by the state. And it is easy for me to say today that I have finally found a world-view for myself which satisfies me.

The End of Nationalism

I have in the meantime become fifty six years old and view things from daily life differently from before. If I die tomorrow, that is good, if I die today, *bueno*, that is also right. I am no longer of absolute importance for the physical existence of my family. In an emergency they will today manage even without me, for, in the meantime, around twenty years after the events, everything has grown older.

The soldier who fell in the war knew that state insurance for surviving family members would protect his family from extreme need, for the laws stated that. But the one who was compelled to war service, who kicked *against* the pricks of the state and was punished for this reason knew that nobody would worry about his family members. At best, in the best of cases, they would be placed as a burden on family relatives. And because the duty of care, the desire to take care of one's own is equally conditioned by instincts, nothing will also change in the attitude of men to these things. But, as a corollary, in times of catastrophes, the attitude of people at least between fifty and sixty to these things will be the same as that which we had and which those people who were before us had.

For the system of society is still the same. So the coming generation may rightly build for itself that organisational form which excludes such complications into a *better* communal life, for the world-view image which comforts there then comes fully by itself and they will be able to live in peace and quiet, and joy will be the content of their lives for the whole knows only the good.

I was speaking about the duty to care. But why then does the individual bear with him such care; only because he wishes peace and nourishment for himself and his family, then he lives in *happiness*. And whether it is a plant or animal, it is the same there too. The feeling and thought of men turns to happiness alone. But stronger men have at all times made use of the care of the individual for himself and his family as one of the chief means of achieving their own personal wishes. And it is the very same thing from the slave-owners in the distant past, as individuals, up to our supposedly modern societal forms, as communal undertakings. The desire for happiness that was already originally present in man as the chief source of his being was, and is, exploited by means of promise and force.

"... I who was plucked out of the being of an all ruling order into the phenomenal form of man that is as passing as a wisp of air" – thus did I write once – "gradually understood the 'Reich' through the formation of my environment. For I was born as a German. I learnt to understand the "Reich" both as something concrete and its conceptual significance; everything that was put into that and what I as a National Socialist felt and wished for."

That significance was then bestowed on daily events which rightly had to be granted to them for the improvement of life. The task of the regional governments, which have only a provincial character, in association with the central authority, is that of making the peoples of the earth happier. The sooner such a thing is achieved the more care is taken for the personal security and independence of the individual and every oppression of him prevented. But, in the case of a tendency to remain unchanged, the masses will, in spite of the finest world-view ideas which the individual may have, fall back into the existential anxiety of the primitive until an external powerful impetus then forces such a solution. So it was up to 1945. But in the course of the last roughly 1½ years I learnt slowly and bit by bit, ever hesitating and regressing, to develop this idea into a global one.

I think that this longing and hoping for a union of reason and life, which is regrettably managed at the moment in different forms with varying vehemence, is not just a matter related to us Germans but is definitely characteristic of all the peoples of the earth. But in it I recognise the core of all strife between man and man and one of the roots of many evils. But if this longing that produces wishful thinking is thought of - instead of in compartmental form - in a global universality and is given expression, then there enters, instead of an effect that destroys everything, a peaceful effort towards the fulfilment of human wishes. Indeed, even the tendency to the existing human egoism does not end up empty handed, for each individual obtains *per saldo*[7] from the peaceful coexistence his own quite personal advantage which allows him to stand with greater convenience than before in the comfortable central point of his own small personal world.

A Cosmic World View

During the last years I have, partly in the quiet of the Argentinean pampas, partly in the unspoiled nature of the rugged primeval world of the Argentinean north, in its Aconquija mountain range, learnt to derive a practical application valid for me from two things.

---

7   on balance

A Cosmic World View

I saw hell, death and the devil because I had to watch the madness of annihilation; for I was harnessed as one of the many horses in the games and, following the will and order of the coachman, could not break out either to the left or to the right. I have further taken a lively inner interest in knowledge that the human mind has up to now wrested from the universe in its efforts "to grasp the stars".

In that peace of the Argentinean places I could go as deep into the workings of a higher order as was possible for me intellectually; and I sought to place myself, my position as a human being, in relation to this by holding the mirror of self-knowledge before myself. And quite of its own accord the reason of *nationalistic* thought was forced into other considerations that finally end in an absolute desire for a universal, *global* solution. And I must say that this result satisfied me.

It is not at all hard, it is really – like everything in Nature – simple. The reflection of the macrocosm in the microcosm, and vice-versa. I heard a thousand times and also understood; but in earlier years I did not derive its practical application. Of course, I am not here alone; for it is superficiality that triumphs. Otherwise, for a long time already, there would have been no more wars, annihilations, hatred and destruction. Since the beginning of the existence of the material "Being" of our worlds - which one thinks one can cognitively date to five billion years in the past - this "Being" has stood in "time".

Since this time even I, who at the moment find myself in the Being condition of man, have existed in some life forms of "Being" following an order of the ruler. Thus I had to wait for five billion years until an all-ruling Natural Order commanded me to take the existential form of man for a short while. I do not know if I was already objectified and present in the phenomenal form of man within the mentioned time period. I do not also know if, in future aeons, I will again obtain such an "order". I think neither the former nor the latter. I know only one thing for certain, that, after the end of my present life form, I have to go through innumerable other life forms of organic and inorganic life as little particles of "Being". I have lived for sixty years. Maybe a little longer, maybe a little less.

How foolish I was to think only in terms of the domain of the "Reich", only in terms of a narrow nationalistic adherence. It is a wonder, better wonderful, that a totally good ruler gave to man, within the realm of his "Being", joy as his highest good. Joy in its thousand-fold forms. Employing joy and again sharing it should alone be the true life's work of man during his earthly life. Everything else is worth little and, when considered rightly, not even egoistic. It is only stupid, nothing else.

The Letter from Pastor Achenbach

I received a letter from a retired Protestant pastor, Paul Achenbach, which he wrote to me on 11 September 1961. It says:

To the accused Eichmann, now in Israel.

On the occasion of a study trip through Israel, Evangelical priests in Germany had commissioned me to inquire of Dr. Servatius if something had been offered to you by way of spiritual counsel. After a telephone call with State Attorney Wechtenbruch I received no further news. From a pastor who lives in Israel and who, in response to a similar request from your former Evangelical home community in Linz, got in touch with Dr. Servatius it transpired that he too had heard nothing more up to my departure from Israel.

Now I do not know if you have obtained information of these negotiations.

Perhaps you have yourself had in the meantime a desire for a talk on spiritual counsel. But I am moved to write to you personally. During my travel through Israel I was also in the courtroom and followed a hearing. Later I took part through the radio and television in the continuation of the trial.

When I heard the accusations in the courtroom and observed the defence counsel and the public I imagined I was taken to the Last Judgement, the judgement day of God. Already now in the courtroom everything was to be observed. But at the Last Judgement our guilt will be visibly uncovered to all the world. Then the Devil himself will be the prosecutor. What will a man then answer if he does not have JESUS as defence counsel by his side. At the Last Judgement everything that is secret will be revealed before God. Nobody goes past the judge's seat of God. So it is good if man recognises, repents and, so far as it is possible, makes amend for, his guilt already in this world. May I remind you of a song verse which you perhaps still remember from your confirmation lessons.

The Letter from Pastor Achenbach

> If the prosecutor indicts me Jesus has already represented me,
> If he dares to examine me, Jesus has prayed for me.
> That my mediator speaks for me that is my trust."

Should it not be possible for you from this point of view to see the entire question of your guilt in the annihilation of the Jews by God in the light of the Bible and eternity? I have heard from reliable sources that you were once a pious young man. If that is true, it is indeed important to ask yourself at what point the course of your life was changed in such a way that you, in spite of your knowledge of the Bible, could fall victim to the fanaticism of the Third Reich. When they intended to annihilate the entire Jewry of the world your superiors perhaps found in you a compliant instrument.

Have you thought of the fact that your being discovered could mean for you, personally, God's judgement but also, if it came to an admission of guilt, at the same time God's mercy? Your readiness to take your life does not remove God's judgement.

I am convinced that no other nation but Israel has the right to hunt for you and bring you to justice; for the Jews are the people against whom we Germans have become guilty to such an extent as never before occurred in the world. God looks for us men always in our guilt. Divided Berlin and Germany I see as God's judgement on account of our guilt against Israel.

Since you are waiting for not only the verdict in Israel but also the judgement of God on your life, activities and actions, you should submit a comprehensive confession of your entire guilt before God and man. Indeed, it was, already in the Old Testament, the case that one who recognised his sin and guilt and repented in the light of God also received forgiveness. A Bible was sent to you for study when you went to Israel. In it you can read what God says of such serious crimes against humanity. I can only hope that you still allow yourself to be spoken to about God and his Word.

You have - as far as I can see - not denied your moral guilt. But you perhaps tried to diminish this. In your responses you based yourself on the oath that you swore. Every oath, even when it is apparently sworn before God, has its limit at the divine commandment and, generally speaking, at humanity. In the conduct of your trial, humanity was granted to such an extent by the bench and the prosecution as was hardly experienced in other hard trials.

False Gods

If I now strive to help you further inwardly, I do that in view of the eternity before which you stand. Through a clear confession and an honest inner disclosure of your and all of our involvement in the frightful things that happened to the Jewish people it might perhaps come to an exoneration for you. If I am not mistaken, you too referred once to the philosopher Kant, but it was precisely Kant who said:

> "Man's conscience is the great confidant of God, It always stands on God's side. It is the great admonisher in man's heart."

One can silence one's conscience but one day the need will arise to answer to oneself. An open, truthful, upright, comprehensive confession before mankind will also be accepted by God in the higher world. Such can have not only for you but also for our divided German nation standing before God's judgement untold effects with regard to a pardon from God. Let me recall to you further some Biblical words:

> "One who touches Israel touches the apple of God's eye."

In the Bible the following sentence has become important to me:

> "One who loves Israel works hand in hand with God."

The serious thing is that the hour of death comes for each of us personally. Then we must stand before the judgement seat of God. We will then be delivered inescapably to God and his judgement. The question of God's chosen people and of what we have done, or not done, to the Jews or to this or another brother will be presented to each. Then God's judgement cannot be transformed into mercy. That is only possible so long as we are on earth, that is, if we repent. But repenting means looking at ourselves as God sees us. One who wishes to find mercy before God - one who loves Germany and wishes to save it from ruin includes himself in the ranks of those who allow themselves to be judged and are ready for expiation. One who loves God and does not wish to anger and sadden Him further turns round even today and confesses his guilt so that the grace of a pardon may befall him and then love and benevolence may be brought to our Jewish brothers, so far as there is still time for us. I commend you to the mercy of your earthly judge as well as to your heavenly judge.

Paul Achenbach

[signature]

The Letter from Pastor Achenbach

To this letter I have the following to say:

To Pastor Achenbach,

I did not know that you had requested to make efforts on my behalf.

Your attempted pressure on me to confess to guilt (whereby you, according to the contents of the letter, doubtless mean *legal* guilt since you speak in *another* place of *moral* guilt) where there is none *I reject as a severe coercion.*

May I refer you to my concluding words and my defence counsel's cross-examination of the prosecution witness, the Evangelical Provost of Berlin, Grüber.

I recommend to you a thorough and pertinent study of sources before you open your mouth in a sermon for the sake of coercion. I fear that, otherwise, your "devil" might be delighted at the "last judgement" that you have made yourself guilty through attempted coercion of a defendant to a false declaration.

Your inquisitorial characteristics are nothing new to me although I must state, for truth's sake, that not *all* Protestant priests are, thankfully, like you; where there is *no* legal guilt I will also not allow myself to be forced to confess such, just because it suits you."

Testament

In the case of my death I request the following:

1. I wish that my corpse be taken by my brothers from Israel to Linz on the Danube, Upper Austria.
2. They are to burn it.
3. The ashes are to be divided into seven parts.
4. 1/7 of the ashes should go to the grave of my parents in the cemetery in Linz on the Danube.
5. 1/7 of the ashes should be scattered in the garden of the house of my wife and sons in Buenos Aires
6. Of the remaining 5/7, one seventh each belongs to my wife Vera, née Liebl, and to my sons, Klaus, Horst, Dieter and Ricardo-Francisco

It should one day be placed in the coffin of each of them, even if they have ended their earthly life.

It may serve as a reassurance to them to know this and to overcome possible fear of death: For death is not worse than birth, and our life awaits thousands and thousands of others.

Adolf Eichmann,

Jerusalem, on the fifteenth of August, one thousand, nine hundred and sixty one. (on the 30th anniversary of my betrothal to my wife)

This testament is to be handed over to my wife Vera, née Liebl, by Dr. Robert Eichmann, Linz on the Danube. For the trouble that I cause even after my death I should be pardoned and I thank the persons who take this trouble.

Adolf Eichmann,

15 August 1961

www.ingramcontent.com/pod-product-compliance
Lightning Source LLC
Chambersburg PA
CBHW070728160426
43192CB00009B/1356